LANGUAGE AND CHANGE
IN THE ARAB MIDDLE EAST

STUDIES IN MIDDLE EASTERN HISTORY

Bernard Lewis, Itamar Rabinovich, and Roger Savory,
General Editors

Israel Gershoni and James P. Jankowski
EGYPT, ISLAM, AND THE ARABS:
The Search for Egyptian Nationhood, 1900–1930

Ami Ayalon
LANGUAGE AND CHANGE IN THE ARAB MIDDLE EAST
The Evolution of Modern Political Discourse

Other Volumes Are in Preparation

LANGUAGE AND CHANGE IN THE ARAB MIDDLE EAST

The Evolution of Modern Political Discourse

Ami Ayalon

In cooperation with

THE DAYAN CENTER FOR MIDDLE EASTERN
AND AFRICAN STUDIES

Shiloah Institute
Tel Aviv University

New York   Oxford
OXFORD UNIVERSITY PRESS
1987

Oxford University Press

Oxford   New York   Toronto
Delhi   Bombay   Calcutta   Madras   Karachi
Petaling Jaya   Singapore   Hong Kong   Tokyo
Nairobi   Dar es Salaam   Cape Town
Melbourne   Auckland
and associated companies in
Beirut   Berlin   Ibadan   Nicosia

Published by Oxford University Press, Inc.,
200 Madison Avenue, New York, New York 10016

Oxford is a registered trademark of Oxford University Press

Library of Congress Cataloging-in-Publication Data
Ayalon, Ami.
Language and Change in the Arab Middle East.
(Studies in Middle Eastern history)
Bibliography: p.   Includes index.
1. Arabic language—19th century. 2. Political
science—Arab countries—History—19th century.
3. Arab countries—Politics and government. I. Title.
II. Series: Studies in Middle Eastern history
(New York, N.Y.)
PJ6075.A89   1987   492'.7'09   86-18068
ISBN 0-19-504140-2

2 4 6 8 10 9 7 5 3 1
Printed in the United States of America
on acid-free paper

To Yael

Preface

Do ideas change reality? Or does reality remake ideas? Or is history what T. S. Eliot called "the endless cycle of idea and action"? Each proposition is arguable. But at whatever point the "endless cycle" may momentarily halt, it is language with which we capture both idea and action. Language mirrors its speakers' understanding of their culture, their past, and their present. As the "cycle" moves on and the historical situation changes, so does language. New words are coined, old words acquire new meanings, their intellectual or emotional "loadedness" accumulating or waning. Usually, such transitions are slow-paced and evolutionary. But sudden, rapid historical change can confuse language and cast a society's accustomed idiom into crisis. This can be the result of domestic upheaval—revolutions, even mere coups, quickly produce their own "newspeak"—or it can follow upon the forceful, perhaps overpowering, encounter with a different culture. It is the latter with which this book is primarily concerned.

Since language reflects the values and experiences of its own speakers, it is signally ill-equipped to convey alien notions with anything like the nuance they have in their natural habitat. The attempt nonetheless to make communication possible is part and parcel of the history of any two cultures meeting—or clashing. To explore the shifts of language is, then, not only just a fascinating pursuit, but indispensable for the proper understanding of such an encounter.

The Middle East had undergone profound transformation as a result of its dramatic encounter with Europe. The society of the region was exposed to a variety of novelties, and its traditional language had to be refurbished if it were to serve the multitude of new lexical needs. The present study seeks to examine the changing Arabic language as a mirror of changing perceptions and values of its speakers. I have chosen to focus on the vocabulary of politics, the field in which the confluence of a rich tradition and strange modern principles has produced perhaps the most colorful aspect of the process. The time span is the nineteenth century, the formative phase of this transformation.

One point seems important enough to be emphasized here at the very outset. When conceptual and linguistic problems result from contact between two substantially different societies, such problems arise in both of them alike. Neither side is at first properly prepared to comprehend, or accurately describe, ideas and phenomena peculiar to the other. Regardless of a possible asymmetry in their motivation to explore one another, neither of them escapes the difficulties inherent in the attempt to understand the opposite side. This has been the case with the cultural interaction between Arabs and the West during the last two centuries. And while I chose to deal here only with one party, it is essential to bear in mind that its counterpart was equally unprepared intellectually for the challenge. This, of course, is a subject for another study.

A number of technical points should be noted. Since the study is based on an analysis of primary texts, bulky notes with numerous references to the sources have been unavoidable. So as not to burden them still further, I have tried to limit references to the most illustrative examples, although normally there would have been many more in each case. Sources in the notes are usually mentioned in an abbreviated form; fuller details appear in the bibliography. Month names are also abbreviated by their first three letters (e.g., Jan = January), except for June and July, which are given in full form. In each note the sources are arranged chronologically. In bilingual sources with a separate page numeration for each language, the reference is always to the Arabic text.

The term "Arab," or "the Arabs," is employed with reference to all those whose mother tongue is Arabic, including Egyptians. This term, though somewhat problematic in a nineteenth-century context, has been preferred for convenience over more accurate but cumbersome formulae. Finally, in a study dealing with the limits of trans-cultural communication, it should be understood that all English renditions of Arabic and Turkish words are, at best, approximate.

Arabic is transliterated in accordance with the system most commonly used in the field of Islamic studies. This does not include quotations from, or references to, sources using other systems; those have been quoted in their original form.

There is no standard system for transcribing Ottoman Turkish in Latin letters. That employed here conforms with rules commonly used in the field, which combine modern Turkish spelling with transliteration from Arabic.

It is a pleasure to acknowledge the help rendered me during various stages of this study by colleagues and friends. First and foremost, Professor Bernard Lewis, to whom I am indebted for sharing with me his vast knowledge of Islamic culture and history and for his unfailing encouragement. Each of our frequent sessions was as inspiring as it was delightful. I consider myself most fortunate to have him as a mentor and friend.

Professors Uriel Dann, Michael Harsgor, Charles Issawi, Herbert Kufner and Roy Mottahedeh read parts of the manuscript and offered many valuable comments; I am grateful to them all. To Professors Itamar Even Zohar, Albert Hourani, Joseph Sadan and Sasson Somekh I am obliged for fruitful discussion of my approach and for many important suggestions. I owe much to Professor Itamar Rabinovich, for his constant support and ever-valuable advice; to Professor Shimon Shamir who, as director of the Israeli Academic Center in Cairo, made my research period there at once gainful and pleasant; and to Mr. Daniel Dishon, for his important help in matters of style.

I wish to offer special thanks to the staff at the Dayan Center of Tel Aviv University, in particular to Edna Liftman and Amira Margalit, for their endless efforts on my behalf, which made my work immensely more enjoyable than it could otherwise have been; to Nancy Lane, Susan Meigs and Valerie Aubry from Oxford University Press, for their masterly handling of the complex operation of turning the manuscript into a book; and to Penny

Beebe, my superb editor—one can hardly wish for a more sophisticated and keen reader.

The research for this study was facilitated by grants from the Princeton Program in Near Eastern Studies, the Ben-Gurion Fund, and the Kaplan Chair in the History of Egypt and Israel at Tel Aviv University. I acknowledge their support with gratitude. I am also grateful to Cambridge University Press for permission to reproduce here a part of an article I published in volume 28 of *The Historical Journal.*

My wife Yael and my son Yaron were the heroes behind the scenes of this project. Without their patience and inducement I would never have brought it to completion.

Tel Aviv   A.A.
June 1986

Contents

List of Abbreviations

List of Abbreviations

BSOAS	Bulletin of the School of Oriental and African Studies
EI^1, EI^2	Encyclopaedia of Islam, 1st and 2nd editions
IJMES	International Journal of Middle East Studies
JNES	Journal of Near Eastern Studies
JRAS	Journal of the Royal Asiatic Society
MEA	Middle Eastern Affairs
MES	Middle Eastern Studies
MW	Muslim World
REI	Revue des Études Islamiques
RMM	Revue du Monde Musulman
WI	Die Welt des Islams

LANGUAGE AND CHANGE
IN THE ARAB MIDDLE EAST

Terminological uncertainties have the same effect on research as fog has on shipping. They are the more dangerous as people are usually unaware of their existence.

Hugo Schuchardt

Introduction

If a time machine had been available to the Egyptian historian ʿAbd al-Raḥmān al-Jabartī (d. 1825), and he had chosen to go and visit his ancestral countrymen of a few centuries earlier, he would have found himself in a rather familiar environment, one quite like his own, politically, socially and culturally. He would have had little difficulty in understanding the life around him and in relating himself to it. Had he, however, preferred to travel ahead in time rather than backward—a century, or even a few decades—he would have been baffled by new sights and strange sounds. Jabartī, a lucid observer of his society and an articulate narrator, would then have faced serious problems in comprehending the circumstances—still more in depicting them. For the changes that Middle Eastern society experienced during the nineteenth century were unlike those that had gradually threaded themselves through prior centuries. The new changes had roots outside the region; they were rapid, intensive and profound.

For many generations Middle Eastern society maintained a sophisticated sociopolitical system, with elaborately regulated relations between ruler and ruled, the elite and the rest of society. It was a slowly changing order, mainly due to its underlying unshaken religious world view. In the nineteenth century, this reality began to change more rapidly. Europe, previously an uninteresting entity, now imposed itself on the Middle East with victorious armies, impressive technology, political and cultural ideas. These novelties generated curiosity among the local leadership and soon became objects of eager emulation. By the end of the century the Middle East had adopted many new principles and practices, and had come to display a growing appetite for more.

Such rapid developments inevitably led to extensive changes in the indigenous vocabulary of state and class. The languages of the Middle East, rich and colorful, and amply adequate for their traditional purposes, were inadequate for transmitting ideas that were alien and largely unintelligible to the region's society. To adapt themselves to the new assignments, the Arabic, Turkish and Persian lexicons changed substantially, like the reality whose transformation necessitated their refurbishment. These languages in transition provide a faithful mirror of the conceptual changes that brought modern institutions into the Middle East. The hero of the present study is Arabic—or, more specifically, the changed Arabic vocabulary of politics.

At the onset of the nineteenth century, when certain Arab observers began to glance at the political play in progress on the European stage, they at first could discern only vague figures engaged in ambiguous activities. They identified what they saw according to their own experience, as a slightly different version of the long-familiar Middle Eastern political system. Several decades elapsed before some of the principles of that strange reality were more accurately perceived.

The process of change involved a very small number of individuals: government officials, translators, travelers reporting their impressions, later also journalists and publicists. Under governmental command or out of curiosity, they set out to examine the alien culture and describe it to their leaders and fellow countrymen. Within this small circle of educated men were a few perspicacious intellectuals who became aware that the phenomena they observed in Western life and politics were profoundly different from those of their own culture. They soon found it difficult, often even impossible, to discuss these phenomena properly with their traditional vocabulary. Arabic, always the pride and joy of its users, suddenly became a deficient instrument: "The Arabic idiom," the Lebanese Buṭrus al-Bustānī suggested in his famous 1859 *khuṭba*, "while abundantly rich in expressing old ideas is in dire want of terms to suit modern needs."[1] Using this "handicapped" language had really become "a kind of burdensome trouble and a sort of affliction," complained a compatriot, Ibrāhīm al-Yāzijī.[2] Another contemporary Lebanese journalist deplored the degradation of Arabic to a state of a "poor language" (*lugha faqīra*):

> If anybody should find [such a definition] presumptuous and insulting to the Arab intelligence, let him take the trouble of translating a speech by a British Parliament member or, better still, render in Arabic the proceedings of a session; an article on European theater; a political study; a commercial report, and the like. Surely he would find himself facing an abyss with every single sentence. He might not transcend it without seriously complicating the language, leaving his readers in disconcertment and doubt.[3]

To attain precision of expression, some of these writers felt, it was necessary to resort to "innovations which would enrich the language and lend it vigor."[4]

Arabic thus became subject to the phenomenon known among linguists as "interference"—the effect of contact between different cultures and idioms. Interference occurs when one language finds itself inadequately equipped for denoting ideas which are current in that of another society. The encounter may affect the morphology and syntax of the exposed language, its phonemic system and, most commonly, its lexicon.[5] It is with this very last aspect of the change that we are here concerned.

There were a number of avenues through which Arabic could meet its challenge. For one thing, it was able to benefit from the experience of Turkish. As rulers of an empire, the Turks had encountered European political ideas and practices at an earlier date and had responded to the resultant problems in articulating them. Indeed many of the terminological innovations of Turkish eventually made their way into the Arabic political vocabulary. The process was facilitated by the fact that a large portion of the Turkish political vocabulary was formed of Turkicized Arabic words; the Turks had long used Arabic as a legitimate source upon which they could draw, just as English and French had drawn upon Greek and Latin, and they persisted with this practice when faced with modern exigencies. In a sense they paved the way for Arab writers, who could now repossess, so to speak, their own linguistic assets, readjusted to serve new needs.[6] Turkish was a ready model not merely for the rejuvenation of Arabic words, but also for the borrowing of foreign terms along with the foreign concepts. This was a convenient and safe procedure which guaranteed an accurate (though not always fully comprehensible) rendition of alien ideas. After all, no local expression could describe a "parliament" more precisely than the loan-word *barlamān;* and *qunṣul* was surely the most exact rendition of "consul." Turkish writers resorted to this technique extensively. They borrowed from French and Italian, to a lesser extent also from English. But their Arab counterparts were less inclined to adopt the method; Arabic had been traditionally averse to borrowing, both due to its conceived sanctity, which was not to be "defiled" by lexical intruders, and because of its special homogeneous morphology, which made loan-words look awkward and unesthetic.[7] The guardians of the language, hoping to preserve its pristine character, preferred to meet the new needs through a variety of other means.

Most of the solutions to Arabic's nineteenth-century lexical problems came from its rich resources. These could be exploited in a number of ways. Writers could derive new words—neologisms—from existing roots, revivify terms from the vast stock of obsolete Arabic expressions to denote new ideas, extend the range of reference of current words to embrace new meanings, or combine two or all three of these methods by way of making verbal compounds. In drawing upon the treasures of their own language, Arab writers were guided primarily by the principle of analogy; what dictated the application of existing or newly remodeled words to novel notions was a conceived sharing or similarity of contents. In the process, new ideas lent their meaning to Arabic expressions, sometimes replacing, but more commonly adding to, their existing import. The result was a broad array of verbal creations with modified and extended range of meaning, featuring various degrees of proximity between their initial content and the new concept they now came to designate. Most of these changes occurred in the course of Arab writers' describing and discussing the novel aspects of European political and cultural life. And when modern-thinking Middle Eastern rulers moved to duplicate some of the foreign concepts, many new ideas entered the region with the names they had acquired through usage in the original foreign context. In the adaptation of political Arabic to its new needs, then, interference took its course primarily on the semantic level. As we shall see, the number of Arabic words whose scope of reference was broadened far exceeded new additions to the lexicon made through borrowing or derivation. Likewise, among the numerous compound neologisms that were created, most consisted of semantically modified components. This makes the subject of this study, the changing language, a rather elusive one. Semantic shift, when wholesale and hasty, is always a problematic development whose stages and underlying motivations are hard to trace, especially so if the users of a language do not fully comprehend the essence of the ideas about which they speak or write. We shall be dealing with the fluctuating meaning of words; and meaning, unlike sound, for example, does not lend itself to exact gauging. An indefinite quality, it varies according to the user, the audience and the circumstances. A vocabulary in transition, therefore, has limitations as a mirror of concepts held by a whole society, especially when the transition is unorganized and brought on by an external force.

Other factors further complicate the picture. An author's choice of word might have been determined by a desire other than to attain clarity and precision. He might have preferred, for stylistic reasons, to express one notion by a number of terms which appeared to him roughly or exactly synonymous. This had been an old practice with writers of Arabic, one which rendered the language ornamentally beautiful at the usually affordable expense of accuracy. But while acceptable and sometimes desirable in traditional writing, such an approach could only create ambiguity in texts dealing with modern ideas that were themselves often imperfectly understood. There were political or ideological considerations as well; an author might choose to employ or avoid certain terms in compliance with the preferences of the government under whose patronage, or censorship, he wrote. Such reasoning often affected the language of Arab writers discussing the affairs of European states, allies or foes of their own governments in Cairo or Istanbul. A writer might also have adhered to certain expressions and rejected others with the explicit intention of making an argument. For example, he might have deliberately applied a traditional name to a modern institution, even when aware of the gap between them, in order to emphasize the latter's precedent in local experience. To a reader of today, these motives are not always readily discernible. But they existed, and they increased the intricacy of the situation. These limitations should not be underestimated. Yet, if the lexicon is less than a precise indicator of perceptions, it nevertheless offers an indispensable view of the changing concepts, and this makes its exploration well worth our while. Words, after all, were the instruments through which novel ideas were communicated. The initial Arab disregard for European civilization, slowly giving way to confused curiosity, then to active exploration, and finally to eager emulation or explicit rejection, are all evidenced in the shifts which constantly took place in the Arabic vocabulary, with its unique colors and resounding tones. Closely studied, it allows us an otherwise unattainable insight into the nature of historic changes in the region. Gaining this distinctive insight is the main purpose of this book.

The period here examined is deliberately loosely defined. In political history, major events offer themselves as visible points of division. Such events, however, do not normally occur in the development of languages. The process through which Arabic was modernized in its encounter with Europe had no crucial turning points. At its beginning, modern political ideas were, to speakers of Arabic, vague curiosities professed by remote peoples, occasionally mentioned by way of digression in texts dealing with more interesting local issues. By the mid-twentieth century such ideas would become of direct concern to the Arab society, which would implement many of them at home and discuss them intensively in daily publications. Between these two points the change, though rapid, was evolutionary. And while a number of events—such as the beginning of organized translation in Egypt, the birth of the Arabic press, more direct foreign impact through occupation and presence, and eventually the emergence of independent polities in the region—were of much significance in accelerating this development, none of them constituted a real watershed in the course of language transformation.

Nevertheless it is possible to identify, if very generally, two sub-periods in the process, distinguishable by their different paces of transition. During most of the nineteenth century numerous avenues of familiarization with modern concepts had been opened and explored, among them the option of experimenting with modern political institutions at home. At that time Arabic was changed haphazardly, through the best judgment of individuals from different parts of the region with no organized communication among them. These men were themselves confused by the abundance of novelties with which they undertook to acquaint their audiences. By the last decade of the century this initial phase of adaptation seems to have run its course. The accumulated linguistic efforts of previous decades began to bear fruits, and the language had come to be equipped with the elementary tools required for handling modern needs with reasonable clarity. Arabic continued to develop and alter, but development from now on was more organized and better coordinated.

The nineteenth century, loosely defined, is, then, the time span covered here. It comprises the important, formative stages of the process of linguistic change: initial unawareness; early piecemeal lexical experimentation; intensified but still unorganized innovation; and the beginning of orderly adjustment. The last stage, in an enhanced version, typifies the evolution of political Arabic in the twentieth century.

For the greater part of the nineteenth century the "West" had been Christian Europe. Its civilizational offshoots across the Atlantic were gradually brought to Arab attention, but they were of little interest to the Middle East.[8] The "region" here is limited to the eastern Arab lands (the *mashriq*), which in terms of nineteenth-century intellectual history meant primarily the two centers in Egypt and Lebanon (the many works published by Egyptians and Lebanese abroad have also been studied). Hardly any political literature was printed elsewhere in this part of the Middle East. Arab North Africa has been excluded:[9] a preliminary exploration has suggested that, in terms of both previous background and nineteenth-century development, the political language of the *maghrib* merits a separate study.

One presupposition made when this study was first conceived was proven invalid at an early stage of research. One could reasonably expect to find significant dissimilarities in the usage of political language between Muslim and non–Muslim writers, or between Egyptian intellectuals and their Lebanese counterparts. The assumption would be warranted by the sociopolitical and cultural diversities throughout the region, as well as by the distinctive backgrounds of the various communities, in their previous and contemporary exposure to Western ideas. The preliminary outline for this study envisaged such differentiation; but the evidence failed to substantiate it. There was, no doubt, a great deal of diversity in vocabulary and usage over the region. Yet, as a part of the central phenomenon explored here, such variations were all but marginal. They were a secondary factor, overcast by the formidable challenge that modern ideas posed to all: Christians and Muslims, Egyptians and Syrians, those who knew more and those who understood less, were all subject to the inhibitory barrier of a language inadequate for its new assignments. In this respect, the differences between a translator from Būlāq and a Levantine traveler to London, between a Beiruti journalist writing from Istanbul and a Cairene exile publishing in Paris, bore little significance.

The preparation of this study consisted basically of three stages. In the first, a broad variety of nineteenth-century Arabic writings were searched, including local chronicles, travel accounts, translations of European books, original Arabic political treatises, a large number of newspapers and periodicals, and numerous dictionaries and lexicons (the sources will be surveyed in some detail below). Arabic translations were compared with the original versions whenever identifiable, which rendered these translations particularly valuable. While not all Arabic works of the previous century have survived, those which are extant do seem to offer a solidly representative sample of Arabic writings and language of the period. References to political concepts, institutions and processes both in the region and abroad were examined, and the terms used in them were collected and classified.

In the second stage I sought to trace the etymological and semantic evolution of each term in an attempt to identify their different layers of content. This frequently proved an amorphous task, involving conceptual difficulties quite like those experienced by the Arabs who tried to make out Western ideas. It was necessary to cross the intercultural barrier of concepts and idiom, in order to grasp the full meaning of each term as understood by people of the Middle East at different times prior to and during the nineteenth century. This "semantic archeology" was conducted by examining the language in selected historical and contemporary texts, and by searching many Arabic lexicons and glossaries from various periods.

Finally, the gathered evidence was studied and analyzed. The findings, many of them rather striking, served as pieces with which the gradually changing puzzle of Arab political perceptions was reconstructed.

The approach and methodology adopted here could evidently produce no more than an introductory study on the subject. Tracing a century-long process and a broad array of notions, it seeks primarily to identify the basic contours and main principles of the change, leaving ample room for further exploration. It intends to demonstrate the potential of this type of evidence in contributing to our understanding of the modern Middle East.

Thanks to an ever-expanding scholarly venture in recent years, most of the important Arab writers of the nineteenth century and their works have become well known. These, therefore, need not detain us long, and we may make do with a quick summary identifying the chief sources on which the present study is based.

Until the time when government-sponsored trips kindled in certain travelers an interest in Europe, Arabic accounts of the continent and its affairs were vague and laconic. A few chroniclers during the first three decades of the century included only passing references to Europe in their narratives. In Egypt, the great classical Muslim historian Jabartī related the story of the French occupation of his country from 1798 to 1801 in two books, *Ta'rīkh muddat al-Fransīs* and *Maẓhar al-taqdīs* (the former fused into the latter), which he eventually incorporated into his *ʿAjā'ib al-āthār*. The minute reporting of local affairs—including French activities and behavior in Egypt, on which he often made illuminating observations—stands in striking contrast to his almost complete disregard for the affairs of France itself, let alone other European lands.[10] The same is true of several other Muslim writers of the time, among them ʿAbd Allāh al-Sharqāwī, Muṣṭafā al-Ṣafawī al-Qalʿāwī, Muḥammad Badīr and ʿAbd al-Salām al-Mardīnī.[11]

Contemporary Christian chroniclers, on the other hand, were more open to the message of Europe. They shared little of the Muslim scorn for the foreign "infidels" and were prepared to examine and discuss them in some detail. Among them was the Lebanese Niqūlā Turk, who wrote about the French occupation of Egypt and Syria. Acknowledging that it could be better understood against the background of developments in Europe, he undertook to include in his *Mudhakkirāt* ("memoirs") a description not only of the French Revolution but also of Bonaparte's ascendancy and wars with European powers. His account represents an important step in the process of abandoning the intentional neglect of the lands beyond the Mediterranean, a process which would soon gather momentum. A compatriot, Ḥaydar al-Shihābī, adopted the same approach, as well as many of Turk's ready descriptions. In his history of Lebanon under the princes of his family, Shihābī occasionally interrupted the narrative of local events to recount current developments in Europe. He wrote in a traditional, very detailed style; most details concerning Europe were quite accurate.[12]

A new era dawned when, at the command of Muhammad Ali, Egyptian students began travelling to Europe. Rifāʿa Rāfiʿ al-Ṭahṭāwī, the *imām* of one such mission to France, soon became an eager student of the new civilization. He was perhaps the most precious product of these missions. Upon his return he zealously devoted himself to conveying the knowledge of the modern world to his fellow countrymen. Drawing mainly upon French books, he wrote on the geography, history, politics and sciences, not only of Europe but of other continents as well, with breadth and depth of detail hitherto unseen in Arabic. In 1835 the Egyptian "School of Translation" was founded (later named "School of Languages"). As its director, Ṭahṭāwī produced and supervised the translation of scores of European books on all subjects, displaying perceptiveness rarely matched earlier or in later years. Aware of the deficiencies of his mother tongue in communicating the new ideas, he labored indefatigably to modify, expand and adapt it to this task, leaving behind him a remarkable lexical inheritance.

Only a few of the items translated at the School of Languages dealt with subjects of concern to us here.[13] These were invaluable in acquainting the Middle Eastern reading audience with the rest of the world. For the first time extensive volumes on European history, geography and politics were rendered in Arabic, projecting rays of light on the hitherto dark land. Ṭahṭāwī's pupils and colleagues—ʿAbd Allāh Abū al-Suʿūd, Muṣṭafā Bayyāʿ, Khalīfa Maḥmūd, Muṣṭafā al-Zarābī, to mention but a few—endeavored to translate works by Voltaire, Montesquieu, William Robertson and others, and sometimes produced their own compilations of material from a variety of European sources. Approaching the task with the meticulous care taught to them by their mentor, they made a significant contribution not merely in providing their readers with a bulk of knowledge about other places, but also in adapting Arabic to dealing with the ideas coming from these places. Until the birth of the private Arabic press in the late 1850s, these translations and synthesized texts represented the primary sources of such information.

Before turning to consider the press, a subject that would carry us through to the end of the period, we may glance at another transmitter of modern enlightenment which for a while was of great importance. A few of the unknown number of independent travelers to Europe during the century recorded their impressions and reactions and published them.[14] Among them were Aḥmad Fāris al-Shidyāq, Fransīs Marrāsh, Nakhla Ṣāliḥ, ʿAbd Allāh Fikrī, Aḥmad Zakī, Khalīl Sarkīs and several others. Their reports were not all of the same quality, but some of them provided vital insight into many aspects of modern life and politics. Often incorporating historical, political and other useful background facts in their eyewitness accounts, these travelers were bound to shoulder some of the burden of modernizing the language. Travel books were especially important prior to the rapid spread of newspapers in the last quarter of the century, by which time they contributed substantially to the change in perception and terminology.

More than any single factor in the nineteenth century, the Arabic press brought the word of other civilizations to the Arabic-speaking public. It also played a central role in molding the language into an instrument fit for the task. An Arabic periodical already existed in 1828, the official Egyptian gazette, *al-Waqāʾiʿ al-Miṣriyya,* initiated by Muhammad Ali. More important were to become the privately owned newspapers which began to emerge in the second half of the century. The first of these, *Mirʾat al-aḥwāl,* appeared in Istanbul in 1855 but closed down after a few issues. The next one, *Ḥadīqat al-akhbār,* began in 1858 in Beirut and soon became an influential organ which lasted for more than half a century. Other Arabic papers sprouted in different centers of the region and outside it. After a slow beginning the pace of their emergence accelerated, and before the century was over hundreds of Arabic newspapers and periodicals could be counted, most of them short-lived, others solidly rooted.[15]

From the start these sources provided an unprecedented wealth of information about the foreign lands. Daily and semi-weekly newspapers offered intelligence on current affairs in foreign countries, including reports on political developments, texts of major speeches, translations of international treaties and other documents, and more. The facts were often accompanied by commentaries, at first taken from the foreign press and later produced independently. Periodicals of lesser frequency included fewer reports on current events, offering instead analyses on a broad variety of topics, from history and economics to physics and veterinary medicine. The few publications which survived the perils of infancy established themselves as popular, respectable, constantly improving creations. Among these were *al-Jawā'ib* in Istanbul; *Ḥadīqat al-akhbār, al-Jinān, al-Bashīr* and *Thamarāt al-funūn* in Beirut; *Wādī al-nīl, al-Ahrām, al-Muqtaṭaf, al-Muqaṭṭam* and *al-Mu'ayyad* in Cairo.

The last third of the century witnessed a rapid expansion of Arabic writings in which modern ideas were broadly discussed. The Middle East became a stage for intensified foreign activity, and in 1882 a European power assumed actual control over a central country in the region. Local rulers, seeking to catch up with other governments in the international power struggle, emulated what they considered a mark of success—European political institutions and practices. But while they convened representative assemblies and promulgated constitutions, they also had to fend off pressures for even quicker modernization and liberalization coming from impatient educated men. The press, the primary medium of reports and comments on world affairs, now became a central arena for open debates engaged in by rulers' agents and the intelligentsia. The chief spokesmen of the intellectual elite—Jamāl al-Dīn al-Afghānī, Muḥammad ʿAbduh, Adīb Isḥaq, ʿAbd Allāh Nadīm, Salīm Naqqāsh, Yaʿqūb Ṣannūʿ, Faraḥ Anṭūn—resorted to journalism as a matter of course to voice their thoughts. They did so wherever allowed, moving from Hamidian Syria and Lebanon to Egypt, and from there to Paris and London. Other men of letters, notably Buṭrus al-Bustānī, ʿAlī Mubārak, Nawfal al-Ṭarābulusī and Nakhla Qalfāẓ, produced original works on modern subjects, based on expanding knowledge of Western countries, their history and culture.

An important question, easier to pose than to answer, is who in the Arabic-speaking countries formed the reading audience? How many people were exposed to the writings which introduced new ideas and concepts? One can assume only two things with reasonable assurance: that their number was increasing as the century unfolded, and that, even by the end of the period, they remained a tiny minority. During the early decades of the century the level of literacy was inconsiderable. Thus, whatever was written and published in Arabic at that time was accessible to a precious few. With the advancement of education more people were able to read, but their number remained small relative to the rest of society. We have only a few clues regarding the circulation of certain periodicals of the time, and these can hardly be used to reach a conclusion.[16] According to one estimate, by the end of the century Egyptian newspapers were read by, or read to, some two hundred thousand people.[17] Even if we accept as true this impressive (but somewhat dubious) figure, the number is still small: with a population of some ten million at the turn of the century, it excludes ninety-eight percent of society as uninformed. This may well have been a proportion typical of other parts of the region as well.

In the present study, the men who wrote and those who read their works, however few, are the ones who count. One need hardly emphasize that they belonged to society's most important political and cultural segments. The authors and their audiences were partners to the phenomenon examined here: the communication of new ideas through an inappropriate apparatus, whose limitations were bound to influence the whole process.

1

Religious Communities
and Nation-States

For many centuries Europe was viewed by the Middle East as a vague and unattractive entity beyond the horizon. Trade and diplomatic contacts with European states failed to change the indifference of the largely Muslim society toward that land. This was so even when the crusaders, mighty forces of Christendom, invaded the Muslim heartlands and remained for two centuries; still more after they left. To people of the Middle East, Europe was part of a basically monolithic outside world—the "abode of war," comprising all non-Muslim segments of humanity. Word on the existence of diverse races, peoples and languages in Europe was brought to the Middle East from time to time, by inquisitive Arab travelers and geographers and by occasional foreign visitors, but it seems to have left little impression. Europe remained a remote land of no relevance, rather than a conglomerate of individual entities with diverse traditions. It was known as the "land of the *Ifranj*," a term typical of the Muslim view of the outside world at the time. *Ifranj*, an Arabicization of "Franks," was originally attributed to that particular people as distinct from other European ethnic groups; by the eve of the nineteenth century, however, it had come to denote Christian Europe at large. Individual nations were scarcely considered.[1] This rather simplistic outlook was also indicative of the Muslim basic self-view, that of an indivisible community of believers.

The powerful European intrusion into the Arab lands following the battle of the Pyramids in 1798 did not immediately alter the Middle Eastern view of Europe. Even the astute Jabartī still displayed much of the traditional disregard for European affairs, despite his country's occupation by the French. For him the invaders were, first and foremost, simply "the unbelievers," *al-kuffār*, who "oppressed this great country and spread throughout it like a poison in a healthy body."[2] A compatriot, Sayyid ᶜAlī al-Ṣayrafī al-Rashīdī, wrote a poem—Jabartī deemed it meaningful enough to include it in his chronicle—in which Rashīdī dismissed the invaders as *jumūᶜ shirk*, "a band of idolators."[3] Another contemporary, the chronicler ᶜAbd al-Salām al-Mardīnī, evidenced the same attitude; he referred to the invaders in the traditional way, as *al-kuffār* or *al-mushrikīn*, "the polytheists." He described the "landing of the *kuffār*" in Alexandria; the "battle [of the Pyramids] between the *kuffār*" and the Muslims"; and the subsequent "settlement of the *mushrikīn*" in Egypt.[4] And a fourth writer, Muḥammad Badīr, derided the *kafūr* (a synonymous variation of *kuffār*), who "thought that trickery and deception would yield victory," but were doomed to defeat by the Lord of the Worlds, *rabb al-ᶜalamīn*.[5]

There were, of course, more specific references to the French. That the invasion was part of an intra-European struggle could not escape as lucid an observer as Jabartī, and he identified the contending powers precisely as "the French" and "the English"—*al-Fransīs* and *al-Inklīz*. Just as often, however, he spoke of them collectively, using the terms *al-Ifranj* or *al-Firanj*—people from the wilderness in the north. The rest of Europe's nations he ignored almost completely. Other writers of the time also used the term *Ifranj* frequently as a name for the heathens coming from across the sea—a little-known and uninteresting lot. The Franks (*Firanj*) are so named "after the city of *Ifransiya*, which is one of their cities, also known as *Ifranja*," Muṣṭafā Qalᶜāwī noted with evident disdain; that city "is the seat of the king of the *Fransīs*."[6]

That the European challenge to the Middle East was more than just another offensive made by some unbelievers against Islam was, however, a fact that could not be ignored for long.

The political leadership and intellectual elite of the Muslim society were soon to realize that Europe, in contrast to its traditional image as "barbarians," now posed at once a powerful threat and an attractive model for emulation. Ignorance and disdain soon gave way to careful inspection of the "land of the Franks." The scene unfolding before their amazed eyes was complex and constantly changing. The political composition of nineteenth-century Europe was only faintly like that of its past. In ever-increasing parts of the continent the spread of secularism was paralleled by the advancing principles of nationalism. Loyalties were redefined: rather than retaining faithful attachment to religion and its institutions, or to monarchs and their dynasties, communities began to identify themselves by ethnic origin, language, history and sentiment. Some of these entities, such as Great Britain, France, Spain, and Sweden, had already become consolidated nation-states long before the nineteenth century. Elsewhere in Europe secularism and nationalism were progressing, generating agitation, revolution and change. During the course of the century new nation-states came into being, including Greece, Italy and Germany. The map of the continent was in flux. An observer of Europe's intricate changes needed a keen eye and, to articulate them, appropriate conceptual and lexical tools.

The initial view of Europe's geopolitical division was rather dim. The Lebanese chronicler Niqūlā Turk—the first to have offered a fairly detailed (if somewhat confused) account in Arabic of the French Revolution and of subsequent developments—mentioned different countries in Europe, which he identified as *bilād,* a generic term for a territory of any type and size, broadly understood as a land. He thus spoke of *bilād Īṭāliyā* (Italy), *bilād al-Nimsā* (Austria), *bilād al-Inklīz* ("land of the English," England), and so forth. At the same time, however, he made frequent references to *al-bilād al-Ifranjiyya,* an ambiguous "Frankish country" whose division appeared to be rather unclear.[7] Even as lucid an observer as shaykh Rifāᶜa al-Ṭahṭāwī—who later would play a leading role in acquainting the Arabs with the rest of the world—found it hard, at first, to determine the exact nature of its components. In his early works, and in other writings of the time, Europe still appeared as a single *bilād.* An individual country such as England or Switzerland was treated as a "region" (*iqlīm*) or "province" (*wilāya*) of *al-bilād al-Ifranjiyya.*[8]

But knowledge drawn from French geography books soon

rendered such terminology unsatisfactory. Europe's political map became somewhat more fixed, and by the early 1840s Ṭahṭāwī and his pupils were careful to use the term *bilād* for single European states rather than for the continent as a whole. Familiarization with the peoples and nations of Europe likewise revealed an aggregate of diverse societies, and the undiscriminating name *Ifranj* was gradually abandoned, losing ground to four interchangeable appellations: *milla; umma; ṭā'ifa;* and *qabīla.* The first two of these were largely synonymous. *Milla,* pl. *milal,* is a word at least as old as the Qur'ān, in which it appears several times with the meaning of religion, referring to both Islam and other creeds. The distinction between a faith and its body of followers being somewhat vague, *milla* came to imply a community of believers as well. With the definite article and no qualifications, *al-milla* meant Islam, the faith and the community—the antithesis of *al-dhimma.*[9] For example, in compound honorifics for Muslim sovereigns and high officials, the term was often used in this sense: common titles such as *tāj al-milla* and *ᶜizz al-milla* were fully interchangeable with designations such as *tāj al-Islām* and *ᶜizz al-Islām.*[10] The term was also applied to other religions. The world, said the twelfth-century historian Shahrastānī, is composed of people of two types: *ahl al-diyānāt wal-milal* (people of religious faiths and religious communities), who include the Zoroastrians, the Jews, the Christians and the Muslims; and *ahl al-ahwā' wal-ārā'* (people of whims and opinions), such as the philosophers and worshippers of stars and idols. Other ways of categorizing peoples are also possible, Shahrastānī suggested, but the one determined by faith is the most valid.[11] It certainly was the most employed, as evidenced, again, by Mamluk correspondence with different European heads of state, in which the former often addressed the latter as "head of the Christian *milla,*" making no distinction between Christendom and individual Christian states.[12]

In the Ottoman Empire, the word—in its Turkish form of *millet*—was used with a similar implication. The Empire's Muslim population, regardless of its ethnic and linguistic diversity, was legally treated as the Muslim *millet.* The term was likewise applied to the Empire's tolerated non-Muslim communities, which by the nineteenth century were organized as semi-autonomous units represented by religious leaders. These included the major religious minorities—the Orthodox Christians, the Armenians and the Jews—with smaller denominations attached administratively to one or another of them.[13] In a less formal manner the term was broadly used to indicate religious groups of all designations; for example, the 1861 *Réglement Organique* of Mount Lebanon provided for a "population census [to be conducted] village by village and *milla* by *milla*," namely, a count by localities and by religious communities.[14] The philosophy of classifying social and political entities by their religious affiliations similarly underlay the Empire's dealings with foreign governments, just as was the case with the Mamluk state. Treating a European sovereign as "leader of the Christian *millet*" was a centuries-old practice that continued well into the nineteenth century.[15] With this classical meaning, reinforced by Ottoman usage, *milla* remained a functioning Arabic term throughout the nineteenth century.

Early nineteenth-century Arab writers who acquired some knowledge about Europe, but who failed to detect the criteria by which its society was divided, continued to designate both the continent and individual nations as *milla*. Their accounts depict a Europe inhabited by the Christian *milla*, the Pope being "head of their religious community (*kabīr millatihim* or *kabīr al-milla al-ʿĪsawiyya*), and consisting of entities like *al-milla al-Faransāwiyya, al-milla al-Inklīziyya* and *al-milla al-Musqūbiyya*. Thus, praising the esprit de corps displayed by the French during the invasion of Egypt, Jabartī noted that their soldiers fought "as if they were following the tradition of the community [of believers] in early Islam, considering themselves fighters in a holy war and . . .regarding anyone fleeing [from the battlefield] as a traitor to his *milla* and an apostate to his faith [*dīn*]."[16] Such was also the case with other nations, in medieval and contemporary times alike: fifth-century Italian city-states, medieval Poland, Louis XIV's France, the postrevolutionary French *nation*—they were all, invariably, *milal*. Writing about the end of the Napoleonic era, shaykh Ṭahṭāwī commented that "the Bourbons re-occupied the throne, the French *milla*'s reluctance notwithstanding." Then a new French constitution was promulgated in 1814, according to which it was the king's responsibility "to declare war and sign peace . . .between his *milla* and other ones." *Milla*, in both instances, was unmistakably the French "nation." But, somewhat confusingly, Ṭahṭāwī also identified the religion of the state as "the Roman-Catholic *milla*." His description, in the same text, of the 1830 French conquest of Algeria as the "mighty victory" won by "the Christian *milla* . . .over the Islamic *milla*" added to the confusion.[17] The ambiguity was typical. The people of Denmark "profess the Protestant *milla*" (*wa-dīnuhum al-milla al-Bru-tistāniyya*), Ṭahṭāwī explains elsewhere; but in the same opus he goes on to describe Norway's assembly (the *Storting*) as the "assembly of *milla* representatives" (*majlis wukalā' al-milla*).[18] In this last example, a new meaning was attached to the term, further complicating the picture. More than designating a religious community, *milla* here indicated a political community enjoying certain political rights—an idea which, as we shall see later on, was incompatible with the traditional concept of *milla*. This new application of the term appeared frequently in the writings of Ṭahṭāwī's colleagues in a variety of similar combinations. Parliaments and representatives were often said to serve as a mouthpiece of the *milla*. Thus, *les assemblées de la nation* in medieval Europe were rendered as *jamᶜiyyāt al-milla;* leaders of the French Revolution became *wukalā'* (representatives of) *al-milla;* the contemporary British parliament was the "assembly of *milla* representatives" (*majlis mabᶜūthī al-milla*); and the same name was applied to the French *Chambre des Députés*.[19] In the same vein, in seventeenth-century Russia it was *la nation elle même* which condemned a prince to death, according to Voltaire, but the Arabic translator ascribed the action to *al-milla al-Musqūbiyya*. Arabic texts from the first half of the century abound in examples of this.[20]

In portraying European peoples as French, English or Russian *milal*, Arab writers depicted societies based on the principles of communal division most intelligible to them and to their readers—those which, determined by religious faith, existed in the Islamic world and in the Ottoman Empire. That all these *milal* formed a part of one Christian *milla* was a perplexing feature of the scene. That some of them were political entities with sovereign characteristics was another source of puzzlement. The use of *milla* with such a variety of meanings attested to the Arab writers' uncertainty concerning the nature of European national entities during the early part of the century.

The word *umma*, pl. *umam,* carried much the same import as *milla*. Arabic seems to have borrowed this term from ancient Hebrew (*umma*) or Aramaic (*ummatā*).[21] *Umma* appears in the Qur'ān numerous times, usually with reference to "ethnical, linguistic or religious bodies of people who are the objects of the divine plan of salvation."[22] Its meaning fluctuated during the stage in which the Prophet endeavored to organize his community of believers, its implication in his own usage being often vague and indefinite. Later, as Islam developed into the dominant factor that shaped the believers' view of the world, the term acquired a clear significance. *Al-umma,* like *al-milla,* meant the Muslim community, united by one faith and sharing one mission. It was the ultimate object of its members' loyalty, a polity—real, and later visionary, as well as a culture. Among classical honorifics attributed to Muslim men of circumstance, one often finds titles such as *awḥad al-umma, dhukhr al-umma, rukn al-umma* and so on, indicating prominence within the only community that counted.[23] *Umma* was also used to designate other nations, likewise defined by their belief, or rather unbelief: non-Muslim peoples of any creed were regarded as *umam al-kufr,* "the infidel communities";[24] and Christians were singled out as *al-umma al-Naṣraniyya* or *al-umma al-ᶜĪsawiyya, umma* often being substituted by *milla* or *dīn* (religion).[25] In this sense *umma* has remained in use to the present day.

There was another, looser meaning to the term. *Umma* was understood more broadly as a group of people at large.[26] In medieval geographical, philosophical and political writings, the word indicated individual non-Muslim peoples, distinguishable by their ethnic origin or language. Masᶜūdī, for example, spoke of such *umam* as *al-Ifranj wal-Ṣaqāliba wal-Nukubard* (the Franks, Slavs and Lombards). Ṣāᶜid al-Andalusī applied the term to peoples like *al-Rūs, al-Yūnāniyyūn, al-Rūm,* and *al-Ṣīn* (the Russians, Greeks, Romans and Chinese). Qalqashandī used it for *al-Jalāliqa* (the Galicians) and *al-Burjān* (the Burgundians?). And Ibn Khaldūn discussed *umam al-Ṣaqāliba wal-Ifranj wal-Turk.*[27] With such a meaning *umma* was occasionally applied even to peoples within the Islamic community, such as the Arabs and Persians.[28] These instances, however, were rare and of small consequence; in the minds of most Muslims *umma* was readily associated with the better known idea of a pious community. The centrality of this last concept must have blurred, to a great extent, the distinction between the two meanings of the term, the specific and the generic; many a Muslim would probably have regarded all *umam* as basically equivalent to his own.

When Bonaparte first ventured to approach the Egyptians,

he addressed them in his famous introductory proclamation as *al-umma al-Miṣriyya*.[29] The "Egyptian *umma*" was, of course, an unwitting concoction of the French oriental experts, who superimposed their newly refurbished concept of nation upon a society accustomed to thinking in quite different terms. The response came in the form of an Ottoman *fermān,* warning the believers about a diabolic French scheme and making clear who was what, in Muslim eyes: Sultan Selīm III stated that the French were plotting to "ruin *ummat al-Muslimīn* which is unified in the unity of *rabb al-ᶜalamīn,*" the Lord of the worlds; the Sultan, "defender of the faith," signed a treaty with Britain ("between the *Inklīz* and *Islām*") to destroy the French *umma*. "Once we have defeated them," the Sultan reassured his subjects, "we shall destroy their Kaᶜba and Temple [*kaᶜbatihim wa-bayt maqdisihim*] and each and every one of their mosques [*jamīᶜ jawāmiᶜihim wa-masājidihim*], then we shall kill them all."[30] The Middle Eastern counterpart of the French *nation* was thus unmistakably established as the *umma* of Muhammad. The notion was clear, and the Sultan knew exactly what kind of emotions he could expect it to evoke.

When writers of Arabic in later years employed the term in a European context, they had to part with this traditional concept. They revived the other, less common meaning of the term and began to use it with growing frequency. Undertaking to discuss foreign issues in some detail, they made frequent references to such peoples and nations as the Prussians (*ummat Brūsiya*), the Greeks (*ummat al-Yūnān*), the Muscovites (*ummat al-Musqū*), and the Teutons (*al-umma al-Tawtūniyya*).[31] At first they intended the term in its looser sense—while such communities were apparently different from the Islamic *umma,* their precise nature was not yet very obvious. The dissimilarities between Sultan Selīm's *ummat al-Muslimīn* and the European *umam* remained to be explored. Later on the foreign notion grew clearer, and the word used to express it became more specific and precise.

As we shall see, *umma* would eventually emerge as the most common Arabic name for a modern "nation," to the exclusion of other designations. However, this would happen only close to the end of the century. Meanwhile, *umma* had to compete with other expressions. A third term used for the same purpose was *ṭā'ifa,* pl. *ṭawā'if.* It stood for a notion much looser than either *milla* or *umma.* Initially *ṭā'ifa* meant a detached portion of a whole and, by extension, a group of people forming a part of a greater body of people. Its size could vary broadly, "from one to one thousand men" according to one classical dictionary, but often to many more.[32] The word appeared frequently in the Qur'ān and Ḥadīth with reference to groups of different size and character, and was used in later times to describe a wide variety of communities. For example, it was applied collectively to the territorial-political fragments of eleventh-century Muslim Spain, whose petty rulers came to be known, somewhat derisively, as *mulūk al-ṭawā'if.*[33] In Ottoman Egypt the term was used to denote professional guilds, town quarters, Sufi orders and religious or ethnic minorities.[34] And in Lebanon it served to designate the various religious communities. Thus, in 1840 the Maronite patriarch called upon members of his community to join "the rest of the *ṭawā'if,*" including "the Druzes . . . the Mutawallīs and . . . the other Christian *ṭawā'if*" in a revolt against the government of the country.[35] *Ṭā'ifa* was also applied to peoples in Europe, at times designated collectively as "the Christian community"—*al-ṭā'ifa al-ᶜĪsawiyya* or *al-ṭā'ifa al-Ṣalībiyya;*[36] and at other times identified by their proper names—*ṭā'ifat al-Banādiqa* (the Venetians), *ṭā'ifat al-Bulghār* (the Bulgarians), and the like.[37] In Mamluk correspondence with European sovereigns such expressions figure commonly. Likewise, the Ottomans used the term (Turkish *ṭā'ife*) in their international treaties and administrative documents, as well as in describing ethnic, religious, tribal and occupational groups of Ottoman subjects.[38] The word could also signify many other things. For example, in early nineteenth-century writings about the West, it was flexibly applied to an ethnic group, a local community, a judicial assembly, a religious school, a political party, a social caste, a military unit, and an order of knights.[39] In principle, therefore, *ṭā'ifa* could be used for any type of collective entity.

As a versatile expression, *ṭā'ifa* offered a convenient choice of name for groups whose nature was inadequately clear. It was used extensively throughout the early decades of the period to designate modern European peoples—*ṭā'ifat al-Ifranj* or *ṭawā'if al-Ifranj*—in general and, more specifically, individual nations, such as *ṭā'ifat al-Fransīs* (the French) and *ṭā'ifat al-Rūm* (the Romans, or Byzantines). According to Muṣṭafā al-Qalᶜāwī, the somewhat mysterious "city of *Ifransiya* . . . [or] *Ifranja*" lent its name to *ṭā'ifat al-Firanj.* And a report in an early issue of *al-Waqā'iʿ al-Miṣriyya* announced the arrival to Alexandria of an Austrian ship "carrying one man from *ṭā'ifat al-Ifranj* and eight Jewish men"—a convenient formula in which the *Ifranj* figured as a singular entity.[40] The term was also applied to pre-modern peoples such as the Vandals (*ṭā'ifat al-Wandāl*), the Visigoths (*ṭā'ifat al-Wizighūṭ*), the Teutons (*al-ṭā'ifa al-Tūnīqiyya*), and the Anglo-Saxons (*ṭā'ifat al-Anklūsaksūn*).[41] Its application seems to have been deliberately loose; there are, for instance, simultaneous references to "a *ṭā'ifa* from among the English," "the English *ṭā'ifa*," and "the English *ṭawā'if*"[42]—a rather perplexing variety which could barely help in clarifying who or what "the English" were. This was likewise the case with the French, designated as *al-ṭā'ifa al-Faransāwiyya*, but composed of such ethnic units as the "Gothic and Norman *ṭawā'if*" and of such social *ṭawā'if* as the clergy, the nobility and the common people.[43] The concurrent description of the Protestants, Lutherans and Calvinists as *ṭawā'if*[44] served to further stall the making of delineated and fixed distinctions.

The last, and most striking, choice of term used to help chart the European ethnopolitical map was *qabīla*, pl. *qabā'il*. The initial meaning of *qabīla* was a group of people related to one another through descent (real or invented) from a common ancestor. In pre-Islamic times the word denoted a tribe, and it appeared in the Qur'ān with this meaning,[45] which has always been the most common application. More specifically, *qabīla* indicated a category in a tribal hierarchical structure, second in size to *shaʿb*, the largest unit.[46] The word was also used, although far less often than with its Qur'ānic meaning, in a broader manner, signifying any group of people—a family, a lineage, a generation, a race.

It was apparently this last flexibility of *qabīla* that made it attractive to Arab writers seeking to describe foreign peoples. During the first half of the century, and in the early years of the second, the word was often applied to European communities of different designations, among them modern nation-states. *Qabīla* could refer to a political faction in ancient Athens, the Basques in Spain, the inhabitants of a Swiss canton, the seventeenth-century colony of Pennsylvania, or the post-revolutionary French nation. In the 1858 Paris international fair, for example, one could see—according to a Lebanese eyewitness—"various *qabā'il* of people," including Americans, Englishmen, Italians, Turks, Arabs and others. Another Lebanese, traveling in Belgium, was fascinated by the country's history as a traditional "battleground" in "wars between the *qabā'il* of Europe in different eras."[47]

Around the middle of the century this term was highly popular. One newspaper spoke of a "Europe unified, despite disagreement among some of its *qabā'il*". The same paper described the 1830 Paris revolt as an "uprising of the *qabīla* against the king", depicted Napoleon III as "the only man capable of winning the love of the French *qabīla*", and referred to the *London Times* as "the English people's mouthpiece"—*lisān ḥāl al-qabīla*. Somewhat inconsistently, it also described Austria as "composed of a number of *qabā'il* with various languages and faiths." Other writers used the term occasionally until the last quarter of the century.[48]

There was another meaning to the word, which seems to have been an innovation by Ṭahṭāwī. He, and later his pupils at the Egyptian School of Languages, used it to refer to emigrants who settle in another country and, by extension, to immigrant colonies. *Qabā'il*, Ṭahṭāwī explained, is a name for a "group of people, men and women, who are sent to a certain place or chose to go and settle there, and who are usually led by a *shaykh* as they go." The word may have been selected to express this idea, for *qabīla* echoed the movement of nomadic tribes in the Middle East. Ṭahṭāwī and his colleagues commonly applied the name to the originally European inhabitants of the New World—*qabā'il al-Ifranj fī Amirīka*. The "United States of America" was accordingly rendered as *al-qabā'il al-mujtamīʿa al-Amirīqiyya* (literally: "the American assembled tribes"); and its war of independence as a "revolt of the large English *qabā'il* . . . against [the government of] their original homeland."[49] Immigrant communities elsewhere—in Canada, Brazil, Peru—were designated by the same name, as were also the French settlers in Algeria in the early years of occupation.[50]

During the decades preceding the birth of the private Arabic press, *milla, umma, ṭā'ifa* and *qabīla* were used alternately with reference to peoples of the outside world, producing a blurred picture of them. An author would often resort to two or three of these words to describe one foreign nation, sometimes in the very same text. In Ṭahṭāwī's *Takhlīṣ al-ibrīz*, for example, the French are at once a *milla*, an *umma* and a *ṭā'ifa*. The first two terms, in singular form, are also used with reference to Christendom; the third is used to denote various groups, classes, factions and parties in France.[51] The Teutons he identifies as "a *ṭā'ifa* of Christians," while his colleague, Muṣṭafā al-Zarābī, considers them as both *umma* and *milla*.[52] European nations, some of them striving to establish or consolidate their own states along newly formulated guidelines, were thus described by a mixture of names that were either too loose or altogether irrelevant. While Europe ceased to be seen by the Middle East as an indivisible *bilād al-Ifranj*, the nature of its constituent parts remained a subject of no more than approximative treatment. At that stage, the concept of secular nationalism was still alien to the Middle East, and none of these terms nor any other existing Arabic expression could properly denote it. A wide gap was thus inevitable between the European idea and its best possible Arabic rendition.

With the inauguration of the Arabic press and the subsequent spread of information throughout the Middle East, the picture began to clarify. A mark of this change was the gradual disappearance of *milla*, *ṭā'ifa* and *qabīla* from writings about the outside world. By the last quarter of the century their occurrence in such texts was rare. Instead, *umma* emerged as the accepted Arabic equivalent of "nation" in its modern sense. It became a key word in accounts on international relations, on the drive for national unity throughout much of Europe, and on the domestic politics of foreign countries. It was used with increasing frequency in association with political sovereignty, typically in reference to national assemblies—*majlis al-umma*—in Europe and the United States.[53]

This growing nontraditional use of the term led intellectuals to seek a redefinition of *umma*. And thus, in 1881, the Azharite shaykh Ḥusayn al-Marṣafī, in his curious *Risālat al-kalim al-thamān* ("Tract on Eight Words,") typically defined *umma* as an entity determinable not merely by faith but also by territory and language. An *umma* based on the latter, he suggested, was the one most worthy of the name, due to the unifying quality of a common tongue.[54] To what extent Marṣafī's statement reflected exposure to modern ideas it is hard to tell; this and other explanations in his book do seem to have been devised, at least to some extent, under foreign influence.

The growing systematic use of *umma* in reference to foreign matters, and the concomitant search for a new definition, would lead to its semantic modification: *umma,* hitherto a community of believers, or simply a community, would gradually acquire the modern meaning of nation-state. The process, however, would not be quite smooth. Acquaintance with Western secular nationalism by a few Arab thinkers at first could not have but a marginal impact on Middle Eastern traditional concepts. The old idea of a Muslim *ummat al-mu'minīn* remained very much alive until well into the twentieth century. It was this very brand of *umma* which men like al-Afghānī and Muḥammad ᶜAbduh, chief exponents of local sentiments during the last quarter of the nineteenth century, were striving to vivify—the one which "Allāh had raised from insignificance and exalted to the highest of ranks," as they zealously preached in the pages of *al-ᶜUrwa al-wuthqā*.[55] In the same paper they spoke with equal frequency (but less zeal) of the English *umma*, the French *umma*, and the other "*umam* of Europe,"[56] a juxtaposition common enough in the literature of the period to have had a seriously confusing effect on the Arab discussion of modern nations, and to have delayed the semantic transformation of the term. This phenomenon may well have hampered the assimilation of the idea itself in the region.

The European idea of nationhood determined by nonreligious criteria became a subject of extensive debate in Arabic political literature around the turn of the century, by men like Muṣṭafā Kāmil, Aḥmad Luṭfī al-Sayyid, ᶜAbd al-Raḥmān al-Kawākibī and Najīb ᶜAzūrī. As the idea gained currency, the term *umma* with its new meaning attained spreading acceptance in the region. It came to indicate the type of community that should, in the view of secularists, supplant the traditional *ummat al-mu'minīn* or, in the view of others, should become a legitimate unit within the eternal community of believers.

2

Sultans, Kings, Emperors

To a subject of the nineteenth-century Ottoman Empire, the notion of government was simple. The Muslim *umma* provided its members not merely with a social and spiritual shelter; it also provided them, as well as its protégés, with a prescribed framework of relationship between the government and the governed. The ruler was to rule and be obeyed; even if a tyrant, he was still to be patiently tolerated, provided he maintained the basic Islamic norms. This was an article of faith, sanctioned by Muslim jurists at least since Māwardī in the eleventh century. The system had functioned successfully, and the validity of its underlying concepts had seldom been contested. The Ottoman sultans, powerful monarchs whose suzerainty was recognized throughout much of the Middle East, enjoyed the unquestioning submission of their subjects. Lesser men of power succeeded from time to time in seizing control over limited territories within the empire. Such princes similarly commanded the obedience of the people in their domains, while themselves continuing to acknowledge the primacy of the House of ʿUthmān. Government was in principle embodied in one man and expressed in one word: *sulṭān*.

This relatively uncomplicated order bore little resemblance to its contemporary Western counterparts. Nineteenth-century Europe and America presented various types of government.

29

Some were republics, a species remotely akin to a system once known but long forgotten in the Middle East. (Republics are discussed separately in chapter 7.) Some were monarchies, but these hereditary governments were not all alike; they differed broadly in their international standing and in their authority at home. The titles of their heads were equally varied. The great majority designated themselves as "kings," sovereigns of kingdoms as large as Great Britain or as tiny as Württemberg. Some actually reigned rather than ruled, sharing power with different political institutions. Other monarchs, claiming a superior status, bore imperial titles. Such were, throughout the century, the Russian czars of the Romanov line and the Austrian kaisers of the Hapsburg dynasty, direct successors of the Holy Roman Emperor. Such, also, were other rulers during shorter periods, in Britain, France, Germany, and Brazil. Imperial titles were regarded as more dignified than royal ones, as they were taken to imply authority and grandeur of the kind once enjoyed by the ancient Roman emperors.[1] Certain sovereigns assumed combined designations, such as Napoleon's "Emperor of the French and King of Italy," or Victoria's "Queen of the United Kingdom of Great Britain and Ireland and Empress of India." Smaller entities, mostly in central and southern Europe, were headed by sovereigns bearing other titles: princes, grand dukes, dukes. Finally, there was the papal state, whose head stood in a category by itself, professing both temporal and spiritual authority. This multicolored assortment of heads of state was a constantly rotating one: patterns of rule were changing, states were forming and dissolving, titles were assumed and abandoned.

For nineteenth-century Arabs hitherto ignorant of European affairs, becoming conversant with the peculiarities of each government was an arduous task. Tracing the identities of the various sovereigns and their diverse titles was probably its simplest part, for the Arabs could benefit, to a considerable extent, from the Ottomans' better acquaintance with Western rulers. But even such a rudimentary grasp was not attained until mid-century. In earlier decades, Arab observers recorded their impressions in a traditional and rather confused manner, projecting Islamic concepts of rulership on contemporary Western politics.

In describing European sovereigns, Arab writers at first confined themselves mainly to two names taken from their traditional vocabulary: *sulṭān* and *malik*. The first of these, *sulṭān,* pl.

salāṭīn, was initially an abstract noun meaning power or authority. Often, though not always, it denoted governmental authority. The term appeared in this sense in the Qur'ān, Ḥadīth and later sources, and has maintained its abstract meaning to the present day. At a certain stage, apparently during the eighth century, *sulṭān* became a designation for men exercising the power of government. At first it was a loose and nonspecific title by which various power-holders, including even petty chiefs, decorated themselves. In the eleventh century the Seljuks assumed it as a regnal appellation. Thereafter it was adopted by other rulers, among them the Khwarazmshahs, the Mamluks of Egypt and the Ottomans. Through its usage over the years, the word acquired a connotation of political authority and military might—as distinct from the religious prestige associated with the title *khalīfa,* Caliph, conceived as Allāh's representative on earth.

For a long time a distinction existed between the terms *sulṭān* and *khalīfa,* which represented two separate functions embodied in two (or more) persons. Centuries of practice reinforced the distinction. Even when the Ottomans, by their late eighteenth-century claim, unified the functions signified by the two terms in one man, some semantic difference remained. The Ottoman monarch now professed a twofold authority: religious, in his capacity as *khalīfa,* and political, as the sovereign sultan of the empire. The title *sulṭān* was not reserved for the heads of the empire alone—princes in Istanbul, and even princesses, often bore it as well (although in these cases the title came after and not before the name). There were also Islamic rulers in Morocco and southern Arabia who simultaneously called themselves *sulṭān* and who were recognized as such by their subjects, and sometimes by others.[2]

By the onset of the nineteenth century, the political title *sulṭān* carried both a generic and a specific meaning. It served, broadly, as a name for rulers of any type, sovereign or not, with much authority or little. When used as such, it was normally qualified by an indication of territory or kingdom. Combined with a personal name, it formed a similarly loose honorific applicable to prominent government officials. In the more specific sense, *sulṭān* was understood as indicating a definite Muslim sovereign, the ruler of one's own province or country—most often the head of the Ottoman Empire. Talking about *al-Sulṭān* in the definite form, one could normally dispense with further clarifications. As was commonly the case with equivocal terms, confusion between the two meanings of the word was bound to occur occasionally; the name *sulṭān,* even while applied generically to a less familiar potentate, would readily bring to mind the best-known ruler bearing that title. Such fluidity in the term's use, seldom posing a problem in earlier times, was liable to create difficulties when non-Muslim sovereigns were first discussed in Arabic in the nineteenth century.

The other term, *malik,* pl. *mulūk,* stemmed from the old semitic root m-l-k, which implied property and, by extension, government. It appears in the Qur'ān both as a title for Allāh, the Heavenly King, and as a designation for certain rulers of non-Muslim peoples. Carrying the latter, earthly implication, the word had borne a derogatory connotation since an early stage in Islamic history, indicating the temporal, unholy facet of government.[3] It represented an antithesis to *khalīfa* and *imām,* which signified piety and righteousness. The Umayyads, to cite a notorious example, were named *mulūk* and their government *mulk* by their opponents, who thus expressed disdain for their worldly-minded government. Considered a term of abuse, *malik* was not officially assumed by Muslim rulers until the early tenth century. At that time the Buwayhids, new sovereigns of the empire, ventured to revive the Sasanian tradition of regnal titles, and included *malik* in their list of designations. They were followed by the Samanids, then by the Seljuks and other dynasties.

The multitude of rulers identifying themselves as *mulūk* gradually rendered the name less majestic again, and it came to imply limited sway over one kingdom among many and subjugation to a supreme suzerain. Consequently, it disappeared from usage in later times; by the heyday of Ottoman power, the name retained little of its former glory and was seldom used. By the nineteenth century, no ruler in the Middle East would choose to be so designated.[4]

Throughout the history of Islam *malik* also served disparagingly as a title for non-Muslim chiefs of all types. There was more than a grain of disdain in the common expression *mulūk al-kufr* or *mulūk al-kuffār*—"kings of unbelief" or "kings of unbelievers," collectively applied to foreign sovereigns.[5] The name was used to designate the "Frankish rulers," *mulūk al-Ifranj,* in general, as well as individual kings such as *malik al-Ṣaqāliba, malik al-Ṣīn* and *malik al-Ḥabasha* (kings of the Slavs, China and

Ethiopia). Such terms were tinged with unmistakable negative undertones, as they emphasized the limits of the ruler's domain, thereby cutting down his prestige. (In contrast, monarchs in the region usually professed sovereignty "of Islam" or "of the Muslims.") The use of *malik* to indicate foreign kings always indicated an inferior kind of power; the word experienced none of the vicissitudes that typified its use in Muslim contexts.

Writers of Arabic during the first three or four decades of the nineteenth century found *malik* and *sulṭān* satisfactory names for the whole range of European rulers. The use of the former for such purposes represented a continuation of past practice; the latter, being flexible, seemed just as fit. The two were used synonymously for all sovereigns regardless of status and title. At that stage the picture of European monarchies was still too vague for a more precise identification.

Thus, *sulṭān* served to designate emperors, including the Russian czar, *sulṭān al-Muskūbiyya;* the Austrian kaiser, *sulṭān al-Nimsā;* and Napoleon I, *sulṭān Faransā*. The 1805 battle of Austerlitz, known as the "battle of the three emperors," accordingly became *wāqiʿat al-salāṭīn al-thalātha.*[6] *Sulṭān* was also used as a title for kings, in pre- and post-revolutionary France, in Britain, Spain, Sardinia, Bavaria and elsewhere. Jabartī, for example, relates that the French people established a new type of regime after having "killed their *sulṭān*"; Niqūlā Turk discusses the historical French-Egyptian enmity, which had persisted "since the times of *al-sulṭān al-ẓāhir* Baybars and the French *sulṭān* Louis"; and Shihābī reports that, in view of the French threat, "the English *sulṭān* signed a treaty with the [Ottoman] *sulṭān* Selīm."[7] The title was collectively applied to the heads of eleven different political entities in Italy—"the Italian states [*mamālik*], ruled by eleven *sulṭāns*"—comprising, in reality, republics, kingdoms, dukedoms and the papal state.[8] The Pope himself, usually called *al-bābā* (an Arabicization of *papa*), was accordingly described as "the *sulṭān* of Rome," an allusion to his temporal sovereignty over that state.[9]

An Arab account of Bonaparte's army further expands the title's range of reference. In the French military, ʿAbd al-Salām al-Mardīnī expounds, "every ten [men] have someone [in command] whom they call *ser ʿasker* ("supreme commander"); [at the head of] every hundred [men] there is someone whom they call *sulṭān* . . . and Bonaparte is the *sulṭān* of them all."[10] By the same token, Kléber, Bonaparte's surrogate *général en chef* in Cairo, was described as "the French *sulṭān* in Egypt."[11] Adjectival derivatives from the word were likewise widespread: Bonaparte's "imperial treasury" was rendered as *al-khazīna al-sulṭāniyya;* the Bourbon "royal family" was *al-ʿā'ila al-sulṭāniyya;* and the *Palais Royal* in Paris was *al-sarāya al-sulṭāniyya.*[12] "Imperial" and "royal" were thus treated, loosely, as indistinguishable pieces of a rather colorless jigsaw puzzle.

This monolithic view was likewise reflected in the application of the title *malik* to foreign rulers. The same variety of European leaders described as *salāṭīn* were equally often entitled *mulūk.* The French Revolution, according to Arab chroniclers, put an end to the reign of "*al-sulṭān* Louis [XVI], the *malik* of France." Subsequently, an army was sent to Egypt under the command of "Abū Nābārta [Bonaparte], *malik* of the Franks," also described as *malik al-juyūsh Būnābārta* ("Bonaparte, king of the armies"). When Pope Pius VII, a few years later, consecrated Napoleon as emperor, the latter was reported to have been "crowned as *malik.*" And when this last event was followed by his assumption of the title "Emperor of the French and King of Italy," the chroniclers spoke of "*al-sulṭān* Būnābārta . . . [becoming] *malik* over the *mamālik* of Italy and over the *mamlaka* of France." In like manner, Peter the Great was referred to as *Buṭrus al-akbar malik al-Mūsqū,* but also as *sulṭān al-Rūsiyā.*[13] The Russian czar, the Austrian kaiser, and the various kings of Europe were all designated by this traditional name, as was the Pope, who was described as *malik Rūma.*[14]

Europe, then, was presented by early nineteenth-century Arab writers as a realm divided among a set of uniform monarchs. In the texts of these early years they bore titles whose meanings were loose and which expressed generically the idea of "a chief," or which connoted specific but irrelevant powers and statuses. The result was an ambiguous portrait of foreign governments.

Along with *sulṭān* and *malik,* Arab writers of this period sometimes introduced into their texts two other regnal titles of occidental origin: *qayṣar* and *imbarāṭūr.* The former, an Arabic version of the Latin *caesar,* was long a recognized item in the terminology designed to discuss foreign monarchs. The word had entered Arabic before the advent of Islam, apparently via Greek or Aramaic, and was regularly used by Arab historians and geographers with reference to Roman and Byzantine emperors. The convenient morphology of *qayṣar*—its compactness and incidental conformity with a common Arabic noun-pattern—facilitated its smooth assimilation into the language. Its plural form, *qayā-ṣira*, was likewise devised according to an existing pattern.[15] The word became an integral part of the Arabic lexicon. By the beginning of the nineteenth century it was familiar enough to serve in interpreting a less-known word—*imbarāṭūr*.

Imbarāṭūr had a particularly interesting history. It entered the Arabic language once in early times, persisted for a while and disappeared, then reappeared in the nineteenth century. Originally a Latin word, *imperator* (from *imperare*, to command, which came to mean to be head of an empire), it was adopted by Arabic during the Crusades, both directly from Latin, in the form *inbarāṭūr* or *imbarāṭūr*, and through French, as *inbirūr*. Between the thirteenth and fifteenth centuries the word was occasionally used with reference to previous and contemporary European monarchs, emperors and kings.[16] However, being awkward by Arabic standards of elegance, it failed to be assimilated into the language. Pre-nineteenth-century Arabic dictionaries make no mention of the term; and in an eighteenth-century Arabic-Persian-Turkish lexicon it appears as exclusively Turkish.[17] With the new exposure to European titulature in the nineteenth century, the word, its awkwardness notwithstanding, was borrowed again. This time it came through Turkish, in which it had been in common use at least since the mid-sixteenth century (see below).

The recourse to these alien words at first did not signify response to any urgent lexical need. During the first third of the nineteenth century, the two names were treated as honorifics rather than titles, serving as little more than extra ornaments. They frequently appeared in combinations such as *malik al-Nimsā al-imbarāṭūr* ("emperor-king of Austria"), *al-inbarāṭūr sulṭān al-Nimsā*, and *al-malik Nābūlyūn* [Napoleon] *qayṣar*. More often than not the writers were content with *malik* and *sulṭān*, and readily dispensed with what seemed to them nonessential foreign niceties.[18]

This fluidity of usage may be better appreciated if we consider the way contemporary users of Turkish dealt with the same matters. To them the subject represented no novelty. Turkish, the language of a state with extensive international ties, had at its disposal an elaborate political and diplomatic vocabulary, including carefully defined titles for foreign rulers. A number of titles were reserved for the Ottoman head of state. The most common of these were *sulṭān*, from the Arabic; *pādishāh*, its approximate Persian equivalent;[19] and *khān* or *khāqān*, a regnal title of Turko-Mongol origin.[20] These titles, especially the first two, were often supplemented by the adjective "of Islam," indicating a claim to sovereignty over the entire community of believers. For centuries the Ottomans used these names exclusively for themselves, the king of France being the only exception when occasionally called *pādishāh*.[21] Other monarchs were referred to by other appellations, to which the names of their countries were always added, diminishing their standing. Thus the Russian czar had at first been called *Rūsyā çārī* (*çāriçesī*, in the case of a woman); after 1739 *Rūsyā imparāṭōrū* (or *imparāṭōriçesī*); and from 1774 *pādishāh*.[22] Heads of the Holy Roman Empire were, at least from the mid-seventeenth century, called *Rūma* (or *Nemçe*) *imparāṭōrū*, a title passed to their Austrian successors;[23] and the same name was applied to Napoleon I (later also to Napoleon III).[24] Only upon those recognized as emperors did the Ottomans confer such designations. European kings were referred to by another name: *kırāl* (*kırālice*, for queens), a modified version of *Karl* (apparently going back to Charlemagne), which came into Turkish via Serbian or Hungarian. It signified a status equivalent to that indicated by the Arabic *malik* and inferior to that implied by *sulṭān*, *pādishāh* and *imparāṭōr*. *Kıral* was used consistently in treaties and correspondence with European kingdoms such as Prussia, England, Poland, Sweden and Sardinia.[25] The Ottomans adhered meticulously to this system of titles, and deviations bore specific significance.

Unlike Turkish, however, Arabic had not been a language of an independent state, except in Morocco, nor had international diplomacy been conducted in it for centuries. Consequently, the language had lost its capacity for making minute distinction among foreign types of government, something that was conspicuous in Qalqashandī's fifteenth-century instructions to Mamluk state secretaries. It now needed to be gradually redeveloped.

It was, again, shaykh Ṭahṭāwī who in the nineteenth century made the first attempt at identifying varieties of rulership in the outside world. In a glossary appended to one of his early translations, Ṭahṭāwī distinguished between three kinds of sovereigns. Most important were those describable as supreme monarchs, *salāṭīn kibār* ("great *sulṭāns*"), who were "like the [Byzantine] *caesars*" (*mithl al-qayāṣira*). They numbered three: The Ottoman, Austrian and Russian rulers. Then there were kings, *mulūk*, whose number in Europe he gave as eighteen. Finally, there existed rulers who fell into neither of these two categories, who were "like kings without being called kings," such as "the Pope of Rome and others."[26] Ṭahṭāwī himself failed to adhere to this promising division, both in the same book and in his other works.[27] His remarks, however, portended a future change. His pupils at the Egyptian School of Languages took further steps in this direction during the second third of the century. It was largely due to their endeavour that the various types of Western governments were identified, at least by name. Translating European history books into Arabic, Ṭahṭāwī's pupils encountered a diversity of foreign sovereign names. Without necessarily fully comprehending the meaning of the names, they faithfully applied a distinct title to each type of ruler. The task created considerable lexical difficulty, which is amply evident throughout their writings. Making great efforts to resolve these problems, they introduced an increasing measure of order into the fluid Arabic titulature of non-Muslim sovereigns.

In the process, "king" seemed the least complex of the notions with which these translators had to grapple. *Malik,* the traditional title for foreign potentates, continued to serve as a matter of course in denoting "king," to the gradual exclusion of *sulṭān.*[28] As there were no rulers in the region itself who would carry that royal name, *malik* came to be understood as, unmistakably, "a foreign king." It persisted in use with this meaning from the beginning of the 1840s to the end of the century and beyond.

Coping with the concept of "emperor" proved somewhat more problematic. A supreme sovereign, or a "super monarch," was of course a familiar idea to speakers of the Arabic idiom; but there existed no tradition of viewing non-Muslim rulers as such, let alone a whole category of them. Some writers found *qayṣar* and *imbarāṭūr* fit for the purpose of naming such rulers. Others, loath to borrow, looked for alternative Arabic names.

One possibility put forward by Ṭahṭāwī was to reserve the name *sulṭān* for emperors, while calling kings *mulūk*. Europe, Ṭahṭāwī said in his translation of a French book, is ruled "by both *salāṭīn* and *mulūk,*" thus rendering a text which read: "L'Europe offre un mélange d'empereurs et de rois."[29] Elsewhere he explained that, while a *malik* reigns over one nation, a *sulṭān* is a sovereign of a number of kingdoms (*ᶜiddat mamālik*); the Europeans call the latter *"imbarāṭūr,* namely a great *qayṣar".*[30] Ṭahṭāwī's solution, however, proved unsatisfactory, because the basic disadvantage of the term *sulṭān*—being, as we have seen, at once generic and specific—rendered it a source of recurrent confusion. Ṭahṭāwī's colleagues and other writers persisted in using the title for European emperors,[31] at the same time searching for a substitute.

Another solution, also a fruit of Ṭahṭāwī's sedulous lexical efforts, was the name *sulṭān al-salāṭīn,* "sultan of [all] sultans." Napoleon, Ṭahṭāwī related, seized power (*tasalṭana*) in France following the Revolution "and was entitled *sulṭān al-salāṭīn.*" The name, he explained, was the equivalent of what the Franks called *imparāṭūr.*[32] The formula was no innovation, for it had been used as a title by Seljuk rulers, and later quite regularly by the Ottomans.[33] *Sulṭān al-salāṭīn* conformed to a common title pattern of Persian origin, implying paramountcy and including designations such as *malik al-mulūk, amīr al-umarā'* and *shāhānshāh.* Choosing a name of this category to denote emperors was thus semantically sensible. But this attempt, like the previous one, was short-lived, since for most of Ṭahṭāwī's Arab contemporaries there could be only one *sulṭān al-salāṭīn,* the Ottoman sovereign; the idea of extending the title to others was objectionable. Thus rejected, it was soon abandoned.

This uncertain groping for a name for foreign supreme monarchs was occasionally apparent in later years as well. One initiative in this direction produced the title *ᶜāhil,* pl. *ᶜawāhil.* Although an old Arabic word—it appears in classical dictionaries with the meaning of "a *malik* as great as a *khalīfa,*"[34] *ᶜāhil* does not seem to have served as a title for any important ruler or dynasty in Middle Eastern history. Nineteenth-century writers who adopted the expression may have discovered it while searching the lexicons. When it first appeared in the newspaper *Birjīs Bārīs* as a designation for Napoleon III, the editor interpreted it in a footnote as the Arabic equivalent of "the Frankish title *imbarāṭūr,* [which means in their jargon] a [monarch] greater than a *malik.*" Thereafter it was used regularly in this newspaper and in a number of other writings to describe European emperors. It was also employed in a feminine form, *ᶜāhila;* in adjectival form, as in "an *ᶜāhilī* state" or "an *ᶜāhilī* decree"; and as an abstract noun, *ᶜāhiliyya,* meaning emperorship or empire.[35] All these experiments came to nothing.

Arabic eventually settled for a solution of a kind it usually tried to avoid: it assimilated the two foreign words *qayṣar* and *imbarāṭūr* as names for emperors, to the exclusion of all other designations. The Egyptian translators, unsatisfied with Ṭahṭāwī's other suggested appellations, often resorted to this pair of terms, however reluctantly. Unlike writers of the previous generation (Jabartī, Turk, Shihābī, and even Ṭahṭāwī in his early writings), they were careful to use these foreign names systematically as distinguished titles of supreme sovereigns. Some of them were meticulous enough to make distinctions such as "*imbarāṭūr al-Rūsiyā* and *malik al-Brūsiyā,*" or "*al-imbarāṭūriyya al-Almāniyya* and *al-mamlaka al-Isbāniyya*" (the Holy Roman Empire and the kingdom of Spain); or to cite correctly Napoleon's title as "*imbarāṭūr al-Fransīs wa-malik Īṭāliyā.*"[36] Adopting their mentor's assiduity, some of Ṭahṭāwī's pupils were careful to distinguish also between lesser sovereigns, designating each kind by a separate name: a Duke came to be *dūq* and his realm *dūqiyya,* a Grand Duke was called *ghrandūq,* and an elector (in the Holy Roman Empire) became *iliktūr* or its Arabic rendition *muntakhib.*[37] While stylistically perhaps undesirable, the usage of such alien names had an important advantage. It helped to convey the foreignness of the circumstances which they represented, and this was more fruitful than rendering them overly and erroneously familiar.

By the time the Arabic press was born, in the late 1850s, the identity and titles of Western sovereigns had been more or less clearly established. Within the next decade references to such rulers became markedly accurate. By that time the situation in Europe itself had been considerably simplified, due to the unification of Italy and Germany and the concomitant elimination of several species of government. Arab writers now used distinct colors consistently in painting the diverse elements of this picture. *Qayṣar* and *imbarāṭūr* came to serve as the most obvious choices of designations for European emperors. Other names became rare exceptions. Certain authors elected to distinguish between *qayṣar,* which they attached to the czar (since both stemmed from the same Latin original), and *imbarāṭūr,* applied to all other emperors. They thus discussed "the meeting between the [Russian] *qayṣar* and the Austrian *imbarāṭūr*," or juxtaposed "the German *imbarāṭūr,* the Austrian *imbarāṭūr* and the *qayṣar* of Russia."[38] Others, indeed the majority of writers, treated the two terms as synonyms and used them interchangeably to describe all emperors, historical and contemporary. The two words were also assimilated morphologically: the plural form *imbarāṭira* was coined, to resemble *qayāṣira.*[39] Also the feminine form, *qayṣara* and *imbarāṭūra;* adjectival derivations, *qayṣarī* and *imbarāṭūrī;* and abstract nominal forms, *qayṣariyya* and *imbarāṭūriyya,* meaning emperorship or empire, came into routine use.[40] The scene of European governments became more intelligible than it had been in the early nineteenth century, when it was dominated by an ambiguous assemblage of various *mulūk* and *salāṭīn.*

While growing more precise, titles of foreign rulers also turned more commendatory. In this process it was once again the translators at the Egyptian School of Languages who made the first substantial contribution. Seeking to produce reliable translations, shaykh Ṭahṭāwī and his colleagues tried to convey the authors' appreciation, even explicit veneration, for their heroes. "The *malik,*" said Muṣṭafā Bayyāᶜ, rendering Voltaire's admiring biography of Gustavus II of Sweden, "was one of those rarely matched great personalities who were born with the necessary traits of leadership . . . [a man of] prominence and brilliant character."[41] "This great *malik,*" said another translator, writing of Louis VI of France, "was perhaps the most diligent and industrious of all French monarchs ever."[42] This favorable tone characterized the texts selected for translation on the command of rulers eager to benefit from their European counterparts' experience. If persistent, such a postive presentation of non-Muslim rulers in Arabic was bound to produce a change in the Arab attitude toward them, and, as a consequence of that change, the import of their regnal titles would improve.

The task fulfilled by the Egyptian translators during the 1830s and 1840s was taken over by men of the nascent Arabic press in the 1850s and 1860s. Borrowing reports from European newspapers, they copied references to foreign monarchs along with their often illustrious honorifics. Formulae such as *jalālat al-malik al-aᶜẓam* ("His Majesty the Great King"), *ṣāḥib al-ᶜaẓama al-imbarāṭūriyya, al-brins Nābūlyūn* ("His Great Imperial Highness, Prince Napoleon [III]"), and *jalālat qayṣar Jirmāniyā*

("His Majesty the Emperor of Germany"),[43] unthinkable at the outset of the century, gradually became standard, and the editors began to employ them even when producing their own commentaries on politics abroad.

The Arab view of European kings and emperors was marked by growing respect as the second half of the century unfolded. To be sure, they were not regarded with universal admiration, yet even among those who came to hold grudges against Europe, few denied its might and achievements. Much of the esteem was associated with the rulers, and so the names designating their position were favorably affected. The royal title *malik,* having lost its pejorative connotation by mid-century, came to reflect the high regard felt for monarchs such as the queen of England and the king of Italy. *Qayṣar* and *imbarāṭūr* gained even more respect, as names for sovereigns "greater than kings in power, influence and authority," whose imperial titles bore "the clearest testimony to their veneration and glory."[44]

Interestingly, however prestigious these foreign titles became in the Middle East, they did not appeal to rulers in the region as names for themselves. The czar and the kaiser, or the queen of Great Britain and empress of India, may have had dominion over larger and richer realms than that of the Ottoman sultan. But their standing could never match that of the Prophet's *khalīfa.* Lesser rulers under Ottoman suzerainty, in Egypt, the Hejaz and elsewhere, acknowledged the sultan's caliphal authority and were content with the ranks he accorded them within the hierarchy of the Muslim state. They too sought no foreign designations. While many names and notions were borrowed from Europe in the nineteenth century, royal and imperial titles were not among them. The distinction between Muslim and foreign sovereign titles was carefully adhered to throughout the period.

In the early twentieth century, as traditional authority continued to decline and European prestige to flourish, Western-style regnal titles were eventually adopted in the Middle East. The caliphate still existed, but the British and the French in fact had the final say on all matters of sovereignty; rulers in the region would therefore realistically do with royal rather than imperial names. *Malik,* its import profoundly refurbished, had acquired enough appeal for it to be assumed as a mark of proud sovereignty by the sharif Husayn of Mecca, in 1916, and then by rulers in Syria, Iraq, Egypt and many other places. The fashion of kingly titles quickly spread all over the region, and by the mid-twentieth century the great majority of its countries had experimented with modern monarchical government. Most of the monarchs would call themselves *mulūk*. Others, notably of the Saudi and Hashimite dynasties, would revive the title *ᶜāhil*, intended to imply superior kingship. The reappearance of such names in the twentieth century, quite like that in the tenth, reflected the powerful impact of a foreign culture on concepts of government in the central Arab lands.

3

Subjects and Citizens

Even before the French Revolution, the governed people in certain European states knew a twofold political status, described by a pair of distinctive designations, "subject" and "citizen." The former signified subordination to a monarch. The latter implied relation to a place and membership of a polity, first a city-state, later a nation-state.

The word "citizen" evolved from the Latin *civis*, meaning a member of the *civitas*, the city (the Greek equivalents being, respectively, *polites* and *polis*). "Citizen" had always connoted a person's civil and political rights. In medieval European city-states, being a citizen meant being free from feudal domination. Later, in fully monarchical times, Rousseau's *Social Contract* spoke of the *citoyen*, key participant in the formation of the "general will," as contrasted with the *sujet*, who shared none of that privilege.[1] When the United States emancipated itself from British domination, its inhabitants ceased to be subjects of the king of England and became citizens of their country. The French Revolution sharpened the distinction by glorifying the *citoyen*, both in the 1789 "Declaration of the Rights of Man and of the Citizen" and in making *citoyen* (or *citoyenne*) a universal proper title of every French person.[2] The idea of citizenship then spread to other parts of the West, especially Western Europe. Sometimes legally still the ruler's subjects, people were acquiring the political status of citizens; monarchs continued to occupy their thrones and bequeath their crowns to their descendants, but the power of government gradually passed to their subordinates. The term "subject" thus slowly lost its old meaning, and the concept of citizenship was striking roots.

With the French Revolution, the Lebanese historian Ra'īf Khūrī noted in 1943, the French "ceased to be *raʿiyya, 'sujets,'* [and became] *muwāṭinūn, 'citoyens'."*[3] One would hardly dispute the clarity of the statement, coming from a keen mid-twentieth century observer. Had the remark been offered to a nineteenth-century Middle Eastern audience, however, it would have sounded meaningless. Until the twentieth century there had been one Arabic expression to indicate the political status of the ruled: *raʿiyya,* pl. *raʿāyā.* Initially a name for a herd or flock of livestock tended by their keeper, the term had been metaphorically extended to denote people, subjects of a ruler. By the same token, the rulers, assumed to be compassionate and caring, were described as *ruʿāt,* "shepherds." The simile was apt; it indicated people's dependence upon and submissiveness to their leader. The essential principle of unmistakable division between the ruler and the ruled remained valid whether the latter obeyed—as they should, and normally did—or rebelled against their masters. The idea of people's participation in government was alien and scarcely compatible with this traditional arrangement. On the eve of the modern era, inhabitants of the Middle East, Muslims and non-Muslims alike, regarded themselves as *raʿiyya* of the Ottoman Sultans, or of other leaders wielding power, such as Muhammad Ali in Egypt.[4]

When Arab writers began to record their impressions of European politics, they considered the name by which they designated themselves to be equally applicable to the governed people abroad. They knew none better. *Raʿiyya,* with its plural *raʿāyā*—the two were employed interchangeably without distinction—was attached, from the beginning to the end of the nineteenth century, to the populace of every country under any type of government. It was used by almost everyone addressing himself to the governed—from the *ʿulamāʾ* of the Egyptian *dīwān,* who solemnly told Bonaparte that the "two peoples, the Egyptian and the French, are but a unified *raʿiyya,"* to Jurjī Zaydān, who in

1898 discussed the political rights and franchises of "the American *ra'āyā*."[5]

Applying *ra'iyya* to the subjects of the autocratic monarchs of Russia, Austria, and certain medieval European states seemed only natural. The czar's government, shaykh Ṭahṭāwī explained, was "extremely coercive [*jabarī*], due to the ignorance of the *ra'iyya*." There, as in the Ottoman Empire, one mark of the monarch's absolute control was the "land tax [*kharāj*] which the Russian king [*malik*] levies from his *ra'iyya*." The account did not seriously distort the subjects' actual status; nor did a depiction of the 1815 Russian-Austrian-Prussian Holy Alliance as a "conspiracy" designed to "consolidate the kings and suppress the *ra'āyā*," or a reference to "the efforts [the Austrian emperor] spends in improving the lot of his *ra'āyā*."[6]

Associating the term *ra'iyya* with constitutional monarchies such as Britain, France or Belgium, where the people were attaining increasing political rights and ensuring them in constitutions, was less appropriate than applying it to subjects of autocratic rulers, especially in writings discussing such issues as the general will and popular participation in government. But if less appropriate, it was no less common. To pick an example, according to one newspaper Lord Derby's resignation from the post of Prime Minister in London in the summer of 1859 primarily "resulted from his attempt to reform election laws and rules, namely, those regulating the voice of the *ra'iyya* in electing members of the House of Commons." In France, to quote another, Napoleon III prior to his ascent to power "used to pronounce his advocacy of the rights [*ḥuqūq*] of the *ra'iyya*." Arabic texts of the nineteenth century abound in examples of this.[7] Still more confusing was the use of the term to portray citizens of nonmonarchical states, such as the United States, where "at the age of twenty-one the *ra'iyya* have the right of casting the ballot and electing their representatives," or republican France, where an "assembly of *ra'iyya* deputies" (*dīwān wukalā' al-ra'iyya*) functioned as a sovereign parliamentary institution.[8]

There was more than something odd—almost a contradiction—in innovative compounds such as *ṣawt al-ra'iyya* ("the *ra'iyya*'s vote") or *wukalā' al-ra'iyya* ("*ra'iyya* deputies"),[9] for traditionally the *ra'iyya* enjoyed none of these political privileges. Rather they had duties, first and foremost that of obeying God and "those who hold authority," *ūlū al-amr*.[10] The latter, in return, were expected to treat their subjects with justice. The new compounds, therefore, combined the mutually exclusive concepts of sovereignty and subjugation. This must have misled many in the reading audience, especially since in local contexts *ra'iyya* was still used in its old sense. When Khedive Ismā'īl, inaugurating the 1866 Council of Delegates, addressed the people as his *ra'iyya*, he clearly meant to imply their subordinate status, traditionally understood. Council members willingly concurred in their reply.[11] When, a decade later, the promulgation of the Ottoman constitution was hailed by the semiweekly *al-Jawā'ib* as a step to secure "the complete freedom and full safety of all the *ra'āyā*, Muslims and others," the editor similarly had in mind the Sultan's old duty of treating his people with justice, rather than a modern concept of people's political rights. Subordination to the Muslim ruler remained a prevalent principle until the disintegration of the Ottoman Empire, and in certain parts of the region even longer. The term *ra'iyya* was associated, above all, with this principle.[12]

Perhaps more intelligible than the idea of popular participation in the government was the concept of civic rights. Civic liberties safeguarded by the state—the protection of one's life, property and honor, and complete freedom of action save when infringing upon someone else's freedom—were neatly compatible with the Islamic view of government. Rulers had always been exhorted to rule justly and display respect towards the *ra'iyya*. And while a ruler's justness was conceived as his duty rather than as his subjects' right, these were in fact two sides of the same coin. That the subjects had a right to proper treatment was, of course, a new notion imported from Europe; but this was actually a logical extension of a traditional concept, a redefinition of an old principle. The idea of civic rights and personal liberties was comprehensible to people in the Middle East, and this was, most likely, their understanding of the European phenomenon which they described as *ḥuqūq al-ra'iyya*, "rights of the *ra'iyya*."[13] It thus was quite easy for Ṭahṭāwī, following half a century of his country's rapport with Europe, to incorporate the concept into his discussion of the Islamic state. As he suggested in his *Manāhij*, his very last opus,

> the *ra'iyya* have rights in the country; these are called civic
> rights [*ḥuqūq madaniyya*], that is to say, rights of the people

living in one state regarding each other. They are also termed 'individual personal rights' [*ḥuqūq khuṣūṣiyya shakhṣiyya*] as distinct from public rights [*ḥuqūq ʿumūmiyya*]. [While the latter deal with] . . . public law . . . and order, civic rights refer to rights of all people with respect to each other, and are designed to protect their property, assets, interests and life.[14]

The idea of the subjects' right to these basic liberties was echoed with increasing resonance in documents issued (rather reluctantly) by the Ottoman court from 1839 on. This was the spirit of the Ḥaṭṭ-i Şerīf of Gülḥāne and of the Ḥaṭṭ-i Humāyūn of 1856. The 1876 Ottoman constitution devoted a special section to the "rights of the subjects," defining civic and individual liberties. The constitution also provided for an elected assembly whose role was widely interpreted as "the defense of the rights of all sectors of the *raʿiyya.*"[15] Yet there was no mention of *political* rights in the document, and the fact that the people could elect their own representatives to a governmental institution was not regarded as such. Rather it was viewed as a manifest of the grace and wisdom of the Sultan, who himself continued to "unite in his person" exclusive sovereignty over the empire.

The distinction made here between civic and political rights was seldom clear to nineteenth-century Arab exponents of these ideas. Much confusion marked the public debate which followed the implementation of the representational principle, first in Cairo in 1866, then in Istanbul a decade later. To a great extent it emanated from the perplexing contradiction between the old inclination to obey the ruler and the new impulse to search for a European type of popular sovereignty. Some twelve years after the inauguration of the Egyptian Consultative Council of Delegates, a spokesman for the council made an illuminating reference to the *raʿiyya* status of his country's people. In an inflamed speech abounding in modern themes such as freedom (*ḥurriyya*), equal rights (*al-musawāt fī al-ḥuqūq*) and nationalism (referring to the novelty of an "Egyptian *umma*"), he boldly stated the council's intention to "defend the rights [*ḥuqūq*] of the *raʿiyya*" and "seek to protect their interests"; he defined these rights and interests as merely "necessary prerequisites for justice [*ʿadl*] and equity [*inṣāf*]"—traits of a properly administered traditional Islamic state. The speech ended with an exclamation, "Long live freedom under the shadow of [the Khedive's] patronage and protection," a formula epitomizing the ambiguous concept of people's "rights."[16]

The word *raᶜiyya* thus continued to carry the old meaning of "subjects" as unmistakably its core denotation. *Raᶜiyya* in that sense could be subjects of a despot, or of a just and caring ruler who would assure their deserved individual rights. But they had nothing to do with the power of government. In addition, the use of the term in foreign contexts lent it the meaning of "citizens," with which it was employed as commonly as with the former, traditional meaning. With this last application it was most often used in denoting citizens of one state residing in another, such as "the Russian *raᶜāyā* in Bulgaria" or "the English *raᶜiyya* in the Ottoman provinces."[17] *Raᶜiyya* was now a flexible term, which inevitably blurred rather than clarified its subject, especially when the subject was a modern political concept in a foreign context.

Toward the end of the century, certain writers had come to feel uncomfortable with *raᶜiyya,* whose old connotations seemed to be incompatible with their new understanding of citizenship. In writings about Europe and about affairs of the Middle East, the term gradually lost ground to other expressions. Of the words replacing *raᶜiyya,* some were initially devoid of any political color. Among them were *al-ahl* and its plural *al-ahālī,* the people; *al-sukkān,* the inhabitants; and *al-jumhūr,* the public. Unlike *raᶜiyya* these words implied no specific relationship between ruler and ruled. Throughout the nineteenth century they were used in discussing affairs at home and abroad with the neutral meaning of "population." Generic and flexible, they provided a convenient choice to authors growing ill at ease with *raᶜiyya,* who tended to use these terms more and more often as the second half of the century unfolded. They employed these words in such politically suggestive compounds as *aṣwāt al-jumhūr,* voices, or votes, of the people; *irādat al-ahālī,* people's will; and *al-ḥuqūq al-ahliyya,* civil rights. The 1876 Ottoman Assembly of Delegates, for example, was said to consist of "elected representatives of the *ahālī.*" Members of the consultative assembly in Transvaal were, similarly, "elected [delegates] of the country's *sukkān.*" And the *Garde National* in Paris became *al-ḥaras al-ahlī.*[18]

Of greater significance was another newly introduced term, *shaᶜb,* pl. *shuᶜūb.* Originally this word had meant a tribal confederacy or supertribe, a people, or an ethnic group, often of non-Arab stock. It was commonly associated with the Persians of early Islamic history (*al-ʿAjam*); the *shuʿūbiyya,* accordingly, was a name for a sect in Iran which had objected to the preferred status of Arabs in Islam.[19] Thus, applied to Muslim peoples *shaʿb* sometimes bore a slightly negative implication, suggesting separatist tendencies detrimental to the unity of the *umma.* When used to describe non-Muslims, it was tinged with the disparagement normally typifying references to foreigners of any kind. *Shaʿb* was a flexible term; an early nineteenth-century chronicler, for instance, discussed "the *shuʿūb* of France," "the French *shaʿb,*" and "the *shaʿb* of Paris" in the very same text.[20] For all its versatility, however, the word did not commonly denote the ruled as opposed to the ruler, nor did it in any way imply political rights or a quest for them. This particular meaning of the word developed with the absorption of the West's modern ideas.

Early Arab accounts of the French Revolution and of Napoleon's government did, however, use *shaʿb* occasionally with this last denotation. This was the word's sense in the description of the French *shaʿb* "arising in total revolt" against king Louis XVI. The word likewise carried this meaning in the account of the king's flight from Paris in "fear of the *shaʿb*" and in the reference to the "will of the French people" (*irādat shaʿb Faransā*) which sometime later brought Napoleon down.[21]

Such usage, uncommon during the century's first half, became far more frequent following the birth of the Arabic press in the 1850s. Newspapers reporting events in Europe and elsewhere discussed issues such as the role "public opinion" (*raʾy al-shaʿb*) played in British politics, the dependence of the king of Sardinia upon his "people's will" (*irādat al-shaʿb*), and the relationship between the government (*ḥukūma*) and the *shaʿb* in the United States. One writer described Bastille Day as the occasion on which the French "*shaʿb* knew its rights and tore down the laws of tyranny." Another aptly defined a republic as *ḥukūmat al-shaʿb bil-shaʿb,* ("government of the people by the people,") as distinct from "autocracy," *ḥukūmat al-shaʿb bi-wāḥid,* ("government of the people by one [person].") A third identified democracy as "a Greek word meaning 'government by the *shaʿb*'."[22] Likewise, the concept of popular sovereignty was expressed in the compound "*shaʿb* representatives (*wukalāʾ al-shaʿb*), which became increasingly common in texts dealing with parliamentary life in the West.[23]

Unlike *ahālī, jumhūr* and *sukkān,* which, even though employed in political contexts, scarcely acquired political connotations in themselves, *sha᷾b* did come to carry a specific sociopolitical significance through its repeated use in conjunction with such terms as *ḥuqūq* (rights), *irāda* (will) *quwwa* (power) and *ṣawt* (voice). It gained acceptance as a name for the governed masses rightfully seeking to make their voice and their will recognized by the government—much like "the people" of socialist jargon.

For the greater part of the period, *sha᷾b,* with this newly acquired sense, seemed irrelevant to the realities of the region and was scarcely used in local contexts. But as the century drew to a close, it began to appear, then became frequent, in texts discussing Ottoman and Egyptian politics. This marked the percolation of the new idea into the thought of Middle Eastern intellectuals. "I am one of the *sha᷾b,*" an Egyptian journalist proudly stated, in an open letter to Sultan ᷾Abd al-Ḥamīd, "and the *sha᷾b* does not wish to die, nor to have its house destroyed":

> If you fail to listen to our voice of reason today, you may one day have to hear a louder voice—the voice [*ṣawt*] of the *sha᷾b.* Woe to him who tries to withstand the *sha᷾b* once it unites, makes a decision and sets out to achieve a noble goal wherein lies its interest! Before that swelling river and mighty stream, Sultans will be but a feather fluttering in the storm.[24]

The spirit was eloquently echoed by Muṣṭafā Kāmil, one of the early exponents of popular sovereignty in the Middle East. "Every *sha᷾b* has sacred rights in its homeland, which no one can infringe," he asserted. "The *sha᷾b* is the only true power [*al-quwwa al-waḥīda al-ḥaqīqiyya*] and the authority [*sulṭān*] to whose will the greatest and mightiest would submit."[25]

Among the terms supplanting *ra᷾iyya* in designating the political status of the governed, *sha᷾b* was thus the most specific, implying rights as well as sovereignty. As such it was closer to the liberal concept of "citizen" than to the traditional idea of "subject." As the nineteenth century led into the twentieth, *sha᷾b* emerged as a common item in the vocabulary of Middle Eastern nationalism—and later also of socialism—a rallying cry capable of evoking powerful emotions.

Largely interchangeable with *sha᷾b,* the term *umma* had a very similar fate in the nineteenth century. Like *sha᷾b,* it initially had a number of meanings, among them a people (loosely defined, and most often foreign) (see chapter 1). Likewise, again, it became a name for the ruled, and subsequently acquired the implication of people's rights and of collective will. Both *umma* and *sha'b* were used to describe a politically conscious public aspiring to have a say in determining its political standing—either through uprising against an oppressive ruler, or by sending representatives to an institutionalized assembly, often called *majlis al-sha'b* or *majlis al-umma,* or else through openly voicing its demand for its deserved sovereignty. "In republican systems," Rashīd Riḍā explained, "government is in the hand of the *umma,* while the president no more than implements decisions of the *umma*'s representatives."[26] Adīb Isḥaq likewise remarked, with his typical perspicacity, that "a democracy" is a kind of system "in which the ruling power is entirely in the hands of the *umma;* the *umma* is hence at once governing and governed."[27] Isḥaq also applied the term to his own people, referring to "the will [*irāda*] of the [Egyptian] *umma*" and to the "views [*ārā'*] of the Ottoman *umma.*"[28] Such usage gained currency among Arab writers of later years. By the end of the century Muṣṭafā Kāmil voiced the concept in his enthusiastic speeches to the Egyptians: the *umma,* he stated, had "the foremost say [*al-kalīma al-ūlā*] in its land . . .the *umma* is master of the land and lord of the country. She elevates whoever she chooses to a ruling position and brings down whoever she wants."[29]

Umma, however, was more often used with the traditional meaning of "a people" or "a nation" as distinct from other peoples or nations, than in designating the governed vis-a-vis the government. The former sense became prevalent to the gradual exclusion of the latter, toward the end of the period, as nationalist ideas were brought to public attention. The word now served primarily in asserting the nationhood of the Egyptian, Arab or, more traditionally, the Islamic *umma,* each facing its outside enemies. The ruled, striving to attain their political rights at home, were more commonly referred to as *sha'b.* The distinction, however, was less than rigorous, and writers in later years sometimes used both *umma* and *sha'b* interchangeably in their works.

All the terms discussed so far treated the governed, subjects or citizens, as a collective. None of them applied to the individual's status within the state. Nineteenth-century Arabic knew no name for a personal political entity comparable to "citizen," *citoyen* or *cittadino.* Nor was such an entity recognized by the region's political tradition. A man was a member of the community, that is, an anonymous part of the only legally sanctioned political corpus. His political fate was accordingly determined by that of the collective. The only way of referring to an individual in a political context was, therefore, through describing him indirectly as "one of the *raʿiyya*," or "one of the *shaʿb.*" Typically, when faced with the post-revolutionary French practice of addressing every member of the republic as *citoyen,* contemporary Arab writers, puzzled by the strange title, commonly rendered it as *al-sitūyān;* even if the title's meaning was grasped, the Arabic repertoire could offer no better name for it. It was not until the twentieth century that a word denoting a person with an individual political status was coined in Arabic.

The new word was *muwāṭin,* pl. *muwāṭinūn,* a derivative of w-ṭ-n which meant to reside or dwell. The noun *waṭan,* from the same root, had long been a name for a place of residence, be it a village, a province or a country. During the nineteenth century, as the idea of patriotism appeared in the region, *waṭan* acquired the sense of *patrie,* a word associated with strong sentiments of loving attachment and loyalty. A "patriot" was described as *ibn al-waṭan,* "child of the homeland," or by the adjectival noun *waṭanī;* both served to denote local inhabitants of the *patrie*—a unit easier to identify in Europe, where it simply referred to any recognizable country, than in the Ottoman Middle East. These terms were used throughout the century with the technical meaning of "resident" as distinct from "alien" (*ajnabī*). Thus, for example, the Egyptian patent law of 1890 was said to be applicable to "anybody in Egypt, whether *waṭanī* or *ajnabī.*" The South African war of a decade later, by the same token, was described as taking place "between the Boers and the black *waṭaniyīn.*"[30]

In addition to having this technical meaning, however, *ibn al-waṭan* and *waṭanī* gradually gained a political connotation during the later part of the period. Being a patriot came to signify conscious identification with the homeland, a virtue highly commended and often quoted as an article of faith. Patriots, moreover, were said to have rights as well as duties in their homeland. The Lebanese Buṭrus al-Bustānī was apparently the first to preach the idea. "It is for *ibnā' al-waṭan,*" he stated in 1860, to claim their *waṭan*'s "protection of their most precious rights [*ḥuqūq*], namely, their life, honor and property, including freedom [*ḥurriyya*] of their civic [*madanī*], cultural and religious rights"; in return, they should devote themselves to the attainment of their country's welfare.[31] The theme of relation between *waṭan* and rights was voiced in later years with ever-increasing frequency and zeal. Adīb Isḥaq went as far as to argue that "there is no *waṭan* without *ḥurriyya;* moreover, they are identical . . .and the *waṭan* cannot exist without rights." Muḥammad ʿAbduh repeated the statement verbatim.[32] This perception seems also to have underlain the occasional rendition of "citizen" or *citoyen* as *ibn al-waṭan* by certain writers and translators.[33] It was this association which led in the twentieth century to the creation of an Arabic name for an individual "citizen."

In the nineteenth century, however, the relation between homeland and personal freedom was scarcely more than a vaguely perceived idea. Adīb Isḥaq himself defined the "freedom" implied by affiliation with a *waṭan* as no more than the traditional "right to fulfil the known duty" (*ḥaqq al-qiyām bil-wājib al-maʿlūm*).[34] Isḥaq and a few other writers of his generation bequeathed to their twentieth-century successors merely an ambiguous clue to the idea. It was mainly the struggle for independence and national assertion in the twentieth century that lent the term its modern implication. Belonging to the *waṭan* came to be regarded as a privileged status, and this is probably what inspired the coining of *muwāṭin* to denote a citizen with political and legal rights. *Muwāṭin* was devised—according to a common pattern of nouns often indicating relation to, or association with, an object—to mean, technically, a compatriot (like *muʿāṣir,* "man of the *ʿaṣr,"* time or era, hence "contemporary"). It thus followed the example of "citizen," initially "a member of the city." Both the European prototype and the Arabic counterpart signified relation to a place, rather than subordination to a ruler as expressed by "subject" and the collectivity of *raʿiyya*. Furthermore, both implied legal status and rights.[35] Yet the traits which "citizen" indicated—individual and political liberty—were not necessarily indicated in full by its Arabic equivalent. These were to vary from one Arabic-speaking country to another, according to their respective political realities.

4

The Sociopolitical Elite—
Traditional Standards of Seniority

On the eve of the modern era, membership in the sociopolitical elite in the Middle East was predicated upon certain clearly identifiable qualifications. These primarily included noble descent, possession of large property, religio-scholarly prominence, sometimes senior age, and the obvious benefits of royal favor and military power. These advantages determined a person's belonging to the *khāṣṣa* or *khawwāṣ*—"the privileged," a loose term applicable specifically to the ruling establishment and, more broadly, to the social and intellectual elite at large. Being so designated distinguished these groups from the rest of society, known, somewhat derogatorily, as *ᶜāmma,* "the commonalty."[1] Such criteria for social division were not unique to the Middle East; they prevailed throughout premodern Europe and, in certain European countries, remained unchanged for most or all of the nineteenth century. In others, however, different standards for political prominence evolved before and during the period, as authority based on representation of the "general will" and sanctioned by popular election gradually supplanted traditional authority. Thus, the parallels between Middle Eastern and European elites, useful if approximate hitherto, were becoming increasingly misleading. The exposure of Middle Eastern society to the different principles of European politics modified its own traditional values defining sociopolitical status. But the change was a slow process which depended upon better understanding of the old characteristics of European leadership and the concepts that replaced them.

As was the case with other aspects of foreign politics, both the traditional European elite and that which developed after the French Revolution were first treated in Arabic texts as equivalents of their Middle Eastern counterparts. Among the Arabic terms extended to depict men of circumstance abroad were several that connoted mastery or possession, such as *ṣāḥib*, pl. *aṣḥāb, dhū*, pl. *dhawū* or *dhawāt*, and *ūlū*, existing only as a plural noun, all meaning possessor or owner, and *rabb*, pl. *arbāb*, meaning lord or master. These were used mainly in compound names with specifying complements, which reflected a concept of politics, government and its institutions as forming a territory reserved for a well-defined category of privileged persons. Just as craftsmanship was the realm of *arbāb al-ṣināᶜa* (literally "masters of the crafts"), and professional corporations the domain of *arbāb al-ḥiraf*, so was politics a matter for *arbāb al-siyāsa;* government belonged to *aṣḥāb al-ḥukm;* and consultative forums, wherever existing, were the designated domain of *dhawāt al-mashwara.*[2] Thus when Bonaparte established the famous *dīwān* in Cairo, its members, notable dignitaries of the traditional elite, were known as *arbāb al-dīwān.* Some time later, when Muhammad Ali ordered the convention of *majlis al-mashwara* (the "Consultative Council"), its members came to be known as *dhawāt al-majlis.*[3] The concept prevailed throughout the greater part of the nineteenth century; as late as 1883 Buṭrus al-Bustānī defined government (*ḥukūma*) as the realm of "*arbāb al-siyāsa,* who are charged with the administration [of the state]."[4] The *arbāb, aṣḥāb* and *dhawāt,* then, possessed an exclusive prominence in society that was universally accepted and uncontested.

Early Arab writers on European affairs, having no criteria other than their own for sociopolitical leadership, characterized the elite abroad as an impregnable circle of notables. They entitled European politicians and diplomats as *aṣḥāb al-siyāsa* ("lords of politics") or *dhawāt al-dawā'ir al-siyāsiyya al-ᶜāliya* ("masters of the upper political echelons"),[5] men of the government as *arbāb al-ḥukm* or *aṣḥāb al-ḥukūma,*[6] political party members as *arbāb al-firqa* ("masters of the group"),[7] and those enjoying the privilege of electing or being elected as *dhawī al-intikhāb.*[8] Members of ruling institutions were similarly identified: senators in ancient Rome were presented as *arbāb al-mashwara al-sinātiyya,* men of the British Parliament were *dhawāt al-barlamān,* and officials of the Paris city council were presented as *arbāb al-mashyakha al-baladiyya.*[9] Even members of forums elected periodically for a limited term, such as the British House of Commons and the United States Senate, were commonly described by such names.[10] These designations were used as a matter of course during the first half of the century, as well as in later years, although as time progressed they occurred less and less often.

The occidental concept of "member" of an assembly or of any collegiate forum involved neither lordship nor mastery. Rather it implied the sharing of functions, rights and duties, as in the case of the various members or limbs of the human body— the original context of the word. "Member," in the sense of "one elected to a parliament," had existed in English since at least the fifteenth century.[11] The extended application of the term to a participant in a collective body reflected a concept of responsibility as something that was distributed, often equally, among its constituents. While the authority of collective institutions and the procedures of becoming or ceasing to be members in them differed broadly, membership in them always involved participation and not mastery. The Ottoman Middle East lacked any similar concept, and although, as we shall see, "member" was used metaphorically in the Middle East before its encounter with Europe, that usage was rare and hardly ever occurred in a political context. Until the middle of the nineteenth century, the most ready local counterpart of the European idea of political "membership" remained that signifying domination by an exclusive few.

Later in the century, this traditional notion gave way to another, expressed by the word *ʿuḍw,* pl. *aʿḍāʾ*. In classical times *ʿuḍw* was primarily used to mean a limb of a biological body. Occasionally, it had additional denotations. For example, in his tenth-century rendition of Plato's *Republic,* al-Fārābī offered an analogy between the most important members of the human body and leaders of the republic (the "ideal state"): "just as the chief member (*al-ʿuḍw al-raʾīs*) of the body is naturally the most perfect member," he suggested, "so also the head of the state is the most perfect of the state's components (*ajzāʾ*)."[12] His example was seldom followed; the word was not used with this meaning in pre-nineteenth-century dictionaries, nor in most of those published during the first half of the century.[13]

With the exposure of the Middle East to foreign ideas, the metaphoric sense of *ʿuḍw* was revived. Already Jabartī employed it occasionally with reference to members of Bonaparte's *dīwān* in Egypt, alongside the more common *arbāb al-dīwān*. He was followed in that by some of the Egyptian translators, and then by journalists who discussed Middle Eastern and foreign politics in the new private Arabic press. Rather than *arbāb* and *aṣḥāb*, men of political institutions in Europe and elsewhere became *aʿḍāʾ al-majlis*, *aʿḍāʾ al-ḥukūma* or *aʿḍāʾ al-ḥizb*—respectively, members of the assembly, the government or the party.[14] Having gained currency in this new sense, the term was then applied to men of local councils established in Egypt under Saʿīd, after the French example; of the Ottoman reform council (*majlis al-Tanẓīmāt*); of provincial and municipal councils in Syria; of Ismāʿīl's *majlis shūrā al-nuwwāb* ("Consultative Council of Delegates"); and of the Ottoman parliament of 1876.[15] Previously the exclusive realm of "lords," politics and political institutions came to be treated as the province of a plurality of "members"; thus the accent was on sharing rather than on mastery.

A related traditional name for men of circumstance in Islam was *ahl al-ḥall wal-ʿaqd*, literally "those who loosen and bind," sometimes modified as *arbāb al-ḥall wal-ʿaqd*, *ahl al-ḥall wal-rabṭ* and similar formulae of the same meaning. Initially *ahl al-ḥall wal-ʿaqd* served as an appellation for those whose right and duty was to appoint and depose a Caliph in the name of the *umma*.[16] More broadly, it was used as a name for people exercising influence in high places, such as senior *ʿulamāʾ*, military commanders and powerful dignitaries. Members of the *dīwān* of Bonaparte's Egypt, to quote a ready example, proudly assumed this title in their negotiations with the French.[17] The nineteenth-century Tunisian statesman Khayr al-Dīn lucidly equated *ahl al-ḥall wal-ʿaqd* with the "persons of knowledge and valor" (*muruwwa*) in Europe who were elected to governmental offices, "except that the former ruled without being elected."[18] Even in this more general sense, the expression carried a distinctly traditional Islamic import, epitomizing much of the Muslim concept of government.

In the earlier part of the nineteenth century, the expression was often used with its loosest possible meaning to describe the social and political elite in Europe. It was applied in a general way to notables, such as the ancient Roman patricians and the highest officers of government in contemporary France.[19] It was also used, rather conveniently, as a vague reference to more specific but not quite intelligible posts and positions; a Russian *ministre,* for instance, was rendered in a translated text as "one of *ahl al-ḥall wal-ᶜaqd*", and the same formula was offered in translating the *magistrats de la ville* (of Stockholm).[20] It was the imprecise nature of *ahl-al-ḥall wal-ᶜaqd,* and apparently also its spoken elegance, that made it attractive to Arab writers, who, in using it, inadvertently built ambiguity into their portrayal of European aristocracy. The later disappearance of the term from usage, in both Middle Eastern and foreign contexts, reflected yet again the changing sociopolitical conventions in the region.

Accompanying the general expressions for the political elite was a wide variety of titles for specific categories. Each carried clear connotations of well-recognized sociopolitical status, with some variations among the titles used in different parts of the region. The usage of this nomenclature in the Middle East was quite consistent. But the influx of alien ideas had a disruptive effect on it. The gap between the available and accepted stock of titles, on the one hand, and the divergent assortment of European leaders and functionaries, on the other, was highly perplexing, especially since the criteria for sociopolitical prominence in certain European nations were undergoing a profound change. This led to unorganized semantic experimentations in Arabic, which resulted in a chaotic picture. Better acquaintance with the foreign scene gradually clarified this confused image. In the process, some titles were abandoned, remaining in the vocabulary of historical writing only. Others were resemanticized, so as to denote leadership defined by new principles. Still more names were newly devised and added to the list of modern appellations.

Perhaps the most common in this group of names was *shaykh,* pl. *shuyūkh* or *mashā'ikh.* Initially this was a title for a man respected for his old age. In pre-Islamic times it had come to denote, by extension, a politically or socially eminent person, whether the head of a family, a tribe or a village. Later it acquired the additional import of a spiritual authority, a mentor, and was applied to figures such as the leader of a Sufi order (*shaykh al-ṭarīqa*), the chief of a religious school (*shaykh al-madhhab*), and the supreme head of the religious hierarchy in the

Ottoman Empire (*shaykh al-Islām*). *Shaykh* was also used for heads of professional guilds, such as the merchants' chief, *shaykh al-tujjār,* and the tanners' chief, *shaykh al-dabbāghīn.* In Ottoman Egypt, *shaykh al-balad* was a title for officials who served as village headmen and, from the mid-eighteenth century on, for leaders of the Mamluk hierarchy who came to play a central role in the country's politics. More broadly, *shaykh* was used as a polite address or reference to respected persons. Talking about *al-shuyūkh* or *al-mashā'ikh* with no qualifications, one would be understood to refer to the dignitaries of the community in general.[21]

Shaykh was thus a title of veneration for one's age, office or personal qualities, connoting preferred social standing and often also high moral values. Its semantic range was broad enough to render it fit for describing a multitude of prominent European identities, in general and specific senses alike. Thus, the exclusively republicanist Paris Convention of 1792, elected by general manhood suffrage, was vaguely referred to as an assembly of *mashā'ikh al-shaᶜb,* "dignitaries of the people."[22] The Pope was the "reverend *shaykh* of the Vatican" (*shaykh al-Fātīkān*),[23] the nominal counterpart of *shaykh al-Islām.* And the president of the republic of Colombia, by the same token, was depicted as *ra'īs shaykh,* literally a "*shaykh*-president."[24] (The author of this last combination resorted to the rhetorical device of hendiadys, namely the use of two partly overlapping terms designed to denote the area of semantic overlap, thereby indicating the expressive inadequacy of each—a highly common feature of a language in transition.)[25] *Shaykh* was often applied to leaders on the local level; mayors of London, Paris, New York and other cities became *shaykh al-balad* (a curious application of the Egyptian title), *shaykh al-madīna* or *shaykh al-nāḥiya*—respectively *shaykh* of a town, a city, a district—and city council members were described as *mashā'ikh al-balad,* in similarity to *mashā'ikh al-aqālīm* (provincial notables) of Muhammad Ali's Egypt.[26] A derivative of *shaykh,* the noun *mashyakha,* was likewise used to denote a city council, as well as another, rather remote idea—that of a republic (see chapter 7). Such names were used frequently throughout the century for foreign functionaries and their Middle Eastern counterparts alike, the latter thus lending their semantic tint to the former.

Late in the century the word was given an additional, more

specific meaning. *Shaykh* became, apparently through a process of loan-translation, the equivalent of senator—originally a Latin word derived from *senex,* old. Senate, in Latin *senatus,* literally a council of elders, was accordingly rendered as *majlis al-shuyūkh,* a new coinage in Arabic. It was not until the last quarter of the century that the need arose to devise this special Arabic term for an institution hitherto identified, inconsistently, by a variety of designations.[27] Only in the 1880s was *shaykh* widely recognized as a term for senator. From then on it came to be applied to senators in ancient Rome, contemporary France, the United States, Italy and other places.[28] The choice of *shaykh* to mean a senator was fortunate, in a sense, for both implied correlation between advanced age and high political standing. Yet each carried other implications, relative to its social and political background. Hoping to avoid confusion, Arab writers sometimes chose to qualify their descriptions by using combined—and cumbersome—formulae, such as *majlis al-shuyūkh* (*al-sinā*), the parenthetical supplement accurately identifying the intended institution.[29] But even such carefully specified titles were not necessarily entirely clear. The occidental term "senate" (*sénat, senato*) was in itself a multicolored name; it stood for a plurality of realities, including councils ancient and modern, appointed and elected. Rendered as a "council of *shuyūkh,*" its already broad range of reference was considerably expanded, since the Arabic word also brought with it a variety of meanings. *Majlis al-shuyūkh* was perhaps more closely analogous to councils whose membership consisted of elderly notables nominated by kings, like those of modern Greece and monarchical France, than to senates whose members were elected by a broad suffrage, as in post-1875 France and in the United States. In Arabic texts of the period it was applied extensively in all of these and other instances.

This elasticity would facilitate the introduction of a new institution entitled *majlis al-shuyūkh* into the region itself in the twentieth century. In its modern Middle Eastern version, *majlis al-shuyūkh,* defined by practically all Arabic bilingual dictionaries as "senate," would, in effect, spell little more than "a corpus of notables." Middle Eastern polities would sometimes borrow other characteristics, functions and responsibilities of European and American senates. At other times, however, such additional qualities would be overlooked: the flexibility of the name would obviate detailed resemblance among the variety of institutions to which it was applicable abroad and at home.

Another word, partly synonymous with *shuyūkh*, was *aᶜyān*, pl. of *ᶜayn*—initially an eye, hence a prime part and, by extension, a senior person. In classical Arabic the term carried a variety of additional meanings which are of no interest to us here.[30] By the nineteenth century it served as a common appellation for men of importance throughout the Middle East. Like *shuyūkh* it was a ready choice of generic reference to all men of elevated status in the region.[31] *Aᶜyān* also had a more specific meaning: it designated that class of people in the Ottoman Empire which, since the late seventeenth century, had gathered influence in the provinces of Rumelia, Anatolia and the Fertile Crescent at the expense of the declining central authority. Being possessors of considerable property, with economic interests and political ambitions, they exercised increasing power, which was often recognized by the government. Benefiting from their membership in the provincial governor's administrative council (*dīwān*), they sometimes acquired actual control over their provinces. Such were, for instance, the ᶜAẓms of Damascus, the Jalīlīs of Mosul, and the notable families of Mount Lebanon, such as Shihāb, Khāzin, Junblāṭ and Arslān.[32]

It is hard to tell whether it was the looser or the more specific sense of *aᶜyān* that was attractive to Arab writers seeking names for the sociopolitical elite abroad. Most likely they recognized the benefit of the term's analogy to a familiar idea and the flexibility it had as a generic expression. "There are three types of government," the Egyptian translator and journalist, ᶜAbd Allāh Abū al-Suᶜūd, explained in 1873: alongside monarchy and democracy there exists aristocracy—*ḥukūma aᶜyāniyya;*

> In French it is called *arīstūkrāsiyya*, and in our places it is described as rule by *ahl al-ḥall wal-ᶜaqd* . . .It means that the country's government is in the hands of a group [of men] who are the *aᶜyān* of the people, the richest and most influential among them.[34]

Ancient Athenian aristocracy, Roman patricians, medieval European feudal lords, Russian boyars, pre-revolutionary French *noblesse* and *gentilhommes,* the British nobility and gentry, even American political leaders—all were described laxly as *aᶜyān*.[34]

Writers may not have had their own Ottoman, Lebanese or Egyptian *aʿyān* in mind in all cases, yet, intentionally or unwittingly, they were imposing upon the foreign notions at least something of the import of a distinct Middle Eastern idea.

Another meaning was added to this supple term in the mid-1870s. At that time an institution was founded in Istanbul, following the promulgation of the first Ottoman constitution, which was named *hey'et-i aʿyān,* or Chamber of Notables. The Chamber, the upper of two forums making up the General Assembly (*meclis-i ʿumūmī*), was composed of *aʿyān* from the different provinces of the empire, who were appointed directly by the Sultan for life.[35] The formation of this institution was a major event which naturally engaged intensive public attention all over the region. *Aʿyān* now came to be readily associated with members of the new Ottoman Chamber, sometimes also of the Ottoman Assembly at large. The term, hitherto seldom used to indicate comparable institutions abroad, consequently became highly common with that meaning.[36] Pliant in this sense as it was in denoting dignitaries and aristocrats, it proved applicable to members of upper councils in all foreign bicameral assemblies, regardless of their status or responsibilities, or the mechanism of their accession to the post. *Aʿyān* could be hereditary British lords; appointed members of the Russian czar's council; partly nominated and partly elected French *sénateurs;* American senators elected by universal suffrage, and others.[37] They all became members of a uniformly identified "council of notables," *majlis al-aʿyān.* Loose and semantically extended, the word would return to the Middle East in the twentieth century with this modern acceptance. Here, as in foreign contexts, it would stand for a variety of realities.

Three other titles of prominence whose nineteenth-century development resembled that of *shuyūkh* and *aʿyān* were *amīr, sharīf,* and *sayyid.* Historically honorifics for local notables, they were used to describe a miscellany of leaders in European political systems, gaining novel meanings in the process. Unlike the previous two terms, however, these terms failed to strike roots and were eventually abandoned. Their history during this period is nonetheless of interest to us, for they offer an instructive insight into the changes that affected the Arab political vocabulary during its modernization.

Most common among these titles was *amīr,* pl. *umarā'.* The semitic root a-m-r initially denoted speech or command—whence *amīr,* an army commander, a usage known at least since the times of the Prophet. That was the sense of the word in the traditional Caliphal title, first assumed by ʿUmar ibn al-Khaṭṭāb, *amīr al-mu'minīn*—"Commander of the Faithful," political and military leader of a conquering people. Historical developments during the first century of Islam led to the extension of the sense of *amīr,* which came to indicate, in addition, a provincial governor as well as a prince. A derivative, the compound title *amīr al-umarā',* supreme military chief, was first conferred by the Abbasid Caliph al-Rāḍī upon Ibn Rā'iq, one of his commanders, in the year 935. This title was soon adopted by the Buwayhids and was often used with that meaning thereafter.[38]

Ever since the early days of the Islamic state, military command had been related to the possession of land; as payment for service favored army officers were granted portions of territory with rights of usufruct or property. The practice was institutionalized by the Buwayhids and was observed in various ways by later Muslim governments including the Ottoman.[39] Consequently, *amīr* acquired the connotation of landowner, while its older meanings remained. In different parts of the Middle East the word came to be understood in one or another of its various senses: in Egypt *amīr* signified primarily a military commander or Mamluk chief; in Mount Lebanon it implied, above all, a powerful, feudal-like landlord and, hence, by local conventions, a senior magnate. In Mount Lebanon the term had a specific significance, as a title for the heads of the area's notable families, the real masters of the region. They were all *muqāṭaʿajīs,* tax-farmers, in a system more similar than any other in the Middle East to classical European feudalism.[40]

For many nineteenth-century Lebanese, and occasionally for other Arab writers, dignitaries of any designation anywhere were properly described as *umarā'.* These writers depicted pre-revolutionary France as the domain of "a feudal government [*ḥukūmat fyūdāl*], namely an *umarā'* government," which was composed of "*umarā'* and possessors of *iqṭāʿ.*" A historical account in *al-Jinān* related that, at that stage in French history, the nation comprised three groups: "the *umarā'* [*nūblis*], the religious establishment [*klayrjih*] and the common people [*tiyīr'itā*]" (the *noblesse, clergé* and *tiers état*).[41] A similar division was reported by the same journal to have existed in Finland, whose society consisted of notables, common people and peasants—"*umarā' Finlānd* . . .the *ahālī* and the *fallāḥīn.*"[42] British lords, "possessors of hereditary *amīriyya*" (lordship), were likewise so designated, both individually and collectively; the Earls of Aberdeen, for example, became *umarā' Abirdīn;* Sir Hamilton Gordon, having been knighted, was reported to have "become an *amīr* among the *umarā'* of Great Britain"; and the eighteenth-century prime minister William Pitt was called *ʿamūd al-umarā',* "the pillar of lords."[43] All these were associated with the House of Lords, an institution commonly known as *majlis al-umarā',* whose constituent "lords spiritual" and "lords temporal" were rendered, somewhat oddly, as *al-umarā' al-rūḥaniyīn wal-zamaniyīn.*[44] Simultaneously, *amīr* was used in the older sense of commander, with *amīr al-umarā'* serving to denote a supreme army chief,[45] as well as in the sense of prince (interchangeably with the loan-word *brins*[46]—see p. 68).

The word *sharīf,* pl. *ashrāf* or *shurafā',* was a specific traditional title for a man esteemed for his assumed distinguished descent. The notion goes back to pre-Islamic times, when the term was used to exalt descendants of notable tribal ancestors. Islam, however, stressed piety at the expense of genealogy as a criterion for social standing. Accordingly, *sharīf* became associated with offsprings of Muhammad and his house, believed to have inherited some of the Prophet's holiness through the generations. By the early Abbasid period the *ashrāf* had come to form a kind of aristocracy, whose privileged status was recognized by the state. They were paid a regular monthly pension and, at least since the ninth century, had had an officer or headman from among themselves, *naqīb al-ashrāf,* who guarded their interests. When the Islamic empire broke up, the *ashrāf* organized themselves in separate communities, each under its own *naqīb.* Under Ottoman rule the *ashrāf* maintained their prominence, enjoying special legal and fiscal benefits, as well as popular respect. In some places they developed a strong spirit of class solidarity, and at times, as in eighteenth-century Aleppo, they came to exercise considerable political power. Their social prestige was not equally high at all times and places, but even where it was relatively low their sharifian background generated some esteem. The independent Sultans of Morocco, lords of the country since the seventeenth century, claimed a *sharīfī* descent, as did the dynasty ruling Mecca from the tenth century to the twentieth and its descendants in Iraq and Jordan.[47]

In addition to this specific denotation, *sharīf* also served as an adjective which meant, broadly, elevated or eminent. It was attributable to a place, such as Jerusalem—*al-quds al-sharīf;* to an object, such as an imperial ("exalted") decree—*khaṭṭ sharīf,* or the Kaᶜba—*al-ḥaram al-sharīf* (literally "the exlated sacred [object]"); as well as to a person of noble rank, character or conduct, in religious or worldly matters.[48]

With this double intent, *sharīf* offered yet another ready choice of a title for privileged classes in Europe. It was used conveniently with reference to notables of all types, from the ancient Roman patricians, through the baronage of medieval England, to the contemporary French *noblesse.* Aristocratic government, by the same semantic token, was defined as *ḥukūmat al-ashrāf.* "If government is exercised by a group of leaders from among the people," one writer enlightened his readers, "then it is [called] an aristocratic government (*ḥukūma aristuqrāṭiyya*), namely, one exercised by the *ashrāf* and heads of the country."[49] (Cf. p. 61 above.) The English nation, another journalist explained, "has always been divided into [two sections]: the *ashrāf* and the [simple] people [*shaᶜb*]"; both are equal before the law, "but the *ashrāf* enjoy a higher level of wealth and standard of living." In Parliament that class was, reportedly, represented by *ḥizb al-ashrāf,* the "aristocratic [i.e. Conservative] party."[50] The name was also attached to individual British lords; lord Alexander Abercrombie, for instance, was described as "one of the *ashrāf* of Scotland"; and Gladstone, having refused the title of lordship, was said to have "declined *laqab al-sharaf (lūrdiyya).*"[51] In a similar vein, the British House of Lords was commonly referred to as *majlis al-ashrāf* or *nadwat al-shurafā',* "council of [aristocratic] dignitaries." This last usage, widespread in the Arabic press, especially during the 1870s and 1880s,[52] enriched an already colorful scene with another component of local traditional characteristics.

A title synonymous with *sharīf* was *sayyid,* pl. *asyād, sāda* or *sādāt.* The word meant lord, master or leader. Like *sharīf* it was an honorific in pre-Islamic tribal society, and it had been carried over to Islam as a title for those claiming direct descent from the Prophet. Likewise, again, it was a common appellation of esteem for a person of distinguished rank or quality, as well as a popular term of polite address. During the early years of the Arabic press, *sayyid* became one of the words enlisted to designate British lords and, more loosely, members of Parliament. *Majlis al-sāda* or *majlis al-sādāt* were used as names for both the Parliament and the House of Lords.[53] Thus in speeches to Parliament recorded by contemporary Arabic journals, the Queen was sometimes reported to have addressed *al-sāda al-ashrāf* (a hendiadys comprising two nouns), and at other times "*al-sādāt* and *al-ashrāf*" or, more accurately "*al-sāda,* members of the House of Commons" (*majlis al-ᶜumūm*).[54] Such instances occurred regularly until the mid-1870s.

The use of the last three expressions was short-lived. Like so many other terms during this experimental phase, *umarā', ashrāf* and *sādāt* were soon found unsatisfactory. They gave way to other terms and came to be confined, once again, to local contexts.

One last term which appeared briefly during this phase of tentative terminological innovations deserves to be considered here. This is *nabīl,* pl. *nubalā',* an old adjective which was given a new meaning as a noun. Unlike the previous three expressions, it had not normally served as a title, nor had it been used in a political sense. Like them, however, it was introduced into the political vocabulary through contact with alien ideas, then withdrawn as unfit. The Arabic root n-b-l implied excellence, ingenuity, nobility of character. The word dates back to the Middle Ages: *Lisān al-ᶜArab* defines *nabīl* as a person possessing "prudence and nobleness" (*al-dhakā' wal-najāba*). Golius's seventeenth-century *Lexicon* likewisė renders it as "*Praestans* (distinguished), *ingeniosus, generosus.*"[55] With the new needs of the nineteenth century the term was refurbished. The semantic proximity and phonetic resemblance between *nabīl,* on the one hand, and *noblesse, nobilta* and nobility, on the other, made it an attractive equivalent of these European terms. During the last quarter of the century it was temporarily added to the long list of expressions denoting European notables of every kind—British lords, French aristocrats, Greek dignitaries and the like.[56] As with similar terms, *nabīl* was used with reference to members of different governmental institutions. Not confined to bodies that harked back to the old feudal assemblies, such as the British House of Lords, it was also applied to those founded on quite different principles, such as the United States Senate. All alike were named *majlis al-nubalā'.*[57]

The names discussed so far were the most common of those

employed with reference to the sociopolitical leadership of Western countries. With the increasing interest in European affairs, their usage with new import grew more intensive. Since Arabic was particularly rich in honorifics and respectful appellations, it was in this section of the changing vocabulary that the greatest fluidity existed. It was therefore this part of Arabic political language that most clearly illustrated the problems of lexical modernization. Many authors were inclined to interchange these expressions, as none of them seemed utterly satisfactory for the new purposes. As late as 1890, no less an authority than Sulaymān al-Bustānī offered this puzzling definition for "senate":

A senate [sinā], in Latin sinātūs, means a council of shuyūkh. It is a name given in some countries to a consultative council, to which they collectively entrust governmental duties. Usually it is composed of the ashrāf class and balances the power of the [simple] people's [jumhūr] class. Among the most famous sinā councils . . . was the assembly of Jews known as Sanhedrin . . . whose members, numbering seventy, were of the aʿyān . . . The name sanhedrin was also given to the assembly of Jewish ashrāf convened by Napoleon I in 1806.[58]

Senators, then, were at once shuyūkh, aʿyān and ashrāf—all sharing the rather vague common denominator of sociopolitical seniority. An equally illuminating example may be quoted from Jurjī Zaydān's al-Hilāl. In an article on ranks and titles in Britain, published in 1894, the English people were said to comprise two categories: the working class, that is, the ʿāmma; and the khāṣṣa, "who are called jintilmān" (gentlemen). The khāṣṣa, Zaydān explains, are further divided into two parts:

The ashrāf form the first class of the khāṣṣa, and bear titles of nobility [sharāf] . . . [members of] this first class form the Parliament [barlamān] or the council of lūrdāt or aʿyān. They are like the distinguished Syrian families of the umarā' and mashā'ikh and muqaddamīn[59] and the rest of them, such as the umarā' of Banī Shihāb and Banī Harfūsh and Banī Maʿn and the mashā'ikh of Banī Talhūq and Banī al-Dahdāh.[60]

The inconsistent terminology in these two brief paragraphs was typical of the difficulties involved in discussing foreign notions, even as late as the turn of the century. Writers whom we usually consider to have been soundly acquainted with modern Western ideas, were groping uncertainly for names and analogies to denote and explain them. Presenting British lords as *ashrāf,* *aᶜyān* and *muqaddamīn,* and equating them with the *umarā'* of Banī Ḥarfūsh and *mashā'ikh* of Banī al-Daḥdāḥ, was surely instrumental in transmitting the broad idea of "aristocracy"; but the comparison could be of little avail in explaining the distinct characteristics of the foreign variant. Acknowledging the restricted expressive potential of each title, Zaydān offered all five of them, seeking to produce a semantic quality that would approximate the original idea. But this wealth of terms could not fully remedy the problem, for the range of reference of all the words put together still fell short of covering certain important shades of the alien concept (for example, the new status of British lords within a redefined political system). Conversely, it added a variety of irrelevant aspects to the idea. Even the high literary competence of men like Bustānī and Zaydān, with their solid grasp of foreign ideas, was of only limited value in crossing the linguistic and conceptual barrier. Much of the resultant ambiguity prevailed throughout the century and beyond. By 1900, none of the terms considered in this chapter had won exclusive acceptance for any particular notion.

Still unsatisfied with what their rich language could achieve in this sphere, Arab writers occasionally succumbed to borrowed words, which, they rightly felt, offered expressive accuracy unmatched by the Arabic substitutes. By far the most frequent foreign words in this category were *lūrd,* pl. *lūrdāt,* for British lords (the House of Lords being, accordingly, *majlis al-lūrdāt*);[61] and *brins,* for prince.[62] Less current were terms such as *sinātūr,* for senator;[63] *bīr,* from the French *pair,* lord;[64] and *shambarlīn,* chamberlain.[65] These were especially useful when employed parenthetically in compounds such as "the council of *aᶜyān* (*lūrdāt*)," indicating an institution of a similar nature but with certain unique alien characteristics. However, the traditional reluctance of Arabic to adopt foreign words limited the use of such expressions to a minimum. Thus, their contribution to clarity was at best marginal, and hence insufficient for preventing some of the more serious errors in the Arab grasp of Western standards of seniority.

5

The Sociopolitical Elite—
Leadership by Popular Election

Perhaps more significant than the Arab difficulty to properly depict ancient Roman senators and British lords was the confusion between old principles of sociopolitical seniority based on descent, wealth or royal favour, and the modern concept of prominence by virtue of popular representation. Almost all the terms discussed in the previous chapter were employed indiscriminately in denoting leaders of both kinds, with the whole gamut of varieties pertaining to each of them. Alongside these titles, however, Arab writers made use of several other terms, designed to convey specifically the idea of representation. These terms helped in removing much, although not all, of the ambiguity surrounding the subject.

In the nineteenth-century Middle East, representation or delegation existed in legal and commercial contexts, as well as in various other aspects of daily life. For instance, people commonly delegated others to represent them in court, and merchants sometimes hired agents to act for them in remote centers of commerce. In political contexts, it was common for the ruler to assign officials to different posts. However, neither representation nor delegation served as part of a mechanism for popular participation in government. To be sure, Muslim rulers were in theory called upon to listen to the voice of the ruled; the head of the Islamic state was expected to rely, in deciding his acts and policies, on consultation (*shūrā*) with members of his community. But the principle had never been institutionalized in a binding manner (this will be examined in more detail in chapter 8). The Islamic state, then, developed no practice of popular political representation; in a system where unquestioning obedience had become an article of faith, none seems to have been needed. Consequently, there was no word for such a practice, nor for those who might personify it.

The idea of persons enjoying sociopolitical prominence as elected representatives of the people was an innovation to nineteenth-century Arab intellectuals. In order to write about and discuss this strange phenomenon, they enlisted terms hitherto used in other contexts and having various meanings. Perhaps most conspicuous of these was *rasūl*, pl. *rusul*, a rather surprising choice of term, which was employed briefly and, apparently, by only one man, namely shaykh Ṭahṭāwī. Originally a participle meaning "a sent [message]," the word came to signify a person bearing one—a messenger or envoy. It was closely associated with the Prophet Muhammad, *al-Rasūl*, the messenger of God to His community. The word also served to designate other prophets and apostles of the monotheistic faiths. Having, in addition, a more secular application, *rasūl* could describe any person sent on a mission of whatever nature. Thus were named French delegates to the Cairo convention of notables in 1800, official French envoys to the Ottomans, and Bonaparte's emissary to al-Jazzār.[1] In the nineteenth century it was used occasionally to denote official foreign ambassadors such as "the French *rasūl* in Istanbul," and the British "Queen's political *rasūl*" in Cairo.[2] The term, however, does not seem to have been very widely used in this secular sense, apparently due to the singularity of its other, more sacred connotation.

To shaykh Rifāᶜa al-Ṭahṭāwī, the basic idea of "delegation" which the term implied made it an apt title for people's political deputies. He used it extensively in his *Takhlīṣ* while discussing the system of representation in post-revolutionary France. Ṭahṭāwī described the lower of the two French houses, the *Chambre des Députés* (*des départements*) as *dīwān rusul al-ᶜamālāt,* and designated a single *député* as *rasūl*.[3] Technically speaking, *député* and *rasūl* carried overlapping meanings, but in the context of French constitutionalism, the former bore an additional significance which the latter did not share. *Rasūl,* on the other hand, brought to the notion a markedly irrelevant import. Evidently, Ṭahṭāwī himself felt less than comfortable with it, for on more than one occasion he deemed it necessary to append to the title an interpretive remark which referred repeatedly to "the *rusul,* who are the *wukalā'* (deputies) of the people."[4] Eventually he abandoned the title altogether in favor of other expressions.

The word Ṭahṭāwī chose to explicate the meaning of *rasūl—wakīl,* pl. *wukalā'—*is equally illuminating. The verb w-k-l denotes, among other things, entrusting, authorizing, delegating, hence the noun *wakīl,* a classical Arabic name for deputy or agent, whether appointed to a long-term post or assigned to a brief mission of any nature. The word does not appear with this meaning in the Qur'ān,[5] but it is common in the Ḥadīth, where it offers a sound authorization for the legal concept of *wakāla.* The concept, which had become a central theme in Islamic Law, deals with mandate, namely the commissioning by a person (*muwakkil*) of a mandatary (*wakīl*) to represent him in a legal or other matter, or to perform some service for him.[6] The term was in common usage in trade and commerce; merchants often appointed an agent, *wakīl al-tujjār,* to represent them in their business, especially if the business was an ongoing enterprise. A *wakīl* could simultaneously represent a number of tradesmen; or a merchant could employ several *wukalā'* at one and the same time. Technical assistants to *qāḍīs* (judges) in medieval Syria also bore the title *wakīl,* as did agents for *multazims,* or tax-farmers, in the countryside of Ottoman Egypt.[7]

In political contexts, *wakīl* had traditionally denoted an official acting on behalf of a sovereign. For instance, officials in charge of the treasury in the Mamluk state, at both the Egyptian center and in the provinces, were called *wakīl bayt al-māl,* "deputy of the treasury," while agents for the Sultan's privy purse were distinguished by the title *wakīl al-khāṣṣ.*[8] As the French occupied Egypt, *wakīl* was accorded as a title to Bonaparte's deputy during the general's absence from the country. It was also used to designate the French inspector of the local assembly of notables—*wakīl al-dīwān.* This last title, according to Jabartī, was actually an Arabic rendition of what the French "called in their language *kumisārī* [*commissaire*], which literally means *wakīl.*"[9] The name also served to describe officials on more limited assignments: when the French undertook to withdraw from

Egypt, their agreement with the Ottomans providing for the move (the al-ʿArīsh agreement of 1800) was reportedly signed by appointed *wukalā'* acting for the two states.[10] The term retained this basic significance throughout the nineteenth century, serving for state functionaries such as treasury deputy (*wakīl al-māliyya*) and deputy of the department of commerce (*wakīl dīwān al-tijāra*) in Saʿīd's Egypt, or commercial inspector (*wakīl al-tafātīsh*) under Saʿīd's successor.[11]

In the Ottoman Empire the word carried much the same meaning and was likewise used at all levels of the state bureaucracy. The Grand Vezir had been known as the Sultan's *vekīl-i muṭlaq,* "absolute deputy" (or, during several short periods in the nineteenth century, *bāşvekīl,* "prime Deputy"); on a lower level, the *vekīl-i ḫarc,* or "steward of rations," was the person in charge of gathering edibles needed for the imperial kitchen and dispatching them to Istanbul. In 1837, when Sultan Maḥmūd II instituted a new forum of officials intended to operate as an imperial cabinet of sorts, he naturally termed that body *meclis-i vükelā,* "chamber of [state] agents," appointed directly by the head of the empire (it was also known as *meclis-i ḫāṣṣ,* or privy council). Some forty years later *meclis-i vükelā* was the appropriate name for a council whose foundation was prescribed by the first Ottoman constitution; consisting of *vükelā-i devlet,* appointed public servants, this new body shared both the title and the character of Sultan Maḥmūd's ministerial council.[12]

In all of these instances, the name *wakīl* and its Turkish equivalent described an official deputy or a commissioned lieutenant. It was more common in single form than in the plural, and when used in the plural, it always referred to small and exclusive groups—for *wukalā'* were never appointed in large numbers. Mid-nineteenth-century Arabic, as well as Turkish, dictionaries confirm this common application of the term, defining it as *ministre, chargé d'affaires, commissaire* or *intendant,* all of which stood for functionaries appointed by their superiors.[13] Accordingly, nineteenth-century texts dealing with historical and contemporary foreign matters applied the name regularly to a broad variety of administrative, diplomatic and military officials. The *vice chancelier du royaume* in seventeenth-century Poland, for example, was described as *wakīl wa-ra'īs efendi al-mamlaka;* the commander in chief of the armed forces in eighteenth-century Russia was *wakīl al-jaysh al-ʿāmm;* the British "Agent and Consul General" in occupied Egypt became "political *wakīl and qunṣul jinīrāl"; and* Austrian ambassadors to other countries were referred to as "political *wukalā'* abroad." Cabinet members in various European countries were designated as *wukalā'al-dawla,* the same name given to their Ottoman counterparts. By the turn of the century, calling the British foreign minister *wakīl al-khārijiyya* was still a common practice.[14]

The title *wakīl,* applicable to an appointed political agent of the ruler but never to one of the ruled, was quite remote from the concept of popular and elective representation. Yet the term itself offered perhaps the best available lexical means for dealing with that phenomenon, once Arab writers became aware of the European notion. Both the old word and the new idea implied delegation, if in different ways, and *wakīl* could reasonably be stretched to accommodate the significance of the novel idea.

One of the first writers to employ the word in this way was the Ottoman imperial historian ʿAṭāullāh Meḥmed, known as Şānīzāde. Describing parliamentary mechanisms in the countries of Europe, early in the nineteenth century, he made reference to consultative councils consisting of two elements: "state servants," *ḥudamā'-i devlet*—a long-familiar notion, and "representatives of the subjects," *vükelā-i raʿiyet* (Arabic *wukalā' al-raʿiyya*)—an innovative compound of two traditionally incompatible nouns. Both groups, he related, convened regularly for deliberation on state affairs.[15] The phenomenon is presented in this text as a successful version of a strange system, and Şānīzāde has much appreciation for it, however disguised. His treatment of it bears clear testimony to the novelty of the idea in the empire.

The combination of *wakīl* and "the people" in a political sense seems to have been introduced into Arabic usage sometime in the 1820s. While the few sources from that decade that have come down to us do not use this combination, it occurs in Elious Bocthor's *Dictionnaire* of 1828–1829. Bocthor suggested the formula *dīwān al-umarā' wa-wukalā' al-shaʿb* ("council of lords and people's *wukalā'* ") as a name for the bicameral British Parliament, and *jamāʿat wukalā' al-mamlaka* ("convention of the country's *wukalā'* ") for the French *États Généraux.*[16] A few years later, shaykh Ṭahṭāwī made use of the new compound while discussing the political system in France. The French provincial delegates (*rusul*), he explained, were actually *wukalā' al-raʿiyya* acting in an atmosphere of utter freedom. As it was impractical for all to participate personally in the work of government,

> the subjects in their entirety delegate 430 *wakīl* for the purpose, sending them to Paris for consultation. These *wukalā'* are elected by the subjects, who commission them to protect their rights and defend their interests.[17]

Ṭahṭāwī, like Ṣānīzāde, was fascinated by the strange idea and, like his Turkish counterpart, regarded it as a complete novelty. In this and other instances in which he discussed popular representation, he was careful to attach the qualifying phrase "of the people" to the noun *wukalā*, drawing his readers' attention to the unusual brand of deputies. When intending the more obvious notion of government officials, however, he needed no qualification. Such was the case with *dīwān al-wuzarā' wal-wukalā'*— "council of ministers and state officials," by which he designated the French cabinet.[18]

Ṭahṭāwī's pupils at the School of Languages were at first as meticulous as their mentor in indicating whose representatives they were discussing at any given time—the government's or the people's. In their translations they spoke of *wukalā' al-raʿiyya*, *wukalā' al-ahālī*, *wukalā' al-milla* or *wukalā' al-ʿamālāt*, as distinct from the conventional *wakīl al-dawla* or *wukalā' al-ḥukūma*.[19] They gave currency to the new usage. And by the time Arabic newspapers began to appear, *wakīl* had become an accepted name for elected representatives of the governed. Thus, a Lebanese press account in 1858 reported that "the Baron Rothschild was elected as *wakīl* to the [British] Parliament," although, being Jewish, he was "not a *wakīl* on behalf of the Christians." Another paper explained that the United States House of Representatives consisted of "members elected by the people, so that every thirty thousand [people] have one *wakīl*."And a third journal, in a historical account of the French Revolution, correctly distinguished between "the *wukalā'* of the common people, the *wukalā'* of the *ashrāf*, and the clergy."[20] The frequent usage of the term by the press turned it into a standard name for the concept of representation, discussed in both its individual and collective forms. Assemblies and councils of elected deputies accordingly became *dīwān* (or *majlis*) *al-wukalā'*.[21] With its new acceptance, it became more common in the plural form, which recalled the pluralistic nature of a representative political system, then in the singular, which connoted the individuality of an authority delegated by the ruler.

The semantic spectrum of *wakīl* was thus extended. It came to embrace a notion formerly meaningless, even though it was incipient in the word's original denotation. Yet, at the same time, *wakīl* also retained its older sense, as we have seen. It came to be employed with both meanings, the old and the new, simultaneously. This was a typical instance of equivocality in partly overlapping but unequally familiar ideas. Aware of a potential semantic confusion, many writers, when using the word, were cautious to specify the kind of *wukalā'* to which they were referring. Many others did not, leaving room for questioning and puzzlement. Typically problematic was the notion of *majlis al-wukalā'*, a highly common designation for elective institutions in the West, such as the British House of Commons, the French *Chambre des Députés* and the United States House of Representatives. The title itself included no clue as to the precise nature of these *wukalā*. The only institution at home bearing that name, the *meclis-i vükelā* in Istanbul (itself a product of European influence), consisted of "delegates" of a very different type; and the formation of such a council in the empire, sharing the title but not all of the traits of the foreign model, would in itself have created ambiguity.

Until the early 1870s, *wukalā'* was by far the most common Arabic name for elected representatives of the people. Then it began to give way to another term, *nā'ib,* pl. *nuwwāb,* a word whose semantic history and modern development resembled those of *wakīl* in many details. The root n-w-b denotes substitution, delegation, or taking the place of another. *Nā'ib* could mean, loosely, any person appointed to represent another in any kind of matter. But it was more commonly used for men nominated to official positions, with an implication of subordination to a superior authority. It thus meant lieutenant, vicegerent or deputy. In the Mamluk state, the title *nā'ib al-salṭana* was applied to the Sultan's deputy and chief administrator (also entitled *al-nā'ib al-kāfil,* the answerable or liable *nā'ib*), and to provincial governors acting in his name in Egypt, Syria and Palestine. During periods of the Sultan's absence from Cairo, a temporary deputy would be appointed in his stead, bearing the title *nā'ib al-ghayba* ("deputy of absence"). *Nā'ib* also served as a title for military commanders of different ranks; the chief commander of the Mamluk army in Damascus was called *nā'ib al-jaysh,* commanding officers of city fortresses in the provinces bore the title *nā'ib al-qalᶜa,* and "lieutenant-commanders of ten" were *nā'ib amīr ᶜashara.*[22] In the Ottoman Empire, the title was used especially in the legal administration, signifying a deputy of a *qāḍī* or *mawla* appointed in any of the subdivisions of their jurisdiction. In their 1850 Turkish-French *Dictionnaire,* Bianchi and Kieffer explained that *nā'ib* "désigne proprement tout vicaire spirituel et judicaire, comme *wakīl* indique tout vicaire temporel, civil et politique."[23] In the Arab provinces, however, *nā'ib* was employed in a political sense as well. For example, the French and Ottoman signatories of the al-ᶜArīsh agreement—depicted, as we have seen, as *wukalā'* of their states—were also described as *nuwwāb* of their respective sovereigns. One article of the agreement allowed for the dispatch of a *"nā'ib* on behalf of the Sublime Porte" to Alexandria, to assist in the French evacuation.[24] In a similar vein, in the preface to his Arabic translation of Machiavelli's *Il Principe,* the Syrian-Egyptian priest Don Raphael praised his benefactor, Muhammad Ali, "the great *wazīr* who is *nā'ib* over the province of Egypt," alluding at once to his elevated post and to his subordination to the Sultan.[25]

In the relationship between the government and the governed, then, *nā'ib*—like *wakīl*—had always been associated with the former. Likewise, and for similar reasons, it had been much more common in the singular than in plural form. Likewise again, it had retained its traditional meaning throughout the nineteenth century, in contexts both local and foreign. *Nā'ib* presented a ready choice of title for men of various statuses and high posts abroad. The ancient Roman imperial governors (French *lieutenants impériaux*), for example, were rendered as *nuwwāb al-qayṣar.* The British viceroy of Ireland was made *nā'ib malik,* or *nā'ib amīr Irlāndā.* The king of Russian-occupied Poland, officially the czar's deputy in that land, was designated as *"nā'ib . . .* on behalf of the Muscovite *sulṭān."* And the pope, "vicar of Christ," was referred to as *"nā'ib* of the Lord Jesus" (or, on one occasion, as "the *nā'ib* of God on earth").[26] The word's traditional import seems to have remained its most obvious and most common for the greater part of the century. By 1870 Buṭrus al-Bustānī, identifying *nā'ib* in his dictionary as "he who replaces another," still chose *nā'ib al-qāḍī* and *nā'ib al-malik* as the only illustrations of the definition.[27]

Largely synonymous with *wakīl, nā'ib* too was to be enlisted
for discussing the once nameless notion of people's representatives in government. The word was occasionally employed by
Ṭahṭāwī, with reference to elected deputies in France, Sweden
and Switzerland.[28] But it gained currency only in the mid-1860s,
especially after the Egyptian Khedive Ismāʿīl chose the term to
designate the membership of a new institution he established in
1866—*majlis shūrā al-nuwwāb,* or Consultative Council of Delegates, a body whose formation has often been considered a major
event in the region's constitutional history. The chamber consisted of seventy-five men, mainly from the countryside, chosen
through an indirect procedure and accorded a strictly consultative
authority. Designed to improve Ismāʿīl's administrative and financial control, and to suit the low level of political awareness,
the electoral system was formulated so as to produce a council of
dignitaries loyal to the Khedive (according to one source, the
members were not elected but, rather, appointed directly by provincial governors).[29] The system ignored members of groups such
as the merchants, artisans, graduates of the new educational net-
work and, of course, the largely illiterate public in general,
"so much so," in the words of one Egyptian historian, "that
[the Council] would have been more properly entitled *majlis
al-aʿyān,*" to wit, council of notables.[30]

Calling these delegates *nuwwāb* was surely a novelty. They
were evidently not ruler-appointed officials in the familiar sense.
They acceded to this position through a procedure that was not
traditional; hence their new status seemed to merit a nontraditional appellation. The title *nuwwāb* could be stretched to denote
the new post, which, in its Egyptian version, was not totally
divorced from old principles. This semantic extension obviously
did not lend the word any implication of actual popular representation. In the Egyptian usage of the time, *nuwwāb* expressed a
meaning that stood somewhere between "official delegates" and
"people's deputies."

Following the foundation of the Khedive's Council, the
name *majlis shūrā al-nuwwāb* (or *majlis al-nuwwāb,* as it came to
be called in 1881–1882), was applied to all institutions of a representative nature in Europe and the United States. Some authors
(not necessarily Egyptians) applied the designation to representative councils in Europe, describing the *Chambre des Députés* in
Paris and the Parliament in London as *majlis shūrā al-nuwwāb.*[31]

More common was the compound *majlis al-nuwwāb*, which quickly grew into a standard designation for such forums. By the mid-1870s, *nuwwāb* had come to replace *wukalā'*.[32]

For about a decade, from the mid-1870s to the mid-1880s, there was yet another word in extensive use with the same meaning. The term *mabʿūth*, pl. *mabʿūthīn*, was a passive participle meaning dispatched or delegated. It was synonymous with *rasūl*, and likewise served as a title for the Prophet, though it did not have the same currency as *rasūl*. Unlike *wukalā'* and *nuwwāb*, *mabʿūthīn* had not served previously as a common name for official agents.[33] In 1876 the Ottoman constitution prescribed the formation of a council of provincial delegates, *hey'et-i mebʿūsān* (Arabic *hay'at al-mabʿūthīn*), the lower house of a new general assembly. The title was thereby applied to people's deputies, elected by male suffrage throughout the empire and intended to represent fifty thousand male Ottoman subjects each (in reality this proportion varied greatly from one province to another). The first council, elected from December 1876 to February 1877, consisted of 120 *mabʿūthīn* from twenty-eight provinces and districts.[34] The extensive press coverage given in the Arab countries to the creation and activities of this institution made the term well known. Subsequently it was extended to denote elected members of representative institutions abroad, and this application continued during the brief lifetime of the Istanbul assembly and for a while thereafter.[35]

At the time when a forum of provincial delegates operated in the Ottoman capital, the concept of popular representation was still novel and largely obscure. Of the three words interchangeably used to express it—*wukalā'*, *nuwwāb* and *mabʿūthīn*, the first two continued to carry the meaning of state agents as well. The third may have offered the least equivocal choice, for its other accepted denotation was the reasonably analogous local version of the same idea. It was also the least common, however, and eventually dropped from use.[36] None of these names could accurately express the idea of popular representation by itself. When the usually articulate Adīb Isḥaq tried to instruct his readers on the notion of *majlis al-nuwwāb* in 1878, he found himself producing a rather awkward explanation; in Europe, he suggested, there "appeared assemblies of *wukalā'*, or *nuwwāb* and *mabʿūthīn*, now known among the Europeans by the name of parliament [*barlamintū*]. These *nuwwāb* . . . are the *rusul* of the

people."[37] Put together, the three expressions—along with *rusul*
which, he felt, would add clarity to his explanation—were expected to convey an idea that would have more dimension than
that expressible by any of them individually. Isḥaq's effort was
typical of the measures taken by a whole generation of writers
who met the challenge of articulating novel concepts by means of
a traditional vocabulary.

As the century drew to a close, there was ample evidence of
Arab confusion about principles of individual prominence in the
West. The persistent adherence to titles like *aʿyān, ashrāf* and
nubalā', even when discussing elected delegates, remained both a
symptom and a source of much ambiguity. The lack of nominal
distinction between Egyptian and European *nuwwāb*, or between
Ottoman and Western *wukalā'*, was another mark of it. Initially,
as we have seen, the Arab difficulty with this subject stemmed
from their lack of experience with popular political participation.
Closer contacts with foreign systems made that concept gradually
comprehensible. As that process was going on, the principle was
implemented in the region itself, but in a modified version which
differed from the original model in certain important respects.
Thus, an interim concept between the traditional notion and the
modern idea was introduced into the Middle East—an inevitable
development, given the broad initial gap between the two societies. This was no more than a preface to a fuller understanding
of the foreign idea which would take place at a later time.

Amidst this confusion, it is possible to discern the emergence
of a measure of order during the last years of the nineteenth
century. Of the titles considered in the previous chapter, *shuyūkh*
and *aʿyān* were gaining growing recognition at the expense of the
rest. Somewhat more systematically than before, these names
were now used to denote the traditional nobility and members of
upper houses in bicameral assemblies. *Shuyūkh* gradually became
the equivalent of "senators," to the exclusion of other meanings
in foreign political contexts. *Aʿyān* was reserved for all other
comparable leaders. Elected representatives of the people, and
members of lower houses in foreign parliaments, came to be
entitled *nuwwāb*, a word which was supplanting both *wukalā'* and
mabʿūthīn. This tendency for greater consistency, while perhaps
not signifying a solid grasp of the popular representative principle, was surely conducive to clarity. It reflected a growing awareness of the prominent role that elected deputies enjoyed within

the new system, and was at the same time helpful in familiarizing the readers with modern criteria of political leadership. In the twentieth century, *shuyūkh* and *aᶜyān* would become common designations for Middle Eastern dignitaries, who in many respects would be more similar than their predecessors to their European counterparts. *Nuwwāb* would become a standard name for members of new institutions seeking to personify an actual, and more intelligible, representative principle.

6

Constitutions, Laws, Legislation

"The best reason why monarchy is a strong government," Walter Bagehot suggested in his *English Constitution,* "is, that it is an intelligible government. The masses of mankind understand it, and they hardly anywhere in the world understand any other." The action of a single will, the fiat of a single mind, he argued, "are easy ideas: anybody can make them out, and no one can ever forget them."[1] More than just the technical leadership of a monarchical state, a position inherited or seized, Bagehot seems to have had in mind an effective rule by one person holding exclusive or nearly exclusive governmental authority in his kingdom. Such a definition would have been applicable throughout most of Europe before the nineteenth century. It applied in the Middle East before and during that century, for such leadership was an inseparable part of the political tradition. With rare exceptions this was the only pattern of rule in the region's history, and none of the normative jurists of Islam had recognized, let alone sanctioned, any other.

That the concept of state was readily identifiable with hereditary monarchy in the Middle East is reflected, for example, in the semantic history of the term *dawla,* pl. *duwal.* Today we take this word to denote primarily a state, that is, the governing authority of a polity, or its body politic. It is also used, more broadly, to mean a nation-state or a country, hence the adjective *dawlī* or *duwalī*, "international". When we dig into the term's past, however, we are likely to expose several interesting sub-layers. *Dawla* is derived from d-w-l, basically meaning to turn, to alternate. One of the initial senses of the word was "a turn of fortune." "*Al-dunyā duwal,*" stated a shrewd eighth-century royal adviser—that is, "life in this world consists of ups and downs." When the Abbasids first introduced their government as *dawla,* they were referring to their "turn of power," destined to follow that of the Umayyads. Their "turn" lasted long enough for the word itself to become identified with the rulers themselves, and *dawla* acquired the meaning of dynasty. It came to have both the sense of turn and that of dynasty, representing a philosophy which held that power was temporary and changeable according to God's will. Further historical developments lent *dawla* the additional meanings of dominion and state, as well as realm, the ruler's kingdom. "Dynasty," "government" and "realm" came to represent basically one and the same identity; speaking of *al-dawla al-ᶜUthmāniyya* or *al-dawla al-ᶜāliya* (Turkish *devlet-i Osmāniye, devlet-i ᶜāliye*), one would be referring to the house of ᶜUthmān, the Ottoman ruling establishment, broadly taken, or the empire under their reign.[2]

Throughout the nineteenth century, *dawla* had been commonly used with all of these meanings, in local as well as foreign contexts[3]—epitomizing, in a way, the Middle Eastern version of "l'état c'est moi." It is interesting to note, in passing, that the occidental equivalents—state, *état, stato*—originated from a very different and much broader notion; derived from the Latin *status,* a neutral expression meaning condition of a person, class or community, they came to denote a politically and legally organized community.[4] We need not, of course, read too much into a single piece of semantic evidence, yet *dawla* surely offers one illuminating instance of the traditional idea of "state" in the region, which was mirrored in a variety of other ways.

In Islam, sovereignty emanated from God and was invested in the head of His community, the Caliph. Government meant *ḥukm muṭlaq,* absolute sway. The ruler exercising it was *muṭlaq al-taṣarruf,* an absolute authority. The only authority to which he was accountable was that of the Holy Law, the *sharīᶜa*—the conceived expression of God's expectations of His community. In the initial Islamic ideal of state, the *sharīᶜa* was to serve as a source of guidance for the ruler and for the whole community. History, however, witnessed an ever-expanding gulf between the ideal and the real. At quite an early stage the Holy Law came to be regarded as a boundary not to be too blatantly transgressed, rather than a source of guidance. And even as a limitation it was not always carefully observed. Theory followed practice; in the writings of jurists such as Māwardī, al-Ghazālī and Ibn Jamāᶜa (of the eleventh, twelfth and fourteenth centuries, respectively), the ideal was modified to fit, then legitimize, existing standards. The *sharīᶜa* was still placed above the ruler, but there was growing flexibility in the practical obeisance to this supremacy. That the community should have an effective ruler was imperative; that he should respect the Holy Law, only desirable.

Absolutism likewise characterized the majority of European monarchies by the eve of the French Revolution. A few of them were to remain absolute throughout most or all of the following century. In others, autocracy had lost ground to other varieties of government, as the power of kings was gradually circumscribed by the rising aspirations of their subordinates. First in Britain in the seventeenth and eighteenth centuries, and then elsewhere—in France, Belgium, Holland, Denmark—in the first half of the nineteenth, monarchies became "restricted," and constitutions were devised to redefine the distribution of authority. Further developments changed these states from "restricted" monarchies into what may be more properly described as "parliamentary" regimes. The difference was of much significance: in contrast to governments, absolute or restricted, which were centered around a king, the newly emerging systems created a sovereignty which lay within institutions elected through an ever-growing suffrage, and in which the monarchs were reduced to little more than symbols. The simple unit of a single ruler and his mass of subjects was thus giving way to a complex order throughout parts of which power was distributed. The constitution was no longer a mere demarcation of royal power. Rather, it became an elaborate definition of a delicate power system, identifying its participants and its rules. It was, in Bagehot's words, a system "unintelligible" to many, one "difficult to know and easy to mistake."[5]

No similar changes took place in the Middle East. The development of "centrifugal" forces in the eighteenth-century Ottoman provinces, which might have portended such an evolution,[6] was cut short by rulers armed with imported, effective methods of control and new instruments for imposing centralization. Government in the nineteenth-century Middle East remained a traditional-style autocracy—the type of regime most readily understood by the obedient subjects of the Sultan, the Pasha or the Bey.

When curious Arab observers first encountered and described European monarchs, their descriptions reflected that traditional concept of monocracy. Two species of monarchical regimes were detected: absolute, the one most familiar and, hence, the easiest to grasp, which they called *malakiyya muṭlaqa;*[7] and nonabsolute, defined as *malakiyya muqayyada,* "restricted monarchy," or *ḥukm muqayyad bil-qawānīn,* "rule circumscribed by the laws."

The Arab treatment of the latter type is particularly interesting. As shaykh Ṭahṭāwī explained in 1843, adopting Rousseau's categorization of government, a restricted monarchical government (*ḥukm mūnarkhī muqayyad*) is the kind of system in which "the king rules according to the laws of the country; adhering to them prevents him from exceeding them to his heart's whims."[8] Thus, in contemporary France "the sovereign is the king, but on condition that he abides by the letter of the law." England offered another example of a "kingdom restricted by the laws which are imposed [*mashrūṭa*] on the king." Other monarchies featured similar phenomena.[9] This was a rather narrow concept of the foreign idea, identifying "constitution" as merely "restriction"; but it was not altogether inept, for at the time of Ṭahṭāwī's writing, in the early part of the century, most European nonabsolute monarchies were indeed little more than "restricted" kingdoms.

Arab writers of later years persistently adhered to this narrow designation, even when the ongoing redistribution of power in Europe rendered the concept obsolete. As late as 1872, England—by then enjoying a parliamentary government which, following two reform bills, represented some two million voters—was still depicted as, only, *malakiyya muqayyada* ("restricted"), in a translated text whose original read "constitutional monarchy."[10] Another contemporary translated account rendered *gouvernement représentatif,* this time in a French context, as *ḥukūma muqayyada,* "restricted government."[11] And in 1897, after a third reform bill in England which doubled the electorate and provided for manhood suffrage, one newspaper characterized Queen Victoria's government as one "restricted [*muqayyada*] by the constitution, so that she cannot slaughter her loyal subjects"—a striking, implicit contrast to contemporary Ḥamīdian despotism.[12] At about that time, the always lucid ᶜAbd Allāh Nadīm thus enlightened his readers on European constitutionalism: the states of Europe, he explained, "established ministerial and consultative councils by which royal power is restricted [*taqayyada*]." The objective was to "save the rulers from erring"; and the step proved successful, in that it restored "people's faith in their kings and ministers."[13]

In this last example, and indeed in the rest of them, the monarch was the indispensable pivot of government, as was the Sultan in the Islamic state. Other institutions and mechanisms were no more than instruments of guidance to the ruler or, at most, maintained certain limitations upon his inalienable authority. Such a view, typical of the writings throughout the greater part of the century, reflected a serious difficulty in grasping the complex alien order. That the law was above the otherwise absolute ruler was a notion long familiar and comprehensible; that a set of agreed-upon principles should seriously cut down the authority of a supreme monarch, even relegate him to a secondary status in his own kingdom, seemed strange and hard to conceive. Such arrangements, hailed in the West as those of mankind's rightful government, were all but unthinkable in Islamic terms.

How were the instruments which confined the kings' absolute power in Europe to be identified? The question confronted Arab writers with a puzzling challenge. They readily confused constitution and law, two different instruments of state, the one designed to determine the rules of political order, and the other to ensure its proper functioning and to regulate the different aspects of communal life. The precise nature of each being inadequately clear, Arab writers during much of the nineteenth century treated them as best they could through the use of two traditional terms, *sharīᶜa* and *qānūn*, thus making a highly problematic analogy to traditional Islamic legal notions.

The Arabic term *sharīᶜa*, pl. *sharāʾi*, carried an import broader than that of "law" or *droit*. It also signified more than a set of laws or a legal code. *Sharīᶜa* was a condensed expression of the special relationship between God and His community. The word had originated in pre-Islamic times, when it indicated a path leading to a source of water, and thus to a source of life.

When it became a legal term, *sharīʿa* was intended to imply a way of life that would carry its followers to salvation.[14] The path was marked by God. It represented His will as revealed to the believers of the early Islamic generations, and man was not to interfere with or modify it in any way. In principle the *sharīʿa* covered all spheres of life, individual as well as communal, spiritual as well as political, even if it was not explicit about some of them. By the late ninth century, the formative phase of defining its principles had come to an end. From then on there was room only for interpretation, through elaboration or extension, but not for change or innovation. Theoretically, "legislation" had become an impossible concept.

The *sharīʿa* prevailed throughout the Islamic lands, its status as the basic legal foundation for the community's conduct never contested. Yet, since new questions which arose from time to time were not specifically answered by the *sharīʿa*, Muslim rulers resorted to extensive "interpretation" of the Holy Law. Some of them went as far as to hold their own will to be legally valid and binding; they would set forth rules and issue regulations with the practical effect of law but sanctioned as interpretations of the *sharīʿa*. These rules were known as *qānūn*.

Qānūn, pl. *qawānīn*, was a Greek word (*kanon*—a rule or measure, whence an assessment for taxation) which was borrowed by Arabic during the early Islamic conquests. At first used as a fiscal term in the context of land taxes, its meaning was expanded during the Abbasid period to denote legal regulations prescribed by the ruler. The practice of administering the affairs of the realm through *qānūns* (or *qānūnnāmes*, "*qānūn*-texts") flourished in the Ottoman Empire, where such laws served as an essential instrument of government. This practice was in no way viewed as legislation; the *qānūns* issued by the Sultans were held as mere "codification," or legitimate extensions, of the Holy Law. The Ottomans, perhaps more than any other Islamic dynasty, treated the *sharīʿa* as the actual law of the state. Under their rule, the *sharīʿa's* legal administration and the *ʿulamā'* enjoyed unprecedented authority and influence.[15] By the nineteenth century, the revealed Law offered the only conceivable basis of a proper legal order in the Ottoman Middle East, with *qānūn* as a convenient complementary tool. While related, these were two distinct conceptions which should not be confused. The Egyptian shaykh al-Sharqāwī, at one time Shaykh al-Azhar, scornfully commented on the French invaders of his country: "They think," he said, "that the prophets Muhammad, Jesus and Moses were but a group of intelligent men [*jamā^cat ^cuqalā'*], and that the *sharā'i^c* attributed to them were in effect *qawānīn* they devised with their minds."[16] To an early nineteenth-century devout Muslim like al-Sharqāwī, such an idea would be nothing short of blasphemy.

The vision of man-made constitutions and laws, equally binding upon the monarch and upon his subjects, at first greatly perplexed Middle Eastern observers. "Most of [the French constitution's] contents do not exist in the book of God, the Most High, nor in the tradition of His Prophet, peace be upon Him," shaykh Ṭahṭāwī readily noticed.[17] Absent as they were from Middle Eastern experience, the conceptual foundations of the strange system and the nature of the relationship among constitution, law and regulation, were difficult to articulate. Puzzled, Arab writers characterized them all as either *sharī^ca* or *qānūn*— an interchangeability they would never have in Islamic contexts. Following the attempted escape of Louis XVI from his palace in June 1791, Niqūlā Turk related, the people in Paris demanded the execution of the king according to "the *sharī^ca* of the republic"—a rather odd combination.[18] Several years later shaykh Ṭahṭāwī tried to explicate: "the French," he said, "call their *qānūn* a *sharī^ca;* they thus refer to 'the *sharī^ca* of such and such a king'." The attempt at clarification did not bring about full comprehension, not even in the case of Ṭahṭāwī himself. When Louis XVIII ascended to the throne, Ṭahṭāwī related, he "produced [*ṣana^ca*] a *qānūn* between himself and the French [people]." This *Charte Constitutionelle* was, according to Ṭahṭāwī, "The *qānūn* by which the French now conduct their affairs and which they take as a basis for their administration [*asās li-siyāsatihim*]." Translating article 1 of this document, however, he chose to render "les Francais sont égaux devant la loi" as "*al-Faransāwiyya mustawūn quddām al-sharī^ca.*"[19]

Writings of later years abound in comparable instances, only a few of which can be quoted here. The martial law declared in Paris during the French Revolution became "the *sharī^ca* known as *sharī^cat mārsyāl*" (an evident misreading of the notion); but the same term was also applied to Napoleon's *Code Civile,* introduced in France and in the European countries by his armies, which was described as *sharī^cat Nābūlyūn.* Newly elected members of the

British Parliament were said to have pledged allegiance "to the king and the country's *sharīᶜa*", while the British Land Act of 1881, an individual piece of legislation, was referred to as "the agricultural *sharīᶜa*" (*al-sharīᶜa al-zirāᶜiyya*). French Lawyers, by the same token, were designated as *fuqahā' al-sharīᶜa*, "[theologian] experts of the *sharīᶜa*." As against this, the French constitution of 1791 was depicted as merely "*qānūn* 91," and that of 1795 as "*qānūn* of the [revolutionary] year 3"; Louis Napoleon's 1852 constitution became *qawānīn al-mamlaka;* and the 1848 struggle of the Prussian people for a constitution was recorded as a quest for "the establishment of a general *qānūn.*"[20]

Specific and accurate in traditional use, but loose and imprecise in foreign application, *sharīᶜa* and *qānūn* reflected profound bewilderment about the foreign idea. Some writers may have felt that the semantic spectra of *sharīᶜa* and *qānūn* did not fully match those of law and constitution. At best, they may have sensed, these Islamic names could express the strange notions approximately. Others may have acquired merely a vague acquaintance with the alien concept and felt no discomfort by such usage. Whatever the case, there was hardly a better alternative at hand.

In addition to the frequent interchanging of *sharīᶜa* and *qānūn,* writers indicated their discomfort or unfamiliarity in several other ways. Many employed the plural form *sharā'iᶜ*—for obvious reasons a highly uncommon usage in Islamic contexts,[21] attaching it to such specific conceptions as the United States Constitution (*sharā'iᶜ jumhūriyyat al-wilāyāt al-muttaḥida*) and international law (*al-sharā'iᶜ al-dawliyya*); or they more loosely applied it to sets of laws and rules such as the ancient Athenian legal codes and the fruits of contemporary French *Assemblée* legislation.[22] Others resorted to the device of hendiadys, seeking to produce a new semantic quality that would perhaps come closer to the intended meaning; formulae such as *al-sharā'iᶜ wal-qawānīn* or *al-aḥkām al-qānūniyya wal-sharᶜiyya,* were applied to the ancient Roman law, contemporary German legislation, and other legal notions similarly difficult to designate more accurately.[23] Occasionally the French word *charte* was borrowed—in Arabic, *shārt* or *sharṭa*—to describe French and other constitutions.[24] And at times still simpler ways out were devised: translating "[chacun des] graves questions constitutionelles" as *mas'ala dhāt ahammiyya,* "a question of importance,"[25] the author avoided the complexity altogether—a convenient and rather common practice during the period. All these attempts created a desultory sense of a subject which, perhaps more than any other, represented the essence of modern sociopolitical philosophy in the West.

To a large extent, the difficulties involved in dealing with European laws and constitutions stemmed from the basic problem of understanding the phenomenon of human legislation. The latter concept, as we have seen, had been absent from Islamic political thought, save for the notion of a limited "codification." The verb *sharraᶜa* which, among other things, meant the prescription of law, was reserved in that sense for God, who "*sharraᶜa* [the Holy Law] to His believers."[26] Muslim writers were reluctant to apply it to people, and rarely did; human beings were not supposed to legislate.[27]

When Arab writers were exposed to the Western phenomenon of creating new legal orders—a constant process of redefining sociopolitical structures and conduct, they tended to view it as a mechanism of "reorganizing" preexisting laws, rather than producing new ones. Projecting their concept of codification on the foreign system, they described legislation as *tartīb al-qawānīn*, "arrangement of [old] laws." An absolute monarch, one writer explained, is one "who has the freedom of *tartīb al-qawānīn* all by himself."[28] Not even an autocrat, then, could enjoy more than the exclusive privilege of "arranging" the laws, let alone assemblies purporting to be "legislative." Such bodies readily became *al-jamᶜiyya al-murattiba*, "the arranging assembly," or *majlis tartīb al-qawānīn*, "the assembly for arranging the laws." A constitution, both the document and the political order based upon it, was accordingly described as *tartīb umūr al-dawla*, literally "the arrangement of state affairs," or simply *tartīb*. Authors thus discussed the French "*tartīb* of the year 1791," the "new *tartīb*" of 1795 or "the *tartīb* of the year 3" in France—all man-made "orders."[29] Other variations reflected the same approach: la puissance législative was rendered as *tadbīr [al-] umūr*, "the administration of affairs," and laws made by legislative forums became "the *qawānīn* which the assembly selected"—*yardā bihā* (as distinct from "created").[30] This kind of usage was common during the first half of the century.

European principles of legislation and of producing documents defining the division of authority gradually became familiar (although not always "intelligible," to use Bagehot's terminology once again). When Ṭahṭāwī adopted Rousseau's classification of governments in 1842, he described the apparatus limiting the power of "restricted" monarchs as "the laws of the kingdom" (*qawānīn al-mamlaka*), which had been "decided upon" (*inḥaṭṭa ᶜalayhā al-qarār*) and which the ruler "does not ignore, nor violate at his heart's whims,"[31] a definition not altogether inaccurate, yet hardly specific and, hence, of limited instructive value.

But thirty years later a colleague, the perspicacious ᶜAbd Allāh Abū al-Suᶜūd, offered this illuminating characterization of constitutional monarchy:

> [The second type is] a restricted [*muqayyada*] or legal [*qānūniyya*] monarchical government, also designated as balanced [*muᶜaddala*] or representative [*niyābiyya*.] In this [kind of regime], the supreme authority is divided between the head of the state and a popular consultative council. This refers to a group of persons elected by each district, namely the inhabitants of all parts of the country, who are [men of] opinion and practice, judgement and knowledge of facts. As representatives of all the people, they offer their views after deliberation on important issues concerning the general order [*tartīb*] of the country, as well as on current matters. They are elected . . . through a direct . . . or indirect process, hence the government is called "representative." The name is appropriate, for [the government] is based on cohesive fundamental order [*tartīb asāsī*] and a rigorous political law [*qānūn siyāsī*].[32]

With this kind of elaborate knowledge came a better grasp of the idea of legislation. It became apparent that ruling authorities in Europe and America were creating laws, not just interpreting them. They were laying guidelines for the conduct of society and prescribing rules defining the relationship between government and governed. Such practice, once recognized, was expressible by the verb hitherto reserved for the creator of the Holy Law—*sharraᶜa*. The word had already occurred in the writings of Ṭahṭāwī who felt rather uncomfortable with it and was compelled to explain that "the legislative authority" in European constitutions "means *tartīb al-qawānīn wa-tabdīl al-aḥkām,*" the arrangement of laws and adaptation of rules.[33] Ṭahṭāwī and his colleagues used the verb sparingly and, it seems, quite hesitantly. As the use of *sharraᶜa* became more common, the word underwent semantic modification, so that rather than recalling the revealed law, it came to imply man-made legislation of all types. During the last third of the century it gained currency as a verb, in the second and occasionally eighth forms, as well as in a verbal-nominal form. Thus, the Christian church was said to have "*sharraᶜat* . . . the separation between spiritual and worldly authority." Abraham Lincoln "*sharraᶜa* . . . the liberation of slaves." And the notion of *corps législatif*—at one time *al-jamᶜiyya al-murattiba*—now became *majlis al-tashrīᶜ* or *al-hay'a al-sharᶜiyya* (or *al-mushtariᶜa*).[34]

Growing common in this modern sense, *sharraᶜa* was coupled in the early 1870s with a synonymous term, *sanna*. Derived from s-n-n, this last verb meant to set an example or standard for conduct, instituting a custom. In Islam it was closely associated with the community's ancestors, whose deeds, commonly referred to as *sunna,* were considered a binding model for later Islamic generations, and became a central component of Muslim Law. The special regard for the tradition of the forefathers had minimized the use of the verb in other contexts, since none after them could have equal authority in originating a custom. If the verb was used in other contexts, it was in order to present the example of a nonbinding custom, and hardly ever in a legal sense. Now, its introduction with a new content in the last quarter of the nineteenth century offered yet another mark of a conceptual change. *Sanna,* like *sharraᶜa,* came to denote legislation in the civilian sense, of the kind practiced by monarchs and legislative assemblies.[35] Both innovations indicated that the alien principle of legislation was growing comprehensible. In the twentieth century they would both become standard names for similar procedures in the region itself.

Better acquaintance with European pluralistic political systems also led to a struggle for, then the adoption of, constitutional arrangements in the Middle East during the last third of the century. One obvious result of this was the better ability to distinguish between law and constitution. *Qānūn,* hitherto rather fluid, came to be limited in its application to the equivalent of "law"—a binding rule on a specific matter established by a legislative or administrative authority. Technically speaking, this was also the traditional sense of the term, the profound differences between a modern-style "law" and a *qānūn* notwithstanding. The choice of this term for the notion was, thus, natural and convenient. The consistent rendering of the former by the latter led to the semantic expansion of *qānūn.* And by the turn of the century it gained wide acceptance in the modern sense, alongside the still current traditional one; in Istanbul the autocratic ᶜAbd al-Ḥamīd continued to prescribe old-style *qānūns,* while in Cromer's Egypt a modern-style "legislative council," *majlis shūrā al-qawānīn,* was already producing "laws" through imported mechanisms. These, like their European archetypes, were similarly called *qānūn.* In twentieth-century usage, the term would retain only this last modern sense, with variations reflecting different legal realities in the region.

"Law" was a relatively simple idea, with at least a technical equivalent in the region's tradition. "Constitution," by contrast, seemed elusive and more difficult to name, even when recognized as a distinct concept. During the last third of the century, Arabic experimented with a variety of designations for this notion, rendered in a multitude of ways. The first constitutional document in the modern Middle East, the 1861 Tunisian constitution, was termed *qānūn al-dawla,* roughly "state law"—a compound neologism, but one with strictly traditional import.[36] Next to be promulgated was the Ottoman constitution, following persistent pressures by liberal patriots and a political crisis. "The word 'constitution' was in every mouth," the British ambassador wrote from Istanbul in May 1876, recording the dramatic events leading to the enactment of the document.[37] One may only speculate which "word in every mouth" the ambassador had in mind, for the notion was novel and still without an accepted name in Turkish—just as it had none in Arabic. Some, in particular "Young Ottoman" intellectuals, were calling for a *meşveret* (Arabic *mashwara*), in this context a "representative government" (see chapter 8). Others may have used the term *niẓām,* referring to a new "order" (a notion to be discussed later on in this chapter). Midḥat Pasha, the indefatigable dynamo of the constitutional movement, was pressing the Sultan for a *meşrūṭiyet,* literally "conditionality," that is, a "conditioned government," or for a *qānūn esāsī (asāsī),* "fundamental *qānūn.*" Six months after the dispatch of the ambassador's account, this last name was chosen to designate the first Ottoman constitution.

In both the Tunisian and Ottoman cases, the word *qānūn* itself seems to have implied an idea broader than simply law. Its conceived meaning here was rather that of a charter. In both instances the term was qualified by an adjective designed to further distinguish it from ordinary *qānūns;* unlike the latter, these constitutions were meant to represent "fundamental" documents, and as such to carry special weight and imply more binding authority. They were more comprehensive, laying elaborate guidelines for a new political and administrative order. Indeed, both resembled contemporary European constitutions in form. In content, however, they still reflected the concept of a traditional-style *qānūn*, namely, a ruling prescribed by the Islamic monarch, whose exclusive prerogatives were plainly evident in every article.[38] Thus, the identification of these new arrangements as a brand of *qānūn* was more than just a technical characteristic. It was symptomatic of the word's underlying traditional concept. The morphology of the name was equally illuminating: the need to render a noun ("constitution") by a noun-and-adjective compound (*qānūn al-dawla, qāūn asāsī*) was a built-in mark of the idea's foreign origin. During the brief fifteen months in which the Ottoman constitution was in effect, and for a few years thereafter, the name *qānūn asāsī* was commonly used to designate both this document and its European counterparts.[39] Then it began to lose ground to another name.

The adjective *asāsī*, implying the "fundamental" nature of laws so designated, was also attached to other nouns with a similar intent. In 1866, Egypt's ruler Ismāʿīl issued an eighteen-article *lā'iḥa asāsiyya*, ordering the establishment of a consultative council in his country. *Lā'iḥa*, pl. *lawā'iḥ*, was a generic term for anything flat, such as a table or board, and hence for anything written—a chart, a decree, a letter, or a law. The Magna Carta, for example, was rendered as "the great *lā'iḥa*."[40] Ismāʿīl's *lā'iḥa asāsiyya* was "fundamental" in that it provided for the foundation of a new institution.[41] The council to which the *lā'iḥa* gave birth offered an important opportunity for practicing parliamentary principles. Its activity resulted in 1879 in a draft constitution which was given the very same name—*al-lā'iḥa al-asāsiyya*. Modified and expanded, it was promulgated in 1882, and came to be known as the first written Egyptian constitution.[42] Like the name of the Ottoman document, *lā'iḥa asāsiyya* was a neologism for a novel notion, and it was likewise somewhat ambiguous. Its article 25, for example, discussed a procedure for the drafting of "*lawā'iḥ* and *qawānīn*"—a hendiadys indicative of the looseness of both in the new context of modern-style legislation. In this and other articles, *lā'iḥa*, frequently interchanged with *qānūn*, was a vague item. *Lā'iḥa asāsiyya* could scarcely be more precise; equally applicable to Ismāʿīl's decree of 1866 and to the 1882 constitution, the name combined a fluid noun with a loose adjective—an illustrative sign of a remaining ambiguity.

One other common word for "constitution" during the last third of the century was *niẓām*, pl. *niẓāmāt*. This, too, was a generic term, meaning standard, order, arrangement or organization of any type. In the nineteenth-century Ottoman empire and Egypt it was readily associated with the new army units of the *Niẓām-i Cedīd* (*al-Niẓām al-Jadīd*) and the *Tanẓīmāt*, the reforms, or new "arrangements," introduced by local rulers seeking to modernize their states. In 1883 it appeared in the name of the Organic Law (*al-qānūn al-niẓāmī*) in Egypt, reorganizing the country's administrative order under the new British occupation.[43] In its etymological and semantic evolution, *niẓām* may have been closer to "constitution" than were any of the other terms considered here; both stemmed from words denoting structure or setting, and both were used to imply political order. Yet such similarity seems to have had little to do with the choice of the former as a name for the latter. Rather, being a loose expression, *niẓām* apparently presented a convenient designation for an idea that was still not wholly clear. The term was used in both the singular and plural forms, as well as through derivatives such as *tanẓīmāt* and the Persian-Turkish *niẓāmnāme*, to describe the French, American and other constitutions abroad.[44] Not quite content with the solution, writers often appended qualifying adjectives to the noun: " '*al-kūnstītūsyūn*' is synonymous with '*al-tanẓīmāt al-siyāsiyya*' " (political *tanẓīmāt*), explained the Tunisian Khayr al-Dīn as best he could. This formula, and the somewhat more common compound *al-niẓām al-asāsī*, having addressed the difficulty in no truly satisfactory way, turned out to be temporary.

Yet another term used to denote "constitution" was *dustūr*, pl. *dasātīr*. Competing with other expressions for ascendancy, it would eventually gain universal acceptance in this modern sense, to the exclusion of all other names. However, this would happen only in the last decade of the century. *Dustūr* was a word of Persian origin, which initially served as a title for a person exercising authority. In the Ottoman Empire it was used as an honorific for the Grand Vezir or other high officials, often in the formula *düstūr-u mukerrem* (*al-dustūr al-mukkarram*, "the honorable *dustūr*").[45] Another meaning was a rule, a regulation or a model, hence also a set of rules—a common usage in the medieval craft guilds. Qalqashandī, for example, bases some of his instructions to state secretaries on precedents he found in "certain *dasātīr*," or books of rules. This was also the sense of the term in *dustūr al-jamʿiyya*, the code of rules of the mid-nineteenth-century "Syrian society," whose individual articles were identified as *qawānīn*. Likewise, *dustūr* (Turkish *düstūr*) was the title of a series of volumes containing state laws and decrees which were published in Istanbul from 1863 onward.[46] The word was commonly used in the compound expression *dustūr al-ʿamal*, "standard," "rule book" or "criteria for conduct"; for example, the Germans were reported to have "chosen the French metric system as *dustūr al-ʿamal* for their measurements."[47]

With the meaning of "a corpus of rules," *dustūr* was extended in the 1870s to denote a Western-type constitution. In 1858 it had occurred in a sense quite close to this. When a Jew (Baron Rothschild) first became a member of the British parliament in that year, he was allowed to omit from his inaugural oath the words "on the true faith of a Christian," and to swear allegiance, instead, to the Royal House "and the Law" (the latter taken in the broadest sense, since Britain had no written constitution). This formula was rendered in Arabic as *innanī uḥāfiẓ ʿalā al-dustūr* ("I shall abide by the *dustūr*").[48] But at that time such usage was rather uncommon and remained so for some time. In mid-1876, a few months before the enactment of the Ottoman constitution, a Lebanese journalist recorded the agitation in Istanbul, where people were "demanding a government based on a *dustūr siyāsī*" or "political *dustūr*"—still a somewhat murky notion.[49] As the constitution was proclaimed, another journalist described it as a "compendium of *al-qawānīn al-dustūriyya*," of the kind hitherto prescribed by the government and published periodically in the *düstūr* series.[50] By that time the word began to be applied to constitutions abroad as well. "John Adams," one author related in 1877, "had an extensive share in drafting the basic laws (*al-niẓāmāt al-asāsiyya*) which were taken to form the *dustūr* of the United States of America."[51] During the French Revolution, another writer recounted a year later, members of the National Assembly announced their intention "not [to] dissolve themselves until they had drafted a *dustūr* for their country. Therefore, their assembly [the *Assemblée Législative*] came to be called *al-jamʿiyya al-dustūriyya*."[52]

Such usage increased thereafter. For a while there was hesitation as authors, somewhat uncertain, chose to reinforce the term *dustūr* by the adjective *asāsī*.[53] But by the 1890s this was no longer deemed necessary. The word gained popular currency, obviating all other expressions. "In the American *dustūr* there is no *qānūn* which would prevent the election [of a president] for a third term," explained an article in *al-Muqtaṭaf* in 1896, making a precise distinction between notions previously often confused. At about the same time, while deriding the Ottoman constitution, which had been suspended for some twenty years and largely forgottten, one journalist referred to "the joke known as *al-qānūn al-asāsī*, that is to say *al-dustūr*," thereby illuminating a common term turned obsolete through another, which had grown more familiar.[54] The concept of constitution was more intelligible, as exemplified by the systematic application of the new word in both nominal and adjectival forms. And as Arab writers were becoming conversant with it, the idea of a constitutional regime began to clarify as well. At one time referred to as "restricted government," this last notion came to be presented as *ḥukūma dustūriyya*[55]—a loan-translation for a borrowed idea, which Middle Eastern states in the twentieth century would seek to adopt under the new name.

7

Government, Autocratic
and Otherwise

In much of pre-Islamic Arabia government was consensual and nonhereditary. Tribal shaykhs held their position by the consent of the tribe's elders, their appointment being revocable at any time. In Mecca a council of clan chiefs, the *mala'*, functioned as a sort of collective political leadership, with a deliberative authority that often had an executive effect. Islam brought theocracy and set new standards for sovereign legitimacy. For three decades after the Prophet's death the old criteria for choosing the community's leaders prevailed, and those who attained power through the familiar process were accorded caliphal authority. But in succeeding years government became hereditary, and before long the theocratic state disintegrated into an array of monocracies. The pre-Islamic and early Islamic practice of making a revocable choice of leaders was abandoned, despite a theory of an elective and consensual caliphate which evolved in Islam. From then on government was inherited—or seized.

Looking back to the conspicuous patriarchal era, after many centuries of autocratic rule, Muslim writers of our time have sometimes been tempted to depict the state of the first four caliphs as a "republic."[1] It is useful to note that "republic" is, and has always been, a very loose term. Meaning literally a "public matter" as well as "commonwealth," it was a designation for

97

polities which, from ancient times until the late eighteenth century, were governed by small oligarchies. Such were the Greek and Roman republics of antiquity, the city-states of medieval Italy, and the Dutch republic since the mid-seventeenth century. "Republic" was also used as a name for monarchies such as that of Poland since the late fifteenth century, where the king was elected by the boards of local aristocracy (the *zemstvos*), or England, where royal authority was confined by the rising power of the gentry and nobility.[2] The term thus implied, very generally, a government in which some of the governed had the privilege of choosing the head of state, or one in which they shared some of his power. The idea of a republic as a state whose head is elected by a broad suffrage, and in which all have a voice in what concerns all, is a rather modern one, largely resulting from the American and French revolutions.

Users of the Arabic idiom had an opportunity to learn about European republics long before these eighteenth-century revolutions. In medieval times Muslim thinkers such as al-Fārābī and Ibn Rushd discussed the concept of a republic as they synthesized the political thought of Plato and Aristotle. They saw no necessity to employ a specific name for the notion, however; republic, or rather the Greek *politeia*, was rendered simply as *madīna*—originally a jurisdiction and, by extension, a town, a city, a polity. Plato's republic, "the ideal state," was accordingly translated as *al-madīna al-fāḍila* or *al-madīna al-kāmila*, the virtuous or perfect state.[3] References to the medieval Italian republics sometime later were more laconic and reflected a decreasing interest in the subject. Arab observers were aware of this peculiar type of regime in Italy and occasionally mentioned it in their writings. They noted, for example, that the Venetians had "a king from among themselves [*malikuhum min anfūsihim*] who is called the Doge [*al-Dūj*]"; that the Tuscans had "no king ruling them but rather notables [*akābir*] arbitrating among them"; and that the Genoese government, by the same token, consisted of "a group [of people] of diverse ranks" (*jamāʿat mutafāwitu al-marātib*).[4] But they too did not care to devise a specific name for this strange system.

The Ottomans, who for centuries had maintained relations with European republican states in war, trade and diplomacy, were more familiar with this European brand of government, and even used a special expression for it, as we shall see. Rulers of

Morocco, likewise an independent sultanate, also had regular correspondence with European republics, which they usually called by the borrowed name *ribublikā*.[5] On the other hand, people from other Arabic-speaking lands, subordinate provinces in the Ottoman Empire, had little chance or inclination to become acquainted with them—until in 1798 the troops of the young French republic made a forceful appearance in their country.

The new idea the French brought with them bore a special significance. More than just a name for a nonmonarchical rule, "republic" now represented the antithesis of the loathsome autocratic order to which the revolution had put a violent end in France in the name of liberty and civic rights. A few years earlier the American Declaration of Independence, denouncing British royal domination and its "absolute tyranny," stated "the right of the people to abolish" oppressive government and replace it with one that would "effect their safety and happiness." Accordingly, the American constitution took care to "guarantee to every State in the Union a republican form of government." The word "republic," Thomas Paine then explained, "means the *public good,* or the good of the whole, in contradistinction to the despotic form, which makes the good of the sovereign, or of one man, the only object of the government"; hence "when a people agree to form themselves into a republic . . . they . . . renounce not only the despotic form, but the despotic principle."[6] This ideology was adopted by leaders of the French Revolution (Paine himself moved to Paris, where he eloquently expounded it). There, the new spirit came to be epitomized in the state's new title, *La République.* It was this spirit which Napoleon later sought to evoke in those countries of Europe which he conquered, establishing republican regimes in them; and it was the one which accompanied the struggle for, and implementation of, the idea in France and elsewhere throughout the rest of the century.

Transmitting an idea representing the essence of the French Revolution to the unconcerned Muslim society in faraway Egypt, which for millenia had known nothing but autocratic rule, posed a serious conceptual and lexical challenge to the French. To meet it they introduced themselves through a pair of terms which they used interchangeably, *mashyakha* (or *mashīkha*) and *jumhūr.*

Before being used in its new sense, *mashyakha* had two common meanings. It served as a plural form of the noun *shaykh,* along with the more current forms *shuyūkh* and *masahā'ikh.* It was also used as an abstract noun, signifying the authority or position of a *shaykh*—as, for example, in *mashyakhat al-Islām*, the position of *shaykh al-Islām*.[7] The translators who came to Egypt with the French expedition seem to have had the former sense in mind when choosing the word for "republic," and the logic by which they chose this name is interesting. At the time of the expedition France was governed by the *Directoire*, a board of five prominent elders. A bicameral legislature, the upper house of which was the *Conseil des Anciens*, was also sharing the authority. It seems likely that in order to simplify the novel idea and facilitate its transmission to the Egyptians, the French orientalists preferred to recall the actual governing body in Paris, rather than refer to the abstraction of republic. They designated their type of regime as "the [government of the] elders," a term evoking familiar associations and designed to generate respect. As we shall see, many in the region indeed came to understand the notion in this sense.[8]

The second word by which Bonaparte's oriental experts described their republic, *jumhūr*, was not of French authorship, but was rather a centuries-old Turkish name for European republics (Turkish *cumhūr*). Initially an Arabic word, *jumhūr* meant a gathering of people, a crowd, a public. The Ottomans employed it in both the sense of public and republic—a striking symptom of the looseness of the latter notion. They applied it to the Venetian, Ragusan and Dutch governments with whom they had dealt for a long time.[9] With the outbreak of the French Revolution the word gained high popularity among Ottoman writers as a name for the oft-discussed French Republic (*Françe cumhūrū*), and for similar governmental systems which subsequently appeared in French-occupied Europe.[10] Because of its Arabic origin the term may have seemed to the French orientalists an appropriate means for conveying the notion to speakers of that language as well. They chose the word to introduce themselves in their very first proclamation to the Egyptians, issued "on behalf of the French *jumhūr*, which is based on the foundation of liberty and equality"; they used it frequently thereafter in their communication with the local leadership.[11]

The initial Egyptian reaction to this idea, as to other concepts imported by the despised French, was typically hostile. Muslim chroniclers who recorded the French invasion took little interest in the strange type of government which the infidel

"Franks" had invented for themselves. Jabartī wrote but briefly and with undisguised scorn of "the [new] order they contrived" (*al-tartīb alladhī ibtadaᶜuhu*). He defined the republic as *jamᶜiyya*, literally an association or grouping, for in this "blameworthy innovation [*bidᶜa*] which they had fabricated . . . they have neither head nor *sulṭān* with whom they would all agree." Having "killed their sultan," the people "unanimously agreed that there was not to be a single ruler; instead, their government, territories, laws and the administration of affairs should be in the hands of the intelligent and wise men among them."[12] Jabartī made sparing use of the names by which the French introduced their republic, usually preferring the generic but clear *dawla* or *mamlaka* to the less intelligible *mashyakha* and *jumhūr*. His compatriot and coreligionist, ᶜAbd Allāh al-Sharqāwī, offered a description that was as brief and disdainful.[13]

This kind of attitude was soon to give way to another, more positive one, as curiosity about Europe replaced disregard. Jabartī's Christian contemporaries, who did not share the Muslim resentment of the foreign "infidels," attached more importance to their new type of government and were prepared to discuss it in greater detail. In their works *mashyakha* was by far the more popular of the two terms under which the idea was brought in. A *mashyakha*, the Lebanese chronicler Niqūlā Turk explained, is the kind of regime in which "the making of decisions and other administrative matters of the country are in the hands of the elders [*masā'ikh*] of the people." Thus, the French republic was little more than "the elders' [government]." Turk spoke of *al-mashyakha al-khamsa*, "the five elders" of the *Directoire* (using the term as a plural of *shaykh* rather than as an abstract noun). By the same token, he reported Bonaparte's Eighteen Brumaire coup as the latter's "assault on the *mashyakha* . . . [in which] three of the *shaykhs* were killed and two remained." To Turk a *mashyakha* signified the familiar notion of oligarchy, and as such the term was just as properly applicable to the government of the British monarchy—*mashyakhat al-Inklīz*.[14]

This initial limited perception of the idea was later reflected in the early writings of Ṭahṭāwī and his pupils as well. "L'Amérique n'a presque plus que des républiques," ran a French text describing the countries and peoples of the world; paraphrasing, Ṭahṭāwī rendered it as *wa-innamā yaḥkumuhā mashā'ikh al-buldān*, "she is ruled by provincial elders." His colleague, ʿAbd Allāh Abū al-Suʿūd, discussing the administrative reorganization in France during the revolution, elaborated on the procedures of "electing [officials] to the posts of the country's *mashyakha,* the courts and the royal services"— *mashyakha* evidently signifying some kind of a supreme council, rather than a type of government.[15]

Closer inspection of the European scene subsequently led to a better grasp of the idea in the Middle East. Yet much of the initial confusion continued throughout the greater part of the century. *Mashyakha* was used extensively until very close to the end of the century as a name for republics both historical and contemporary.[16] Its appearance continued to indicate a measure of uncertainty regarding the precise nature of "republican" governments. For, along with republic, *mashyakha* also served to denote such notions as an electoral region (the power-base of a *shaykh*), a city council (the mayor being "*shaykh* of the *mashyakha*"), a provincial council, a rural community in the provincial administration of Russia, the abstract notion of knighthood in Britain, a convention of prelates in the Vatican, the government of a country (*mashyakhat al-bilād*), the Paris Commune, the French *Directoire,* and, in the more current sense, the leadership of Islamic institutions such as al-Azhar.[17] Such a versatile expression could scarcely convey a clear idea, let alone one of foreign origin. The common denominator of these various though closely related meanings was that of elders' ascendancy, a principle long known in the Middle East, where it was exercised in rather different circumstances. *Mashyakha,* then, loosely indicated the sense of an oligarchic government without a monarch, a meaning relevant to some old and some new, but not all, republics.

Meanwhile another term was gaining growing recognition: *jumhūriyya,* a word derived from *jumhūr,* which itself disappeared from use with this meaning soon after the departure of the French, who had brought it. *Jumhūriyya* was devised in Turkish in the late eighteenth century, when it served to mean republicanism, the abstraction of the republican idea (Turkish *cumhūriyet*). Soon its semantic spectrum was broadened and it came to denote republic, the actual form of government as well. The Turkish *cumhūriyet* remained for decades less popular than *cumhūr* in conveying this latter meaning, and it seems to have acquired general acceptance only in the second half of the nineteenth century.[18] In Arabic, on the other hand, *jumhūriyya* became current much sooner; borrowed by Ṭahṭāwī in the early 1830s, it almost immediately took the place of *jumhūr*, alongside *mashyakha*.[19] When the term *jumhūriyya* was first introduced, the interpretation attached to it reflected conceptual difficulties similar to those inherent in the word *mashyakha*. A republic, Ṭahṭāwī explained, is a system in which the subjects (*raʿiyya*) are governed by their notables (*kibār*); "this is republican government [*ḥukm al-jumhūriyya*], as the notables are called *mashā'ikh* and *jumhūr*."[20] Calling a republic *jumhūriyya*, then, could be justified if notables were identified as *jumhūr*. By a similar logic, Ṭahṭāwī's colleagues used *jumhūriyya* in the sense of oligarchy (translating *oligarchie des ducs* as *ḥukm jumhūriyyat al-dūqāt*), and aristocracy (rendering *les parties . . . aristocratiques* as [*al-*] *aqsām . . . al-jumhūriyya*).[21] In this sense *jumhūriyya*, just like *mashyakha*, signified little more than government by dignitaries. It was apparently assumed to be different from the region's own type of rule, yet the nature of the difference remained to be clarified.

Toward the middle of the nineteenth century the word *jumhūriyya* was growing more common, gradually superseding *mashyakha* as a name for an alien idea still largely unclear. At that stage writers often felt the need to interpret the newer term through reference to the older, in formulae such as "*jumhūriyya*, that is to say *mashyakha*." At other times they rendered "republic" by the hendiadys "*mashyakha and jumhūriyya*,"[22] or by the somewhat awkward combination *mashyakha jumhūriyya* (the former a noun, the latter an adjective), which reflected the looseness of both.[23] This uncertain interchangeability of two distinct terms, though perplexing, was better than the earlier identification of "republic" as, merely, *mashyakha*, which portrayed a reality quite confused in itself. While the principle of popular political rights was making impressive strides in Europe (especially after 1848) and America, participation in government still remained the privilege of small sociopolitical elites. At mid-century, "republicanism" was more of a rallying cry than a fulfilled concept, a slogan that was still a novelty in the largely artistocratic polities in the West. To spectators in the Middle East this evolving idea was largely unfathomable.

By the birth of the Arabic press, neither *mashyakha* nor *jumhūriyya* was established firmly enough to exclude the other. In 1859 they both seemed unsatisfactory to the Lebanese editor of the important daily *Birjīs Bārīs* ("Paris Jupiter"), who was induced to seek a third possibility. Searching the classical dictionaries, he came up with the curious expression *fawḍā,* hitherto a common term for "anarchy." He selected it, so he explained, on the basis of its definition by Fīrūzābādī's fourteenth-century authoritative Lexicon (the *Qāmūs*) as "an egalitarian [*mutasawūn*] people without a chief," living in "full cooperation, equality and mutual conformity." The writer toyed with the word for a few months, speaking of Napoleon III as *ra'īs al-fawḍā,* of Switzerland as *dawlat al-fawḍā,* and of the United States as a polity whose "regime is a *fawḍā* known as 'the Union' [*al-ittiḥād*]."[24] Then he abandoned it and returned to *mashyakha.* The term *fawḍā* lost this novel use and remained current with the previous meaning of anarchy or, more specifically, absence of leadership.[25]

This mid-century episode stands as a lively illustration of the problems faced by Middle Eastern intellectuals trying to familiarize their local audiences with western concepts. It shows a serious difficulty in conveying, if not in grasping, the profound meaning of the idea. The editor offered no reference to the principle of political freedom and popular participation in government, which was the essence of modern republicanism. Instead of devising a new expression that would reflect the principle, or borrowing the alien word that would designate it precisely, he used a term denoting the idea only in its technical and least significant aspect. The writer soon became disenchanted with his own choice, and reverted to a word that was equally unsatisfactory, as we have seen.

With the development of the Arabic press, the term *jumhūriyya* struck roots.[26] During the last quarter of the nineteenth century it won widespread currency, despite the puzzling occasional appearance of *mashyakha.* The consistent adherence to a single term for expressing the idea was useful in eliminating some of the confusion surrounding it, as was the fortunate choice of the particular term itself. For, unlike *mashyakha,* which brought to mind the traditional elite of elders and dignitaries, *jumhūriyya* was associated with "the people." It helped convey the notion of relation between public and government as distinct not only from monarchy but also from oligarchy. "There is a difference," the Egyptian journalist ʿAbd Allāh Abū al-Suʿūd explained in 1873, between "a government by the *aʿyān* and *ashrāf,* known in French as *arīstūkrāsiyya . . .* and *ūlīgārshiyya,*" on the one hand,

and *jumhūriyya,* on the other. While in the former, "the management of the country's affairs is in the hands of the *a'yān,* the richest and the most influential,

> in a *jumhūriyya* the administration of the country's affairs is in the hands of the people. This means that they rule over themselves, without the government of a king or a *sulṭān* or a group of *a'yān.* It is antithetical to both monarchy and oligarchy, and requires equality of all members of the country's community in their civil and political rights, as well as the absence of privileges.[27]

Jumhūriyya, then, recalled the people as the backbone of the government. It implied, in Adīb Isḥaq's words, *ḥukūmat al-sha'b bil-sha'b*—"government of the people by the people."[28] A newly devised name for a newly encountered idea, *jumhūriyya* seems to offer as good an answer to the terminological challenge posed by "republic" as could be found.

Yet consistency in usage and a successful choice of term were, in themselves, no guarantee of a quick or thorough grasp of the idea. On the contrary, many instances in which the word figures with a variety of meanings attest to its fluidity. To quote a striking example from al-Bustānī's definition of the term in 1882:

> The Hottentots in Africa are to this very day in a state of *jumhūriyya,* or more precisely *fawḍā,* for they live in equality and freedom [*bil-tasāwī wal-ḥurriyya*], having neither ruler nor leader.[29]

Another instance of this vagueness was the common lack of discrimination between "republic" and "democracy"—two related yet not entirely identical concepts. This confusion is a typical characteristic of nineteenth-century political Arabic which merits close consideration.

Technically speaking, "democracy" was not a name for a specific form of government. Rather it indicated certain qualities of the political system. More common in adjectival than in nominal form, it designated a state, monarchical or otherwise, that was based on equality of political rights. Literally, democracy meant "people's government," and in that sense it was hardly a precise term. During the nineteenth century, when there was an increasing struggle in much of Europe for political freedom, "democracy" became largely interchangeable with "republicanism" (this synonymity is still preserved in modern Greek, in which *demokratia* is the name for both notions). Democracy was also used loosely as the equivalent of a "parliamentary," "constitutional" or "representative" government. Broad though its range of reference was, to the Middle East the term, and the concept behind it, was an innovation.

To assert that the notion of democracy was a novelty in the modern Middle East is not to pass judgment on the degree of political freedom in Islam. This is of little relevance to our purpose, and its discussion might take us far afield from the issues with which we are concerned.[30] Regardless of whether or not Islam was democratic in theory or practice, it is a fact that there was no equivalent to the word "democracy" in premodern Middle Eastern languages. Muslim thinkers had often been occupied with such issues as justice (*ʿadl*) and oppression (*ẓulm*). Whether or not their society and polity were "democratic" was a question of little meaning to them.

On the other hand, Muslim philosophers took an interest in Greek political writings which discussed democracy, among other theoretical themes. In medieval Arabic translations, Plato's "democratic polity" was rendered as *madīna jamāʿiyya* (or *jummāʿiyya*), a corporate or collective state. Al-Farābī described it as "the state whose people are totally free to themselves, doing whatever they please . . . and none of them has sway over the other." The philosophers were somewhat critical of that system; to them the excessive freedom of the common people was a danger that could lead to the overwhelming of good by the powers of evil. Democracy was thus an imperfect system and a corrupt version of the "virtuous state."[31] But the thinkers who applied Platonic criteria in their discussion of politics seem to have been on the fringes, rather than in the center of Islamic political discourse. Later even this marginal interest faded away. By the time it was rediscovered by Middle Eastern intellectuals, the word "democracy" had acquired new connotations. Arab observers, confused by the flood of novel notions, did not associate the new variant of "democracy" with its forerunner, and thus did not use the term employed in the medieval translations for modern democracy.

Nineteenth-century Arabic writings include very few references to democracy as a distinct idea. Since the notion was initially amorphous, writers of Arabic, like many of their European contemporaries, tended to confuse "democracy" with "republic" or "republicanism." They employed the same word, *jumhūriyya*, to denote both. *"Dīmuqrāṭiyya* means *jumhūriyya*, namely government by the *jumhūr*," Ṭahṭāwī remarked in 1843. Elsewhere he elaborated:

> *Dīmuqrāṭiyya* means that the subjects rule over themselves, whether by means of their [own] assembly or through [an assembly] of their representative notables. In the past [i.e. at the time of the revolution] the government of France had been of this type, but this [system] had not succeeded there. This system is, in fact, a kind of republic [*nawᶜ min al-jumhūriyya*].

Ṭahṭāwī's colleagues offered similar explanations, defining democracy as a "republic of the people" (*jumhūriyyat al-ahālī*), a literal tautology, or "government by the people" (*ḥukm al-jumhūr*).[32] This confusion persisted until late in the century. In 1882, Buṭrus al-Bustānī thus summarized the failure of Cromwell's republican Commonwealth in England:

> The English in the days of Cromwell attempted to set up a democratic government [*ḥukūma dīmuqrāṭiyya*]. Having lacked the necessary virtues, they got into turmoil and became wary. So they returned to their former state.[33]

A report on a popular demand in Italy for a "government by the *jumhūr* (*dimuqrāṭ*)," an English-Arabic word list identifying "democratical" as *jumhūrī*, and a description of democratic (or liberal) principles underlying the organization of the French national bank as *mabādi' jumhūriyya*—all attested to this fluidity.[34] Multilingual dictionaries of Arabic throughout the period reflected the confusion, using *jumhūriyya* to define both "republic" and "democracy."[35]

Difficult to distinguish even in their land of origin, "republic" and "democracy" were thus perceived as one and the same idea by Arab observers at the end of the nineteenth century. They felt no need to produce separate Arabic words for them; *jumhūriyya*, like the Greek *demokratia*, seemed to properly express both. "Democracy" represented an unimportant variant of "republic," one that was seldom discussed during the formative century of modern Arabic. This is probably the reason why the shapers of the language, who diligently devised Arabic names for so many other imported concepts, failed to offer one for democracy and eventually settled for the foreign word *dīmuqrāṭiyya,* despite its inelegance by traditional standards of style.

There was, however, one exceptional attempt, brief but highly illuminating, to offer an Arabic name for democracy. In 1871 the Jesuit Lebanese weekly *al-Bashīr* proposed the curious form *raʿāʿiyya* as an appropriate equivalent to "democracy." *Raʿāʿiyya* was an abstract noun derived from *raʿāʿ,* meaning mob or riffraff. The paper related that *"raʿāʿiyya* imposed itself on the [French people, following the French Revolution] to the extent that they had no escape from it"; described a "democratic republic" as *jumhūriyya raʿāʿiyya;* and identified the German "Social Democratic Party" as *al-ḥizb al-ishtirākī al-raʿāʿī.*[36] Having a somewhat derogatory connotation, the term may have reflected the editor's critical attitude toward the idea—one that is reminiscent of the medieval Muslim view of the philosophers.[37] It is also reminiscent of the use of *fawḍā,* at one time an appellation for "republic"; not only were both absent from the region's political experience of recent centuries, but they were also largely incompatible with principles underlying its political realities. Like *fawḍā, raʿāʿiyya* turned out to be short-lived. It was one of many neologisms that failed to strike roots and soon disappeared, leaving the field to the loan-word *dīmuqrāṭiyya.*

During the last third of the century, the word "democracy" and its adjectival derivatives were employed with increasing frequency by Arabic newspapers regularly reporting events abroad. They were used mainly in names of political movements and organizations, notably of those in the United States, where the use of "Republican" and "Democratic" as designations for rival parties signified that these were not two sides of the same coin, but rather, possibly, two different coins. Thus, *"al-jumhūriyyūn* (the Republicans) defeated the *dīmūqrāṭiyyīn* (the Democrats)," an Egyptian journal reported in 1896, leaving little room for confusion between the two.[38] Such differentiation no doubt helped to increase Arab consciousness that democracy was perhaps something other than just "a kind of *jumhūriyya,"* as Ṭahṭāwī once suggested.

By the turn of the century, both "republic" and "democracy" had come to convey the alien, yet now more familiar, notion of a "people's government." Certain specific aspects of it, as well as much of the underlying social and political philosophy, still remained to be explored. Now the notion was introduced into the Middle East itself. *Jumhūriyya* and *dīmuqrāṭiyya,* in nominal and adjectival forms, came to be employed most commonly in official names of states, parties and organizations, and in the jargon of documents such as constitutions and political manifestos. In titles readily betraying a foreign origin—the former word being a neologism, the latter a loan-word—the two terms seldom represented more than nebulous concepts applicable to a broad range of realities. Most of these bore little resemblance to their European counterparts carrying the same names. The appearance of such "republican" and "democratic" bodies in the Middle East was possible only with titles taken to denote imprecise notions—as were *jumhūriyya* and *dīmuqrāṭiyya.*

The extension of the idea to the Middle East (and, for that matter, to other Third World countries) eventually led to a clearer distinction between the concepts of republic and democracy. While the latter retained the implication of political freedom and rights and popular franchise, "republic" gradually turned into a mere technical name for all governmental systems with a nonhereditary head of state, popular participation in government being a possible but not imperative characteristic. A republic, therefore, would no longer be necessarily a government by the public; it could be anything else, as long as it carried the symbolic feature of a head elected in some, even very limited, way. Expanded to embrace Middle Eastern and Western republics alike, *jumhūriyya,* loose and imprecise, would surely be just as applicable to the Islamic patriarchal caliphate.

8

Instruments of Modern Politics— Parliaments and Parties

In pluralistic polities, where governmental authority is distributed among a number of forces, parliaments and parties are two essential instruments of politics. Parliaments serve as forces through which authority is exercised. Parties constitute organized channels of popular political activity and competition for governmental positions.

In the history of Western government, parliaments have taken on different forms, varying considerably in their power, composition and representative quality. In autocratic regimes parliaments have often been merely advisory councils of nominated officials, having no power of their own. In democratic republics, parliaments have been elective and broadly representative assemblies, enjoying legislative power and control over the executive. Parliamentary institutions can be large or small, unicameral or bicameral. They can all be identified as either an assembly, council, or parliament—generic names which indicate certain common characteristics of form and function. They often also bear proper names, such as Congress, Cortes, Diet and Reichstag; each of these refers to a distinct entity with individual traits and a unique course of development. Technically speaking, such bodies have not been exclusively a European phenomenon; they have had equivalents in the Middle East and elsewhere. In

Middle Eastern villages, cities and professional guilds, there have been councils of various designations which administered communal affairs. Similar forums have also existed on the state level, operating as government agencies with different degrees of authority. In Arabic, as in occidental languages, there developed a set of generic expressions to denote such bodies. In the nineteenth century these names were taken to designate their European technical equivalents. In the process they were modified and acquired new meanings.

During the first five or six decades of the nineteenth century, three Arabic terms were current for all types of collective governmental bodies at home and abroad: *shūrā* (or *mashwara*), *dīwān*, and *majlis*. The first of these is of particular significance, its usage in modern contexts symbolizing much of the difficulty with which this study is concerned. It is perhaps most profitably considered last. Of the other two, *dīwān* was by far the more common during this part of the period. Thereafter it lost ground to other expressions, among them *majlis*.

Dīwān, plural *dawāwīn*, expressed a notion with familiar historical connotations and a specific contemporary import. Apparently of Persian origin,[1] the word initially meant a register, hence also an administrative office. As early as the Umayyad period, *dīwān* was used to indicate one among several bureaus, for example, *dīwān al-kharāj* (the office assessing and levying land taxes), *dīwān al-rasā'il* (office of correspondence) and *dīwān al-khatam* (office of the seal). *Dīwān* was used with this meaning under the Abbasids, Buwayhids, Seljuks, Fatimids, Ayyubids and Mamluks, then by the Ottomans.

In the Ottoman Empire *dīwān* (Turkish *dīvān*) stood for a variety of entities. At the highest level it was a name for the Imperial Council—*dīvān-i humāyūn*, until the mid-seventeenth century the central organ of government of the empire. The decline of this body thereafter was marked by the gradual transfer of its functions and influence to the Grand Vezir's office and his "afternoon council," the *ikindi dīvānı*, which became the seat of effective authority. In the provinces and smaller administrative units there were local *dīvāns*, councils of appointed officials who assisted the governors in running indigenous affairs. Finally, as in earlier Islamic states, *dīvān* was a name for governmental departments in Istanbul, such as *dīvān ül-defteri ül-sultānī* (the imperial registration bureau) and *dīvān ül-rūznāme* (the office in charge of administering the imperial treasury); the latter institution was a branch of the former.[2]

When Bonaparte organized his control of Egypt, he created a central council in Cairo consisting of Egyptian notables, instead of the former Ottoman officials, which he entitled *al-dīwān al-ʿāmm,* or "general *dīwān.*" It was first made up of one hundred eighty men, ten of whom formed an executive committee of a sort, and then was replaced by an assembly of sixty. With the general *dīwān,* similar councils of a local nature were established in Cairo, Alexandria and the provinces.[3] Bonaparte's purpose was, in his own words, to "attempt to accustom the notables of Egypt to the ideas of assemblies and government."[4] As a first step toward that end, the *dīwāns* were invested with the authority of deliberating on local matters and representing the population before the French military governor. Yet, while intended as a novelty, these councils could hardly have been regarded by Egyptians as more than a slightly modified version of the long-familiar Ottoman *dīwāns* in their country, especially since French supervisers were regularly present in the general *dīwān's* sessions and represented the real authority, that of a foreign power.

In the turbulence following the departure of the French, Bonaparte's administrative experiments were soon forgotten. Under Muhammad Ali the term *dīwān* again acquired its more traditional sense. Muhammad Ali used the name extensively for new governmental departments which he intended to be the equivalents of European ministries: *al-dīwān al-khidīwī* (in charge of interior affairs), *dīwān al-jihādiyya* (war), *dīwān al-irādāt* (finance), *dīwān al-baḥr* (marine affairs), *dīwān al-madāris* (education and public works), and the like. His son Ibrāhīm, who invaded Syria and Palestine in 1830–1831, convened in the large towns there *dīwāns* of a somewhat different type, akin to the Ottoman provincial councils. They consisted of appointed notables who were to assist Egyptian officials in running local affairs.[5]

With its use in pre-Ottoman and Ottoman administration, and in Bonaparte's and Muhammad Ali's Egypt, *dīwān* had been given a broad range of reference. Technically the word was applicable to state bureaus of all functions and to any deliberative or consultative body. Broad though it was, however, the term also implied certain specific characteristics. *Dīwāns* were not sovereign institutions. Rather they were subordinate to a ruler or governor who set the limits of their responsibilities. Their members, always from the *khāṣṣa,* were in every instance nominated by the head of the state or his deputy. Whether administrative departments or provincial councils, *dīwān*s were commonly thought of as government agencies whose authority stemmed from their representing the Sultan.

When Arab observers began to write about institutions of government in Europe, they identified a variety of bodies that appeared to be properly describable as *dīwān*s. Such were royal courts, privy councils, and ministerial councils nominated by monarchs. It seemed only natural to present the French pre-revolutionary royal cabinet (the *cabinet de Tuileries*) as "*kābīnat al-Tūlirī,* namely the *dīwān* of this palace, that is to say the *dīwān* of the king." In the French post-Napoleonic monarchy, the privy council was, likewise, *al-dīwān al-khuṣūṣī;* the royal secretariat became *dīwān sirr al-malik* (literally "council [in charge of] royal secret [affairs]"); and the *Chambre des Pairs,* of nobles appointed by the king, was *dīwān al-bīr.* By the same token, the Polish king's court of the seventeenth century was depicted as "the most magnificent of the *dawāwīn* of Europe next to the *dīwān* of the king of France"; the Austrian and French cabinets were referred to as "the *dīwān*s of Vienna and Paris"; and the one in London was described as *dīwān al-ḥukūma,* "the *dīwān* of [the British] government."[6] The application of the word to such bodies was not seriously misleading; like Middle Eastern *dīwān*s, they were all institutions nominated by monarchs to whom they were answerable and whose authority they represented.

But there were numerous other—and more interesting—instances in which the term was used with reference to assemblies that, by contrast, were elective, representative and sovereign, at least in part. Such, for example, were the British Parliament and its lower house (the Commons), both of which were variably designated as *al-dīwān al-ʿāli* (supreme), *al-dīwān al-ʿumūmī* (general or common) or simply *dīwān Lundrā,* the London *dīwān.*[7] Such also were the French pre-revolutionary *États Généraux,* the 1792 *Convention Nationale,* the *Corps Législatif* of the Consulate regime, and the post-Napoleonic *Chambre des Députés;*[8] the Danish *Rigsdag* ("the Copenhagen *dīwān*");[9] and the United States Congress and Senate (sometimes identified, nonspecifically, as *dīwān al-mashyakha* or *dīwān al-jumhūriyya*).[10]

This variety of governmental forums differed in constitution, authority and place within the state system. Used to describe them all, *dīwān* was evidently intended in its broadest possible sense to mean assembly or council. As we have seen, however, the word had its traditional semantic limits, and even with its most general purport it could only be associated with bodies of the type known in the Middle East. These shared few characteristics with European and American "*dīwāns.*" Many writers were probably unaware of the gap. Others, conscious of it, and of the risks inherent in stretching a word beyond its familiar confines, tried to circumvent these risks by qualifying the term; they used such formulae as *dīwān al-rusul, dīwān wukalā' al-ra'iyya* and *dīwān al-a'yān wal-nuwwāb* to indicate the popular or representative nature of these bodies, thereby creating compounds of traditionally incompatible components.[11]

This last lexical solution proved unworkable. As Western parliaments became a subject of daily Arabic press accounts, *dīwān* was eventually deemed unfit for the purpose. It gradually gave ground to other terms, in contexts both foreign and local. By the last quarter of the century the word had lost the meaning of assembly. It remained in use only as a name for governmental offices and administrative subdivisions.

Of the terms that replaced *dīwān,* the most common was *majlis,* plural *majālis. Majlis* was used infrequently in the early decades of the period; but by mid-century it had gained widespread currency. Unlike *dīwān,* which was applicable to specific institutions with definite traits in the region, *majlis* was initially a very loose expression. Its literal sense of "a sitting place" was extended to include the person or persons therein, regardless of the circumstances, a usage which occurs in the Ḥadīth.[12] The word was employed more broadly to indicate a place for meeting or sitting together, hence also a group of people convening in one place, as well as their session. In the Middle East such gatherings were sporadic and temporary occasions. Thus, *majlis* carried an import of something transient: it denoted an event more than an institution. Such were *ad hoc* assemblies of high officials convened by Ottoman Sultans for special consultation on urgent matters, known as *majlis shūrā* or "convention of the *shūrā*" (they will be considered further below). Such also were unofficial meetings of elders in the professional guilds of Egypt, who assisted the *shaykh* in administrative matters.[13] Jabartī, who described the activities of Bonaparte's *dīwān* in Egypt in great detail, often referred to its sessions as *majlis,* as he did to its convention place, "the *majlis* of the *dīwān.*"[14] The first in the Middle East to establish a *majlis* of a more permanent nature at the state level was Muhammad Ali in Egypt. In 1824, seeking to replace the bureaucratic administration by a deliberative system, he doubled the two chief offices, *al-dīwān al-khidīwī* and *dīwān al-jihādiyya,* by establishing a "supreme council" for civil affairs—*al-majlis al-ᶜāli,* and a "council of military affairs"—*majlis al-jihādiyya,* respectively. These were advisory forums which discussed matters presented to them by the Pasha and made decisions by majority rule (the former of the two also had certain judicial powers). In 1829 Muhammad Ali began another experiment with a consultative assembly, *majlis al-shūrā,* presided over by his son Ibrāhīm. Composed of high officials, religious dignitaries, and some one hundred village heads, the assembly met annually to consider and make recommendations on domestic state affairs. A number of other councils were thereafter founded under similar titles, in which the name *majlis* was attached to permanent institutions.[15] Then, with the Tanẓīmāt in the Ottoman Empire, the casual conventions of the consultative *majlis al-shūrā* were gradually supplanted by a more regular deliberative activity in a series of new councils. In 1837, Sultan Maḥmūd II founded the *meclis-i vükelā* (or *meclis-i ḫāṣṣ*), a privy council of ministers. It was followed, the next year, by a *meclis-i valā-i aḥkām-i ᶜadliye,* Supreme Council of Judicial Ordinances. Before long the state witnessed a wide proliferation of official councils, including a system of local "administrative councils" (Turkish *meclis-i idāre,* Arabic *majlis al-idāra*) in the provinces, which replaced the provincial *dīwāns.*[16]

Introduced along the model of European councils, these *majlis*es were intended to serve as new instruments of government in place of the old. Indeed, in form and modus operandi, Western assemblies and Middle Eastern *majlis*es had much in common. This apparent resemblance made it acceptable to designate both the prototype and its local variants by one name. During the first three or four decades of the century, *majlis* stood for an innovative notion and was far less current than the long-familiar *dīwān.* It was occasionally used to describe institutions such as the thirteenth-century Imperial Court in the Holy Roman Empire, the Royal Court in seventeenth-century Sweden, assemblies in ancient Athens and Rome, the French *Chambre des Députés,* and the contemporary British Parliament.[17] Applicable also to Muhammad Ali's Consultative Assembly and to similar forums in Istanbul and the Ottoman provinces, *majlis* was no more than a generic term for governmental and administrative agencies of all kinds. Loose and devoid of associations with specific traditional institutions, it thus had a convenient advantage over *dīwān*.

With the growth of interest in foreign matters, and the multiplication of councils and assemblies in the Middle East itself, the term *majlis* became more popular. Eventually it gained ascendancy over all its synonyms, but this did not happen until the last quarter of the century. Meanwhile, in the early years of the Arabic press, a number of other terms were in use.

One curious expression at that time was *dār al-nadwa* or *nadwa*. In pre-Islamic Mecca this was the name for the convening place of the *mala'*, the council of tribal leaders which administered the city's public affairs. *Nadwa*—from n-d-w, to meet or assemble—meant gathering; *dār*, meaning house or abode, indicated the convention place. While current with this meaning in daily speech and in literature, *nadwa* was not used to designate any important political institution in Islamic history. The political sense first attached to it in the nineteenth century was drawn straight from its pre-Islamic usage. Like many other words, this too seems to have been provided by the medieval lexicons. *Dār al-nadwa*, the Lebanese journalist Rushayd al-Daḥdāḥ remarked when introducing the term in 1859, "is the hall [*qaṣr*] in which the people's leaders in every country met to deliberate [public] affairs. This was [originally the name for] the place in pre-Islamic Mecca where notables of [the tribe of] Quraysh gathered for consultation."[18] During the 1860s al-Daḥdāḥ used the name regularly to designate the British Parliament and both of its houses—*nadwat al-ʿāmma* and *nadwat al-shurafā'*; the French *Parlement*; the United States House of Representatives (*dīwān al-nadwa*); and comparable institutions in Belgium and Holland.[19] Writers in later years occasionally employed the expression for these and other assemblies—historical, like the fourteenth-century French *États Généraux*, which was called "the *barlamān* known as *dār al-nadwa*"; and contemporary, like the British Parliament, which was referred to as "*dār al-nadwa*, or *al-barlamint*." The term was at times used to describe the convention place, as in the report on a "meeting of the British lords and people's representatives at *dār al-nadwa*"; and at other times to indicate the institution itself, as in reference to "members of *dār al-nadwa* in London."[20] The word was used with this intent through to the end of the century. Other authors resorted to the term *jamᶜiyya*, a derivative from j-m-ᶜ, to gather, to assemble. In the nineteenth-century Middle East it was primarily associated with nonpolitical, voluntary forums established to further social and educational goals, such as *al-jamᶜiyya al-Sūriyya* ("the Syrian Society," founded in Beirut in 1847), *cemᶜiyet-i ᶜilmiye-i Osmāniye* ("Ottoman Scientific Society," Istanbul, 1861) and *jamᶜiyyat al-maqāṣid al-khayriyya* ("the Benevolent Society," Cairo, 1880).[21] *Jamᶜiyya*, like *majlis*, was generic rather than specific. It was applicable to associations of any type, as well as to short-term gatherings: "on the third day [of the month] a *jamᶜiyya* took place in the *dīwān*," runs a typical text in Jabartī's chronicle, evidently referring to a meeting.[22] A versatile expression, it was chosen as a name for such institutions as the French *Convention* (*jamᶜiyyat al-kūnfānsyūn*), *Assemblée Constituante* (*al-jamᶜiyya al-murattiba*), and *Assemblée Nationale* (*al-jamᶜiyya al-waṭaniyya*), the Russian Council of Notables (*jamᶜiyyat al-ashrāf,*) and the United States Congress (*jamᶜiyyat al-wilāyāt al-muttaḥida*).[23] There was also a slightly modified version of the term—*jamāᶜa*, stemming from the same root and similarly indicating a group or gathering of people. This variant in the name was occasionally applied to the French *Chambre des Députées*.[24]

During the last third of the century, *jamᶜiyya* was sometimes attached to political bodies in the region itself, and for a while seemed to be striking roots with this meaning. The municipal assembly of Istanbul, for example, was given the name *cemᶜiyet-i ᶜumūmiye*, "general assembly." The same name in Arabic form (*al-jamᶜiyya al-ᶜumūmiyya*) was attached to the Egyptian assembly founded in 1883, following the British invasion of the country. This last assembly consisted of cabinet ministers and other members, both appointed and elected. It operated in Egypt for thirty years. When dissolved in 1913, it gave way to another *jamᶜiyya*, which was a kind of "legislative assembly"—*al-jamᶜiyya al-tashrīᶜiyya*. However, *jamᶜiyya* lost this meaning after World War I, and retained only its older and looser sense of association or society.

Yet another option explored by Arab writers during the early years of the press was loan-translation of the French *chambre* or Italian *camera*, extending the name of the assembly place to the group of people occupying it. The Arabic equivalents were *qāᶜa,* a hall, and *awḍa,* a room (the latter was more common with this meaning in Turkish than in Arabic). In like manner, the Italian word was sometimes borrowed untranslated, the Arabic form being *qamira.* During the 1860s and 1870s these words were very common in designating not only the French and Italian, but also a variety of other assemblies. The British Parliament, for example, was referred to as " *'al-barlyamint,'* namely the general *qāᶜa,* " and its two houses became *qāᶜat al-shurafā'* and *qāᶜat al-ᶜumūm,* Lords and Commons, respectively. Members of these bodies were, accordingly, *aᶜḍā' al-qāᶜa.* The United States House of Representatives was, similarly, *qāᶜat al-nuwwāb;* the Prussian Upper House (*Herrenhaus*) was presented as *qamirat al-aᶜyān;* and the *Chambre des Députés* in Paris was entitled "the French *awḍa.*"[25]

These last locutions further complicated an already confused description of Western parliaments. As the century unfolded into its last third, the plurality of Arabic names used for the purpose was still producing an inconsistent and vague understanding of these forums. Often one source would employ a variety of terms, sometimes in the very same account, as designations for one institution, creating a real puzzle. To pick an example, reporting the move by the United States Congress to abolish slavery, a contemporary Lebanese weekly informed its readers of "the decision made by the [United States'] general *majlis*es" (*majālisihā al-ᶜumūmiyya*). Discussing the matter further in the next issue, the paper referred to "the reform decided upon by the supreme *majlis* and the *qāᶜa* of representatives of the United States of America, which held its convention at the *jamᶜiyya;* the majority of votes . . . of the two *majlis*es [*al-majlisayn*]" supported the resolution.[26]

The perplexity such descriptions reflected, and undoubtedly evoked, was due not only to the multiplicity of expressions. It resulted also from the indefinite semantic scope of each. Of the terms discussed so far, three also came to serve, around the same time, as interchangeable names for another novelty, related but not identical to parliament—the international conference. Between the late 1850s and late 1870s, writers who used *dīwān, majlis* and *jamᶜiyya* with reference to European and American parliaments, attached these terms almost as often to events such as the 1815 Congress of Vienna—*majlis Wiyāna,* the 1858 Paris

Conference—*jam'iyyat Bārīs,* and an international conference in Paris in 1860—*dīwān nuwwāb al-mulūk.*[27] This is not to say, of course, that those employing the terms with such equivocality were unable to distinguish one forum from the other. Rather, the confusion is best seen as another illustration of the difficulties in devising new names for the new notions. The whole set of terms related to parliaments was then still extremely amorphous, with a semantic scope broad enough to cover at once permanent assemblies and transient conferences. With such a broad range of meaning, *dīwān, majlis* and *jam'iyya* could be applied to both local councils and foreign ones, while still allowing for considerable differences between them.

We now come to the most interesting expression selected by Arab writers to describe European-type parliaments. *Shūrā* or *mashwara,* two interchangeable variations of the same term, added a special texture to the Arab portrayal of modern political institutions. *Shūrā* denoted an idea deeply entrenched in the region's tradition, and while not the most common name used for the new purpose, it nevertheless recurred with high frequency in texts throughout the century (somewhat less so at the end than at the outset). Its very presence in these writings was of much significance, because of its historical connotations.

There is little need to dwell here upon the meaning and evolution of *shūrā,* which has been the subject of extensive scholarly treatment. A few brief remarks will suffice. The word signifies counsel or consultation, a practice recommended by the Prophet and by Muslim jurists.[28] As a political institution *shūrā* dates back to the times of 'Umar, but 'Umar's *shūrā* had no organized sequel. Muslim sovereigns at times sought the advice of their subjects. Consultative forums carrying the name *shūrā* are known to have existed in medieval North Africa and Spain (especially in the judicial system and municipal administration), in the Qarmatian state in tenth-century Bahrain, and in Mamluk Egypt.[29] The Ottomans, who brought the notion of consultation from their pre-imperial past, were notable for their more systematic practice of the principle (Turkish *meşveret*); Ottoman Sultans took counsel with broad circles of their subordinates, especially during the eighteenth and early nineteenth centuries.[30] Yet no apparatus for this purpose was ever prescribed or created. *Shūrā* or *mashwara* remained a theoretical recommendation to the ruler; whether or not to make use of that device was left to his discretion.

As a name for a political institution, *shūrā* was more specific
than terms such as *majlis* or *jamʿiyya*. While the latter two words
implied certain organizational qualities, *shūrā* further indicated a
definite function, and hence also the precise limits of authority.
Shūrā was universally understood to mean an institution consultative in nature and totally dependent on the ruler whom it was
meant to serve. It is these specific traits that make the term so
important for our analysis. From the beginning of the encounter
with Europe to the end of the century, writers of Arabic every-
where applied the term as a matter of course to Western governmental councils and assemblies of all types. It was used independently, or in compounds such as *dīwān al-mashwara, majlis shūrā
al-umma, jamʿiyyat al-mashwara, shūrā al-dawla*. Muhammad
Ali's official organ, *al-Waqāʾiʿ al-Miṣriyya*, regularly discussed
the Pasha's own *majlis al-mashwara* alongside institutions such as
the British Parliament and the French *Chambre des Députés*,
which were referred to by the same name or very similar ones.[31]
Ṭahṭāwī, more closely acquainted with Europe's political structures, attached the name to such diverse bodies as the ancient
Roman senate, the Swiss Federal Assembly, the General Assembly in Mexico and the United States Congress (the latter he described by the somewhat awkward expression *mashwarat dīwān
ʿumūmī*).[32] So did his colleagues, the translators, who regularly
resorted to *shūrā* and *mashwara* in rendering *Sénat, Assemblée
Générale, États Généraux* and *Parlement*.[33]

Writers in later years continued to apply the term to all
institutions, from the Russian czar's council[34] to the House of
Representatives in Washington.[35] The British Parliament and
both of its houses were all described as *shūrā* or *mashwara*, and
their membership often referred to as *arbāb-* or *aʿḍāʾ al-shūrā*[36]—
as were the *Assemblée Nationale* and its two components in republican France,[37] the Swiss Assembly,[38] and numerous bodies
elsewhere. Consequently, *shūrā* became a synonym for *majlis* and
jamʿiyya; it was applicable to all governmental and administrative
forums, regardless of function and authority.

Most Arab writers who used the term to designate institutions abroad in the second half of the century intended to convey
no specific characteristics; they simply employed *shūrā* to technically indicate a form of organization. Yet if *shūrā* had acquired
this indefinite acceptance, it had also preserved its traditional
specific meaning. That was especially so when the word was used

in local contexts, as a name for new bodies that appeared in the Middle East at that time. Muhammad Ali's *majlis al-mashwara* of 1829 and the local councils organized by his son Ibrāhīm in Syria and Palestine under the name *dīwān al-mashwara* have already been mentioned. Khedive Ismāʿīl went a step further by using the term in 1866 for an institution that had the novel quality of being elective, if only indirectly—*majlis shūrā al-nuwwāb,* "Consultative Council of Delegates." Following the British invasion, the latter was supplanted by the *majlis shūrā al-qawānīn,* with a partly nominated and partly elected membership. Meanwhile, in Istanbul, Sultan Maḥmūd II in 1838 set up the Consultative Council of the Sublime Porte, *dār-i şūrā-yi bāb-i ʿāli,* in an attempt to abolish the Grand Vezirate and redistribute its authority. In 1868 Sultan ʿAbd al-ʿAzīz inaugurated a body called *şūrā-yi devlet,* "Council of State" (probably modeled on the French *Conseil d'État*), composed of appointed officials who were to assist the Sultan and his ministers in legislative matters. (The former of the last two bodies was short-lived. The latter became the most important civil administrative institution, next to the Council of Ministers.) Lesser bodies in Egypt, Istanbul and the Ottoman provinces were likewise characterized as *shūrā* councils: Muhammad Ali's *majlis shūrā al-madāris* (council of education) and *majlis shūrā al-aṭibā'* (medical council), and the Ottoman *şūrā-yi ʿaskerī* (military council), were such instances, and there were numerous others.[39]

There were differences of all kinds among these various institutions. But one feature of major importance was common to them all: none of them enjoyed more than consultative authority. They were all deliberative in nature, and their ideas were to serve as advice which the ruler would adopt or reject. Their foundation having been prompted by the Western example, these forums also at the same time represented a vivification of old principles and practice. Their description as *shūrā* was not accidental; it marked the traditional delimitation of their authority.

Shūrā thus came to denote two rather distinct ideas. It meant one thing when used in a local context; it meant quite another when applied to institutions abroad. This dual acceptance, as we have seen in a great many instances, was a likely source of ambiguity under the circumstances of rapidly changing concepts. Readers would likely mistake fully sovereign Western parliaments for councils with limited advisory power, as both had come to carry the same name. The term was also likely to delude those who wanted to believe that true European-type parliaments had actually been brought into the Middle East or, on the other hand, that the foreign notion corresponded to an old Islamic principle which had always been there.

This latter argument became common toward the end of the century among proponents of a trend of thought known as Islamic Reformism. Among them were Young Ottoman thinkers, notably Nāmik Kemāl, and such perceptive men as Muḥammad ᶜAbduh and Rashīd Riḍā. Seeking to show that modern ideas were compatible with Islamic principles, they suggested that parliament and *shūrā* were two slightly different versions of the same notion. Both, they maintained, were instruments allowing the voice of the ruled to be heard in government.[40] The argument was designed to serve a twofold purpose: to make parliamentary government more palatable to Muslims, and to make Islam more acceptable to liberals and modernists. The selection of the term was thus motivated by a polemic approach, more than by misunderstanding. Yet, even if these apologists were aware of the differences between the two notions and chose to minimize them only for the argument's sake, they surely contributed to the general lack of specific understanding. The identification of *shūrā* with parliament, for whatever reason, must have had a detrimental effect on the assimilation of the latter concept in the Middle East. The ensuing confusion prevailed throughout the nineteenth century and continued well into the twentieth.

Toward the end of the century, *majlis* was emerging as the chosen name for parliaments and other modern-type assemblies at home and abroad. In the early 1870s it became more popular than other Arabic words used to designate such institutions. By the end of the decade it had come to exclude the rest of them, with exceptions that were growing ever rarer. The word often required qualifying complements, as in *al-majlis al-ᶜāli*, usually a cabinet or senate; *majlis al-umma*, usually a national assembly; *majlis al-shuyūkh, majlis al-nuwwāb* and so forth. *Majlis*, a nonspecific term with no traditional political connotations, conveniently became the accepted Arabic equivalent of "assembly" and "council." It could denote any such institution in or out of the Middle East.

During these late years of the period, another linguistic phenomenon, hitherto marginal, was growing very popular: the usage of loan-words as names for foreign councils and assemblies. Most common among them was *barlamān*, from the French *parlement*. This word was used interchangeably with *majlis* to indicate parliaments in Britain, France, Italy, and sometimes in places where the assemblies had originally carried other titles (as in Bismark's Prussia or imperial Germany).[41] Similarly, the term *sināt*, or *sinātū*—an Arabicization of the French *sénat* and Italian *senato*—was applied to all senates. Along with *barlamān* and *sināt* came a variety of proper names such as *kūnjris* (congress), *kūrtis* (Cortes) and *rashstāgh* (Reichstag). These appellations appeared in great abundance during the last quarter of the century, illustrating, as loan-words always do, the limited capacity of Arabic for handling the terminological challenge all by itself. More important, they attested to the growing awareness of the distinction between these foreign bodies and the local traditional ones. It was this awareness that later made *barlamān* not only popular but also attractive; in the twentieth century it became a name for institutions which sprouted all over the region in emulation of the foreign model.

The other instrument of modern politics to be examined here is the political party. Organizing in parties, in the very general sense of groupings or associations, has always been an effective method of political action, in the West as well as in the Middle East. Here, however, "party" is considered in a narrower sense, that of one among several political groups competing for power within a parliamentary system of government. An essential aspect of the word "party" is thus its very literal significance, that of a part of a whole. Parties are permanent bodies (as distinct from *ad hoc* gatherings), with an ideology or program, organization and leadership. By the beginning of the nineteenth century such bodies had already been active in Britain, France and the United States. Later they developed elsewhere. As we shall see, the difficulty of distinguishing between the general and the specific meanings of the word marked the Arab perception of the idea throughout much of the period.

In the Middle East, where a distribution of governmental authority among several components did not exist, political parties were likewise nonexistent. There were often power struggles among groups. But in a system accepting the monarch's supreme authority, such groups showed little resemblance to European political parties seeking greater influence within a representative system. It was only in the last quarter of the nineteenth century that a group calling itself a "party"—adopting the name from the European example—appeared in the region. But even that group cannot be viewed as more than a precursor of political parties in the modern sense. Multiparty systems as a political phenomenon would emerge in the region only in the twentieth century.

In examining the idea we shall be concerned mainly with one term, *ḥizb,* plural, *aḥzāb.* The initial meaning of this word was part or portion. With this denotation it was used, for example, to indicate one of sixty portions into which the Qur'ān was divided, to facilitate its recitation.[42] From this meaning was derived another, that of a group of people, a clan, a faction or a company. It was often used for a group of supporters of a man or a cause; hence *ḥizb Allāh,* the "Party of God" in the Qur'ān, which responded to the Prophet's call.[43] Sometimes the word carried a negative connotation, implying division and factionalism incompatible with the Islamic call for unity. At other times it was neutral and synonymous with *ṭā'ifa, jamᶜiyya* and *jamāᶜa,* indicating any group of men.

During the greater part of the nineteenth century it was mainly with this last, neutral and loose sense, that *ḥizb* was used in the Middle East. The word was applied to such entities as the Holy Alliance in post-1815 Europe—"the *ḥizb* known as *ṣānt alyāns,"* the Catholics and Protestants of France and Britain— "the religious *aḥzāb,"* and the "*ḥizb* of Armenians who were opposed to their Patriarch [and who] broke away from him."[44] These distinctions, of course, had nothing to do with political parties. *Ḥizb* was also used with reference to political groups within pluralistic polities which did not operate as organized parties, strictly speaking. Niqūlā Turk, for example, described the execution of Louis XVI in Paris, in January 1793, along with "a group [*jumla*] of people from among the government [*arbāb al-dawla*], who belonged to the [king's] *ḥizb*"; and as "only a few people of the king's *ḥizb* survived, the *ḥizb* of the republic gained considerable strength."[45] Here, evidently, the term signified little more than a group of loyalists. Similarly, "it is rumoured that a large *ḥizb* of American Congress members wishes to launch a war against England," one newspaper reported, meaning a group of politicians.[46] Writing of the past, one author likewise noted that following the defeat of Hannibal by Scipio, turmoil in the Roman Empire became widespread "and the *aḥzāb* within it multiplied." Here, again, the reference was to factions.[47] With such a nonspecific political meaning the term was also used as a verb (in the fifth form), to indicate short-term joint action of groups seeking to further a cause. In sixteenth-century England, according to one text, Queen Elizabeth accused Mary Stuart of having "*taḥazzabat* (joined forces) with her enemies to assassinate her." In contemporary Naples, there appeared "*taḥazzubāt* (factional associations) of people against the king of Italy." And by the same token, Garibaldi was described as "one of the famous *mutaḥazzibīn* [those joining together] to advocate the idea of a Socialist International."[48]

While using *ḥizb* flexibly, nineteenth-century Arab writers also chose the term to designate specific political parties abroad. *Ḥizb* was thereby given a more accurate meaning, which it carried along with the older, generic one, which it eventually replaced. The change began with the emergence of the press,[49] in which an increasingly consistent attribution of the term to political parties in Europe and the United States gradually lent it precision. Such party names were either borrowed—for example, *ḥizb al-tūrī*, *ḥizb al-libirāl*, *ḥizb al-radikāl*, *ḥizb al-kunsirfātīf* (the Tory, Liberal, Radical and Conservative parties);[50] or, more commonly, loan-translated in such awkward compounds as *ḥizb muḥibbī al-ḥurriyya* ("party of freedom lovers," the Liberals), *ḥizb al-muḥāfiẓīn* ("the Conservative Party") and *ḥizb mā warā' al-iḥtifāzī* ("the Ultra Conservative Party").[51] As was the case with other items of the political vocabulary, the process of modernizing this term was slow. Authors occasionally interchanged *ḥizb* with other generic terms: *ṭā'ifa*, *firqa* (division, unit), *qism* (part) and *fi'a* (group), or sometimes simply *ahl* ("[group of] people"), were applied to such entities as the Conservative Party—*al-firqa al-muḥāfiẓa*, the Liberal Party—*ahl al-ḥurriyya*, and the Democratic Party—*al-fi'a al-dhīmuqrāṭiyya*.[52] These further attested to the fluidity of the notion.

By the time the first political *ḥizb* appeared in the Middle East, the term had come to carry a double meaning, being at once loose and precise. The Egyptian *al-ḥizb al-waṭanī*, known as "the patriotic (or national) party"—established in late 1879 by a group of ex-ministers amid a tense political atmosphere—has often been described as "the first political party in Egypt." More accurately it was a grouping of men who combined to express the country's desire for independence, an *ad hoc* association organized loosely, for whom attaining parliamentary representation was not at all a goal. When these politicians were joined by army sympathizers, the latter were depicted, just as loosely, as *al-ḥizb al-ʿaskarī*, the military "party," or rather, "group of supporters."[53] Aḥmad ʿUrābī, who also joined the *ḥizb* and became its leader, later offered an illuminating definition of it. Accused in court of illegally heading a "*ḥizb* within the government system," he argued that *ḥizb* was no more than a general name attached to a patriotic association. Egypt, he insisted, was "inhabited by various ethnic communities [*ajnās*], each of which may be regarded as a *ḥizb*. Furthermore, the country's [entire] population forms a *ḥizb* by itself." Every people, ʿUrābī suggested, "have *aḥzāb* which concern themselves in preserving their country's independence and defending its rights."[54]

ʿUrābī's argument may have been apologetic. But the point was surely valid: *ḥizb* was then still an uncertain term; and the *ḥizb* he himself headed was an association of an ambiguous type, a movement. It was doubtless "patriotic" and "nationalistic." But it was not a political party as understood in the context of political pluralism. This loose sense of *ḥizb* was still reflected in a statement in 1899 by a compatriot, Jurjī Zaydān, who lamented the "division of every country and every people and every community [in the Islamic lands] into [so many] *aḥzāb* (factions) and *firaq* (groups) that only God can enumerate them."[55]

Of the two meanings which the word implied in foreign contexts, it was thus only the older, more general one that was applicable in local contexts as well. *Al-ḥizb al-waṭanī* of 1879 seems to have foreshadowed political parties in the Middle East in name more than in substance. That "party" turned out to be short-lived, with no immediate successor. The next appearance of *ḥizb* in the region would again be in Egypt, in the twentieth century. This time it would carry the name in its newer sense, the sense which was acquired through its application to political parties in Europe and the United States.

Conclusion

"A perfect translation is impossible," Luis Lozano, a professional translator, once observed. "We cannot project our perceptions into the minds of other people and arouse in them images identical to our own. Even the simplest object, a tree, for example, will evoke in one person a particular species, shape, size, color, and surroundings which can never coincide with those imagined by another person." It is relatively easy, however, to translate abstract ideas, Lozano went on to say; "since no one can picture in a material way such concepts as friendship, justice or freedom, there cannot be much discrepancy when referring to these terms in any language."[1] As the evidence produced in the present study clearly demonstrates, there is ample room for confusion even in the rendering of abstract notions. Such a confusion is liable to occur in translation from one language to another when both belong to the same civilization; it is the more likely when the translation is designed to cross an intercivilizational barrier.

The difficulties facing Middle Eastern writers who engaged in such a task were tremendous. Confronted suddenly with an alien system of ideas, Arab authors were caught unprepared. Lacking the conceptual training, even the lexical tools, required for the purpose, their situation was much like that of a jazz band ordered to play a classical symphony. The developments dis-

cussed in the previous chapters bear testimony to the unprecedented magnitude of the challenge and to the depth of the crisis it
generated. They also testify to the admirable efforts invested by
the educated Arab elite who had to meet that challenge.

As we have seen, the most natural (and hence most common)
way of addressing the problem of inadequate repertoire was
through analogy. Arab writers, at times unaware of the foreign
ideas' distinct nature, and at others aware of it but lacking appropriate Arabic terms, introduced many novel concepts through
words denoting their approximate Middle Eastern equivalents.
Thus, nations and nation-states in the West were treated as *milla,
ṭā'ifa* and *qabīla;* European emperors were entitled *malik* or
sulṭān; citizens were described as *raʿiyya,* and their appointed or
elected leaders as *shuyūkh, aʿyān* or *mabʿūthīn;* parliaments were
presented as *dīwān* and *mashwara,* and their members as *arbāb*
and *aṣḥāb;* and man-made constitutions became *sharīʿa.* Technically, such analogies lent new layers of meaning to old Arabic
words, layers which seemed to be compatible with their preexisting content. This kind of solution had the obvious advantage of
rendering the new ideas intelligible, no doubt an important pre-
requisite for their assimilation in the region.

But analogies, by definition, are of limited designative capacity; they are useful for general orientation, but are not designed
for precise identification. When an *analogous* instance is presented
as *identical* with another, through the application of one name to
both, proximity substitutes for exactitude, and discrepancy is
likely. When Ṭahṭāwī explained that "the Protestants . . . are to
Catholic Christianity what the Khawārij are to Islam," his was an
analogy carefully qualified by an explicit reference to the respective Christian and Muslim contexts; it did not pretend to offer
more than a rough idea of the Protestants and, moreover, sought
to prevent confusion between them and their Middle Eastern ana-
logue. But when, on the other hand, Ṭahṭāwī's colleague rendered
a "décret rigoureux contre les Protestantes" as *al-fermān al-ṣaʿb
al-ṣādir fī ḥaqq al-muʿtazila* ("the rigorous *fermān* issued with regard to the *muʿtazila*"), in which the Protestants are identified
outright as a medieval philosophical school in Islam, he made
confusion between the two unavoidable.[2] The latter example is the
more typical of the analogies used by nineteenth-century Middle
Eastern observers of the West. The resultant discrepancy may or
may not have reflected misconception on the part of the writer,

but it was always liable to produce one in the reader's mind. And when names devised through this method gained popular currency, confusion was perpetuated.

The ambiguity produced by imprecise analogies had two inevitable effects. First, it interfered with the Arab understanding of principles underlying political patterns in Europe, and was therefore largely responsible for the confused view Arabs had of Western civilization in general. Second, and perhaps more important, by making Arab observers acquire an approximate, rather than accurate, notion of the new ideas, it eventually influenced the way in which such ideas were implemented in the region itself. Analogies, both lexical and conceptual, facilitated the adoption of new patterns through making them more comprehensible; but at the same time they also contributed to the creation of modified—and often substantially different—versions of foreign ideas in the Middle East. One may therefore argue that the gap which emerged between European political models and their Middle Eastern applications, ascribable, of course, to many other factors, may also be attributed to the lax way in which the foreign ideas were presented and interpreted in the region during the first formative century of exposure to the West.

Better acquaintance with foreign concepts gradually led to dissatisfaction with the usual method of conveying modern knowledge. Certain Arab writers, while still using analogies regularly, were careful to add explanatory remarks indicating the limits of the comparisons. Others turned to explore alternative lexical paths. They dug in classical dictionaries, bringing back to life words long forgotten, such as *ᶜāhil* and *dār al-nadwa;* revived archaic meanings of words, as was the case with *fawḍā* (used to denote republic); devised neologisms, such as *jumhūriyya, raᶜāᶜiyya* and *mu'tamar;* and, rather reluctantly, resorted to outright borrowing of foreign words, such as *lūrd, barlamān, sharṭa* and *dīmuqrāṭiyya.* The discontent which gave ground to these efforts marked an important development, for it signified growing awareness of the dissimilarities between traditional and modern ideas. Such differences seemed to warrant that a distinction in name be made between the foreign and local ideas. Symbolically, some astute authors even found it difficult to properly render in Arabic the very word "politics"; they felt ill at ease with using the traditional term *siyāsa,* meaning management of state or of other affairs (and nowadays the accepted word for "politics"), sensing that the Western variant of politics was something else. Some of them thus preferred the alien (and awkward) term *būlītīqa* or *būlītīqiyya*. *"Būlītīqa* means *siyāsa,"* shaykh Ṭahṭāwī remarked, for *"būlītīqa* is all that concerns the state and its government"; but in a European context, he noted, *būlītīqa* had additional specific characteristics: "the *Ifranj* use the term to imply the caution and prudence of state leaders, their keeping of state secrets, their handling of documents and their addressing [official] matters."[3] Such traits may have been shared by Middle Eastern leaders as well, yet Ṭahṭāwī felt that, in the European version, they carried a certain additional spirit which the word *siyāsa* could not quite properly convey. This kind of keen awareness was an essential condition to a more precise understanding and rendition of the new concepts coming to Middle Eastern attention.

However, the growth of such awareness was necessarily slow and protracted, a fact clearly reflected by the lexical evidence. The second and third quarters of the nineteenth century, in particular, were a period of haphazard lexical experimentation and much fluidity—a period, to use Jaroslav Stetkevych's words, in which Arabic was "tortured" and often strained "beyond its point of tolerance," and one typified by extensive "disharmony between concept and term."[4] Numerous expressions were tried. Some struck roots; many others were abandoned after a while. Certain new words were semantically sounder than the previous analogical terms they replaced, but as such they were often less understandable to the audience. Evoking no familiar associations in those who came across them, they remained enigmatic, obscuring as much as they clarified. Such, for instance, was the case with *jumhūriyya,* which replaced *mashyakha* as a term for republic; the newer expression was more accurate (or, rather, less erroneous), yet to many it spelled little but mystery. Such was also the case with most of the loan-words, which conveyed the alien ideas precisely but must have left many people perplexed about their exact, or even approximate, meaning.

The Arab deciphering of modern Western concepts, and the verbal tools created to transmit them, came a long way during the nineteenth century. An Arab intellectual in 1900 examining a political text from 1800, or even an account from the early years of the press in the mid-1860s, would have found many ideas to have been ambiguously presented and numerous expressions to be obsolete, if not altogether unrecognizable. By 1900 the Arabic political vocabulary had become considerably richer, not so much in the number of words as in the expanded designative ability of many old terms. Yet this is not to say that all, or most, of the obstacles to a smooth communication of modern ideas had been removed. As we have seen, much confusion was still evidenced— and produced—by imprecise language even at the end of the period: at that stage, *raʿiyya* was still an acceptable word for citizens, *aʿyān* was a common title for lords and congressmen, *mashyakha* continued to occur in texts discussing republics, and elected representative assemblies were often referred to as *majlis shūrā*. Following several centuries of "Muslim discovery" and another century of "Arab rediscovery" of Europe, there remained much to be discovered, comprehended and assimilated; and Arab intellectuals of the late nineteenth century bequeathed this task to their successors in the twentieth.

In the twentieth century, the process of Arab familiarization with modern ideas was accelerated by closer contacts between Europe and the Middle East. The channels through which knowledge was brought in, first the press and then the electronic media, constantly improved. The emergence of separate Arab political entities, and later of independent states, permitted extensive practice of the modern principles at home. Ideas hitherto known to a few intellectuals became public property, and the adaptation of Arabic to new needs was more orderly, passing from translators and journalists to language academies. The Middle East became a stage for what seemed to be modern-style kings and republican governments, citizens with political rights and their elected representatives, parliaments and political parties, constitutions and civil legislation, nation-states and inter-Arab diplomacy. More precisely, these were *malik* and *jumhūriyya*, *muwāṭin* and *nuwwāb*, *majlis* and *ḥizb*, *dustūr* and *tashrīʿ*, *umma* and *muʾtamar*. Most of these terms, common in 1800, had been resemanticized by 1900 so that they now meant very different things. Reminiscent of, yet distinct from, their past traditional referents, they were also analogous to, but not identical with, their Western counterparts. With their historical import and modern meanings, these words faithfully reflect the dual composition of the Middle Eastern variants: Western concepts superimposed upon traditional foundations and then refashioned.

Yet despite the better grasp of modern ideas and the coordinated lexical efforts, some ambiguity concerning modern principles of politics seems to have remained. Many Arabic words continue to designate both the Western and the Middle Eastern versions of the same ideas, blurring the distinctions between them. This must adversely affect the Arab interpretation of politics abroad (and hence, indirectly, interfere with the dialogue between the Middle East and the West—although the rapid development of communication helps to minimize the problem). In addition, each of the ideas imported into the region has come to take on many local forms. The proliferation of states gave ground to a plurality of political realities; and in the Arabic language which serves them all, many political terms have come to carry a whole gamut of connotations, changing their meaning from one Arab context to another. For instance, the term *umma,* in the newly acquired sense of nation-state, means one thing when used with reference to Egypt—*al-umma al-Miṣriyya,* a context in which it brings to mind primarily a glorious past, a unique communal homogeneity and a proud national revival; but the word means something quite different when applied to the Arab nation—*al-umma al-ʿArabiyya,* implying a fragmented community sharing a dream of future unity. The Lebanese *umma,* the Palestinian *umma,* and every other *umma* in the Middle East, each lend a specific color to the term, which also continues to bear its old meaning in references to the Islamic *umma.* To give another example, the post-1952 Egyptian *jumhūriyya* has little in common with the post-1967 *jumhūriyya* in the Popular Democratic Republic of (South) Yemen which, in turn, bears no resemblance to the Lebanese *jumhūriyya.* All three, of course, are quite unlike the political systems in France or the United States, which speakers of Arabic designate by the very same name.

It goes without saying that the intercivilizational language barrier has been equally detrimental to Western efforts to fathom Middle Eastern ideas; the lesson the lexical evidence in this study seems to teach us applies to both cultures alike. The most accurate way of describing political institutions and processes in the Arab countries is, of course, by using the Arabic terms. Any substitute would be at best approximate. If, for instance, we designate a *majlis al-umma* as "parliament," we risk imposing upon the subject a variety of irrelevant connotations which might badly distort it. This is even more true in the discussion of Middle Eastern realities in earlier centuries, when the gap between traditional Islamic concepts and modern Western vocabulary was incomparably broader than it is now. This might sound trivial. Yet, numerous instances in recent scholarship repeatedly confirm that these points cannot be overemphasized. The semantic exploration of modern Arabic is still an undeveloped field. The utilization of semantic evidence in Middle Eastern historical research is even less advanced. As already indicated in the introduction, the present work does not purport to offer more than a preliminary statement on the subject. Even within the limited territory of political concepts investigated here, much remains to be done, and many other ideas untouched by this study still need to be explored. Areas other than politics—social attitudes, economic notions, religio-philosophical views—would likewise benefit from this kind of examination.

In the grand play of modern Middle Eastern political history, where relations with another culture have played an immense role, language has been of crucial importance in every sense. This, apparently, is as true of the twentieth century as it is of the nineteenth.

Notes

Introduction

1. Quoted by Krymskii, p. 498. I am grateful to Mr. Z. Keinan for translating extensive sections from this invaluable book.
2. Al-Yāzijī, p. 7.
3. *Ḥadīqat al-akhbār,* 22 Dec 1858, p. 2.
4. Bustānī, quoted by Krymskii, p. 498.
5. The classic book on the subject is Weinreich's *Languages in Contact.* See also Haugen, "Analysis."
6. Lewis, *Islam in History,* pp. 283–84.
7. See further in A. Ayalon, "*Ḍimūqrāṭiyya.*"
8. See A. Ayalon, "Arab discovery."
9. Except for Khayr al-Dīn al-Tūnisī's highly instructive treatise, *Aqwam al-masālik,* which was popular throughout the Arab lands.
10. Cf. S. Moreh's introduction to Jabartī's *Mudda;* Abu Lughod, pp. 20–23.
11. See bibliography.
12. On Turk and other contemporary Christian Lebanese see Philipp, pp. 165ff.
13. For a nearly complete list of these translations see Shayyāl, *Ta'rīkh al-tarjama . . . fī ʿaṣr Muḥammad ʿAlī,* appendixes 1–3.
14. See Pérès, "Voyageurs"; idem, *L'Espagne,* pp. 72–87; Louca, pp. 197ff.; Zolondek, "Travelers"; Abu Lughod, pp. 69ff. (with a partial list of travelers and references to their biographies on pp. 72–75).
15. The most important work on the Arabic press of the nineteenth and early twentieth centuries remains Ṭarrazī's *Ta'rīkh al-ṣiḥāfa al-ʿArabiyya,* in four volumes (Beirut, 1913, 1914, 1933). See also: Hartmann; al-Jundī; Ḥamza; ʿAbduh;

134

Khaddūr, pp. 43–85; Muruwwa, pp. 129ff.; Hourani, *Arabic Thought,* especially pp. 245ff.; Ahmed, pp. 17–34; Krymskii, pp. 480ff., 568ff., 601ff.

16. Certain periodicals occasionally provided lists of their representatives in different locations, over an area sometimes spreading from Java and Bangkok to Paris and Moscow, including, of course, many of the Arab cities of the Middle East. See e.g. *al-Jinān,* 1872, p. 291; *al-Jawā'ib,* 7 Nov 1877, p. 8; *al-Naḥla,* Sep 1879, p. 16. *Al-Jawā'ib* seems to have been the newspaper with the broadest circulation during its lifetime; see Ṭarrazi, vol. 1, p. 61; Hourani, *Arabic Thought,* pp. 98–99. For estimates on the circulation of certain Egyptian newspapers around the end of the century see Hartmann, pp. 12, 18; Lutfi al-Sayyid Marsot, p. 159; Rizq, p. 24.

17. "We often see servants, donkey-rearers and others who cannot read, gather around one who reads while they listen. The streets of Cairo and of other towns in the region are full of this. . . . The subscribers for Egyptian newspapers . . . now number over twenty thousand. This is [merely] the number of subscribers. The readers' number, however, reaches perhaps 200,000, since a single copy of a newspaper is touched by many hands, and is read by tens or scores of people." *Al-Hilāl,* Oct 1897, p. 131.

Chapter 1

1. See Lewis, *Muslim Discovery,* especially chapter 1; idem, "Ifrandj," *EI²;* Kahane, "Lingua Franca." For the use of *Ifranj* or *Firanj* as a proper name for the Franks see e.g. Masʿūdi, *Murūj,* vol. 2, pp. 145ff.; Qalqashandī, vol. 5, pp. 412ff. However, Qalqashandī himself, like others, often confused the notion of "Franks" as an individual people with that of Europe in general—cf. ibid, pp. 404ff., 420, 421. Similarly, Ibn al-ʿIbrī, pp. 57, 60, 227, 237, 244, 257–59; Ibn Khaldūn, pp. 72, 77, 83.

2. Jabartī, *Maẓhar,* p. 7; see also pp. 9, 12.

3. Ibid, p. 149.

4. Mardīnī, passim.

5. Badīr, p. 1.

6. Qalʿāwī, fol. 52b; Jabartī, *Mudda* and *Maẓhar,* s.v. *Firanj* in the indexes. Occasionally, however, Jabartī quoted texts mentioning other European peoples, such as the Muscovites and the Venetians. For similar contemporary references to the *Ifranj* see e.g. Shihābī, p. 193 (designating Bonaparte as "king of the *Ifranj*"); *al-Waqā'iʿ al-Miṣriyya,* 1829–1830, no. 30, p. 3; no. 31, p. 2; no. 37, p. 4 (reports on the arrival of ships carrying passengers *min ṭā'ifat al-Ifranj*); Badīr, passim. I am grateful to Dina LeGall for bringing the texts by Qalʿāwī and Badīr to my attention.

7. Turk, pp. 5, 6, 78, 98.

8. E.g. Shihābī, p. 550; *al-Waqā'iʿ al-Miṣriyya,* 1829–1830, no. 121, p. 1 (reference to *iqlīm Isbāniya*—the "region of Spain"); Ṭahṭāwī, *Takhlīṣ,* pp. 61 (*al-bilād al-Islāmiyya* vs. *al-bilād al-Ifranjiyya*), 69; idem, *Qalā'id,* pt. 1, p. 15, and pt. 2, p. 104, and *Kanz,* pp. 5, 6 (references to various European countries as *wilāyāt*). *Wilāya* was a loose term which, by the nineteenth century, was commonly understood as the Arabic equivalent of both the Turkish *vilāyet* ("country" in general, as well as "province") and *eyālet,* a more specific term for a "province."

9. E.g. Ṭabarī, vol. 3, pp. 813, 883.
10. See e.g. Qalqashandī, vol. 6, pp. 42, 49, 61, 67, 73, 130ff.; vol. 7, pp. 263, 270, 276, 302, 387. See also Ḥasan al-Bāshā, *Alqāb, p.* 62; Fāris al-Shidyāq, *Bakūra,* p. 309, where he offers *milla* (along with *dīn* and *diyāna*) as the Arabic equivalent of "religion."
11. Shahrastānī, *Milal,* vol. 1, pp. 10–11; vol. 2, p. 61.
12. E.g. Qalqashandī, vol. 6, pp. 90, 94, 173ff.; vol. 8, pp. 36ff. See also Ibn Khaldūn, p. 233.
13. Shaw, *History,* vol. 1, pp., 58–59, 134–35, 151–53; Gibb and Bowen, pt. 2, pp. 207ff; cf. Braude, pp. 69–72.
14. Ṭarabayn, p. 379.
15. Ferīdūn, vol. 1, pp. 12–13; *Muᶜāhedāt,* vol. 1, pp. 5, 181–82, 214, 240; vol. 2, pp. 3, 56, 97, 196, 214; vol. 3, pp. 85, 221; Cevdet, vol. 6, p. 236; Shihābī, pp. 187–89 (quoting Ottoman *fermāns*); Bianchi, *Dictionnaire,* and Handjèri, *Dictionnaire,* s.v. *nation;* Lewis, *Emergence,* pp. 334–36.
16. Jabartī, *Mudda,* pp. 20–21.
17. Ṭahṭāwī, *Takhlīṣ,* pp. 141, 142 (cf. Duverger, pp. 81–82), 253, 271.
18. Ṭahṭāwī, *Qalā'id,* pt. 1, pp. 41, 94; see also his *Takhlīṣ,* pp. 141, 142 (cf. Duverger, pp. 81–82), 271; idem, *Taᶜrībāt,* p. 58.
19. E.g. Zarābī, *Qurra,* vol. 1, pp. 105–6 (cf. Desmichels, vol. 1, p. 192); Bayyāᶜ, p. 6 (cf. Voltaire, *Charles,* p. 34); Naᶜām, p. 86 (cf. Marquam, pp. 146–47); Qāsim, pp. 247, 250, 344, 345, 368, 370; Maḥmūd, vol. 1, pp. 45, 341 (cf. Robertson, *L'Histoire,* vol. 1, pp. 75–76; vol. 2, p. 375); Aḥmad Ṭahṭāwī, *Rawḍ,* p. 265 (cf. Voltaire, *Pierre,* vol. 2, p. 174).
20. For these examples see, respectively, Aḥmad Ṭahṭāwī, *Rawḍ,* p. 265 (cf. Voltaire, *Pierre,* vol. 2, p. 174); Qāsim, p. 250. For similar instances from the first half of the century see e.g. Jabartī, *Mudda,* p. 7 (Bonaparte's proclamation); idem, *Maẓhar,* p. 20; *al-Dīwān al-khuṣūṣī,* p. 3; Shihābī, pp. 441, 484 (cf. *Correspondance de Napoleon Iᵉʳ,* Paris, 1856, vol. 11, p. 444); *al-Waqā'iᶜ al-Miṣriyya,* 1829–1830, no. 121, p. 2; Ṭahṭāwī, *Takhlīṣ,* pp. 72, 155, 253, 271; Zarābī, *Qurra,* vol. 1, pp. 16, 66 (cf. Desmichels, vol. 1, pp. 26, 119); Bayyāᶜ, p. 54 (cf. Voltaire, *Charles,* p.75); Qāsim, pp. 24, 248, 358, 371.
For examples from a later part of the century see *Wādī al-nīl,* 23 Apr 1869, p. 16; 30 Apr 1869, pp. 45, 46; 16 June 1869, pp. 359–60; *al-Jarīda al-ᶜaskariyya al-Miṣriyya,* 1865, pt. 2, p. 7; Abū al-Suᶜūd, *Dars,* pp. 2, 13; *Thamarāt al-funūn,* 20 July 1875, p. 1; *al-Ṣadā,* 5 June 1876, p. 1; Mubārak, vol. 3, p. 1052; Fikrī, p. 173.
21. Horovitz, pp. 190–91; cf. Jeffrey, p. 69.
22. R. Paret, "Umma," *EI¹.* Cf. also Massignon, *L'UMMA,* p. 151; Van Nieuwenhuijze, pp. 11ff; Wendell, pp. 24–77.
23. E.g. Qalqashandī, vol. 6, pp. 38, 45, 48, 50, 52, 53, 62, 65, 130ff.
24. E.g. Qalqashandī, vol. 4, p. 468; vol. 7, p. 67; Ibn Khaldūn, p. 253.
25. E.g. Qalqashandī, vol. 6, pp. 95, 174, 176, 177; vol. 8, pp. 36ff.; Shihābī, p. 187 (quoting an Ottoman *fermān*).
26. S.v. in *Lisān al-ᶜArab.*
27. E.g. Masᶜūdī, *Murūj,* vol. 2, pp. 144, 145, 148, 152; idem, *Tanbih,* pp. 22, 50, 60, 67f., 120, 125, 156; Ṣāᶜid al-Andalusī, *passim;* Qalqashandī, vol. 1, p. 371; vol. 5, pp. 379, 404, 414, 420, 421; Ibn Khaldūn, pp. 72, 73, 76, 77, 83, 404. See also Ibn al-ᶜIbrī, p. 64f.

28. E.g. al-Tawḥīdī, pt. 1, pp. 70ff.

29. Jabartī, *Mudda*, pp. 8, 10; see also the extensive discussion of this question in Wendell, pp. 84ff.

30. Shihābī, pp. 187ff.

31. E.g. Ṭahṭāwī, *Takhlīṣ*, pp. 69, 155; idem, *Qalā'id*, pt. 1, pp. 29, 42, 83, 100; pt. 2, p. 8 (cf. Depping, p. 14); idem, *Kanz*, p. 33; idem, *Taʿrībāt*, p. 52; Zarābī, *Qurra*, vol. 1, p. 16 (cf. Desmichels, vol. 1, p. 25); Qāsim, pp. 3–5, 270.

32. S.v. in *Lisān al-ʿArab*, and in Lane.

33. ʿInān, *Duwal al-ṭawā'if*, passim.

34. Raymond, vol. 2, pp. 505–7, and s.v. in the index.

35. Nawwār, p. 325, and passim.

36. E.g. Qalqashandī, vol. 8, pp. 42ff.; vol. 11, pp. 396, 403.

37. E.g. ibid, vol. 5, pp. 404, 405, 416, 417.

38. E.g. Ferīdūn, vol. 1, pp. 12–13; *Muʿāhedāt*, vol. 1, pp. 5, 53, 84, 149, 155, 181, 213, 240; vol. 2, pp. 56, 97; vol. 3, pp. 85, 210, 221; Cevdet, vol. 5, p. 273; Shihābī, p. 187 (quoting Ottoman *fermāns*).

39. For these examples see: Ṭahṭāwī, *Takhlīṣ*, pp. 146, 252; idem, *Qalā'id*, pt. 1, p. 79; pt. 2, pp. 99, 100 (cf. Depping, pp. 222, 224); idem, *Taʿrībāt*, p. 264; Abū al-Suʿūd, *Naẓm*, pp. 182, 186, 197; Zarābī, *Qurra*, vol. 1, p. 16 (cf. Desmichels, vol. 1, p., 26); Bayyāʿ, p. 17 (cf. Voltaire, *Charles*, p. 43); Qāsim, pp. 138, 141, 152.

40. Qalʿāwī, fol. 52b; *al-Waqā'iʿ al-Miṣriyya*, 1829, no. 30, p. 3, and see similarly no. 37, p. 4.

41. E.g. *al-Dīwān al-khuṣūṣī*, pp. 3–4; Jabartī, *Mudda*, pp. 36, 60, 85, 86, 87; idem, *Maẓhar*, p. 20; Sharqāwī, pp. 3, 75, 81; Qalʿāwī, fol. 52b; Turk, p. 108; Shihābī, pp. 187–88, 190, 217; *al-Waqā'iʿ al-Miṣriyya*, 1829–1830, no. 116, pp. 2–3; no. 120, p. 1; no. 121, p. 1; no. 125, p. 2; Ṭahṭāwī, *Takhlīṣ*, pp. 72, 252; idem, *Qalā'id*, pt. 1, p. 68; pt. 2, p. 3; idem, *Taʿrībāt*, pp. 37, 52, 58, 85, 91, 263; Zarābī, *Qurra*, vol. 1, pp. 16, 86 (cf. Desmichels, vol. 1, pp. 26, 154); Qāsim, pp. 7, 138, 141, 146, 243, 244, 253. For later instances see: *Ḥadīqat al-akhbār*, 4 Sep 1858, p. 1; Ṭarābulusī, p. 462; Qalfāẓ, *Ta'rīkh Buṭrus*, p. 32; *al-Ustādh*, 23 Aug 1892, p. 27.

42. E.g. Jabartī, *ʿAjā'ib*, vol. 3, p. 187; *al-Waqā'iʿ al-Miṣriyya*, 1829–1830, no. 121, p. 1; Naʿām, p. 84 (cf. Marquam, p. 143).

43. E.g. Jabartī, *Mudda*, pp. 36, 60, 85, 86, 87; Ṭahṭāwī, *Takhlīṣ*, p. 252; Abū al-Suʿūd, *Naẓm*, pp. 182, 186, 197; Bustrus, p. 58; Qalfāẓ, *Ta'rīkh Buṭrus*, p. 32; Qāsim, p. 244.

44. E.g. Qāsim, pp. 138, 150, 152.

45. Qur'ān, XLIX:13, *wa-jaʿalnakum shuʿūban wa-qabā'ila*—"We have made you peoples [nations] and tribes". For the use of *shaʿb* see chapter 3.

46. *Lisān al-ʿArab*, s.v. q-b-l; Qalqashandī, vol. 1, pp. 308ff.; J. Chelhod, "Ḳabīla," *EI* ².

47. E.g. *al-Waqā'iʿ al-Miṣriyya*, 1829–1830, no. 121, p. 1; Ṭahṭāwī, *Qalā'id*, pt. 1, p. 27; pt. 2, pp. 100, 104 (cf. Depping, pp. 224, 232); idem, *Kanz*, p. 57; Zarābī, *Bidāya*, p. 120; Naʿām, pp. 85–86 (cf. Marquam, pp. 145–46); Bustrus, p. 58; Ṣāliḥ, p. 117.

48. *Birjīs Bārīs*, 13 Oct 1859, p. 3; 26 Oct 1859, p. 4; 9 Nov 1859, p. 4; 23 Nov 1859, p. 4; 7 Dec 1859, pp. 2, 4; 18 Jan 1860, p. 4; July 1860 (bilingual edition), p. 4; Ṣāliḥ, p. 117; Tawfīq, *Riḥla*, pt. 3, p. 2; pt. 7, p. 6.

49. See further in A. Ayalon, "Arab discovery."

50. Ṭahṭāwī, *Takhlīṣ*, p. 148 (cf. Duverger, p. 85); idem, *Qalā'id*, pt. 1, p. 14; pt. 2, p. 102 (cf. Depping, p. 228); idem, *Kanz*, p. 117; idem, *Taʿrībāt*, pp. 102, 105, 264, 275, 277, 293, and appendix, p. 85; Abū al-Suʿūd, *Naẓm*, pp. 181–82; Naʿām, pp. 84–87 (cf. Marquam, pp. 143–47); Qāsim, pp. 307, 358, 373, 375; see also *al-Bashīr*, 22 Oct 1870, p. 61.

51. Ṭahṭāwī, *Takhlīṣ*, pp. 69, 141, 142, 146, 155, 203, 252, 253, 271.

52. Ṭahṭāwī, *Taʿrībāt*, p. 85; Zarābī, *Qurra*, vol. 1, p. 16 (cf. Desmichels, vol. 1, pp. 25–6).

53. *Al-Jinān*, 1871, pp. 452, 490, 493; 1874, p. 626; 1885, pp. 8, 27; *al-Jawā'ib*, 6 Feb 1878, p. 4; *al-Janna*, 1 Mar 1881, p. 1; *Dā'irat al-maʿārif*, vol. 9, p. 146; *al-Muqaṭṭam*, 5 Mar 1889, p. 3; 19 Oct 1893, p. 3; 9 Jan 1894, p. 3; 30 Nov 1895, p. 3; 10 Feb 1896, p. 3; 3 June 1897, p. 3; 12 Apr 1898, p. 3; 17 Mar 1900, p. 1; Fikrī, p. 256; *al-Hilāl*, Feb 1894, p. 349, and May 1898, p. 661; *al-Ra'y al-ʿāmm*, 7 Nov 1894, p. 308; 19 June 1897, p. 163; *al-Rajā'*, 19 Apr 1895, p. 1; 10 May 1895, p. 1; 17 May 1895, p. 1; 21 June 1895, p. 1. Another meaning of *umma*—"the people," as distinct from "the government," is discussed in chapter 3.

54. Marṣafī, pp. 4–5. Interestingly, as examples for an *umma* defined by territory he cites *al-umma al-Miṣriyya* and *al-umma al-Ḥijāziyya*. See also Delanoue; Wendell, pp. 135–40.

55. 25 Sep 1884, pp. 188ff., and passim.

56. *Al-ʿUrwa al-wuthqā*, 1884: 3 Apr, pp. 102, 105; 10 Apr, pp. 126, 127; 24 Apr, pp. 132, 133; 22 May, p. 220; 28 Aug, p. 151; 25 Sep, pp. 186, 197, 198. See also Haim, "Islam and the theory"; Wendell, pp. 167ff. For more examples of the use of *umma* with this modern meaning see *Ḥadīqat al-akhbār*, 16 Oct 1858, p. 1; 9 Apr 1859, pp. 2–3; 9 Jan 1862, p. 1; Marrāsh, *Riḥla*, p. 34; *al-Bashīr*, 11 Nov 1871, p. 573; *al-Jinān*, 1871, pp. 452, 490, 493; 1872, pp. 112, 113; 1874, p. 626; 1885, p. 27; Ṣāliḥ, p. 53; *al-Jawā'ib*, 6 Feb 1878, p. 4; Isḥaq, *Durar*, p. 100; *Al-Waṭanī al-Miṣrī*, 29 Sep 1883, p. 6; *al-Laṭā'if*, vol. 2 (1887–1888), p. 197; vol. 7 (1892–1893), p. 442; *al-Fayyūm*, 9 Feb 1895, p. 100; *al-Rajā'*, 29 Mar 1895, p. 2; *al-Mushīr*, 25 Apr 1896, p. 674; *al-Ahrām*, 9 July 1896, p. 2; *al-Ra'y al-ʿāmm*, 19 Apr 1897, p. 168; *al-Muqaṭṭam*, 12 Mar 1898, p. 1; *al-Mawsūʿāt*, 23 Aug 1899, p. 241.

Chapter 2

1. For a discussion of empires and emperors, the concept and the terms, see Koebner, *Empire*.

2. For a more detailed account on the semantic development of the term, see J. H. Kramers, "Sulṭān," *EI¹*; Ḥasan al-Bāshā, *Alqāb*, pp. 89, 323ff.; Arnold, pp. 202–3. Cf. also Qalqashandī, vol. 5, pp. 447–48, and s.v. in the term index. Unlike the Ottomans, Moroccan rulers often attributed this title to heads of Christian European states, in treaties and correspondence; for some representative examples see De Castries, ser. 1, pt. 3, vol. 1, pp. 100–1 (*Īzabīlā bint al-sulṭān Anrik* of England, 1569); ser. 1, pt. 3, vol. 2, pp. 18, 157, 210, 479–80; ser. 1, pt. 3, vol. 3, pp. 285, 426, 436; ser. 1, pt. 5, vol. 1, pp. 50, 282; ser. 1, pt. 5, vol. 2, pp. 399–400.

3. In the Bible at one time the idea of king (Hebrew *melekh*) and kingship was unmistakably a negative one; cf. the angry response of the Prophet Samuel to the People of Israel's demand for a king.

4. For a more detailed account see Madelung, pp. 84ff.; Mottahedeh, "Some attitudes"; Ḥasan al-Bāshā, *Alqāb*, pp. 73–74; idem, *Funūn*, pt. 3, pp. 1139–42. The Persian equivalent of the term, *shāh*, and its derivatives *pādishāh* and *shāhānshāh*, continued however to be used by the Ottomans and by other Muslim sovereigns.

5. E.g. Qalqashandī, s.v. *mulūk al-kufr* in the term index.

6. E.g. Ṣabbāgh, p. 1; Turk, pp. 5, 47, 173, 217; Shihābī, pp. 321, 505, 508, 599; Ṭahṭāwī, *Takhlīṣ*, p. 116; idem, *Qalā'id*, pt. 1, pp. 28, 36, 42; idem, *Kanz*, pp. 25–27, 30, 31, 53, 76.

7. For these examples see respectively: Jabartī, *Mudda*, p. 46; Turk, p. 24; Shihābī, p. 187. For similar examples see: Jabartī, *Mudda*, p. 11; Turk, pp. 1, 2; Shihābī, pp. 187, 213, 214, 219, 236, 430, 439, 440, 460, 505, 506, 508, 601, 610, 640; Ṭahṭāwī, *Takhlīṣ*, pp. 259, 260.

8. Shihābī, p. 219. See also Turk, p. 5.

9. Shihābī, pp. 219, 320.

10. Mardīnī, p. 392.

11. Turk, p. 95.

12. E.g. Shihābī, p. 458; Ṭahṭāwī, *Takhlīṣ*, pp. 106, 198, 253, 255.

13. Bayyāᶜ, pp. 15–40. In the latter part of the book the language becomes much more consistent.

14. E.g. Ṣabbāgh, p. 1; Turk, pp. 2, 4, 47, 217; Shihābī, pp. 193, 214, 219, 430, 437, 440, 441, 447, 448, 450, 451, 460, 464, 466, 480, 489, 504, 505, 506, 610, 640; *al-Waqā'iᶜ al-Miṣriyya*, 1829–1830, no. 91, p. 1; no. 110, p. 3; no. 113, pp. 2, 3; no. 114, p. 2; no. 116, pp. 2, 3; no. 120, p. 1; no. 121, p. 1; no 126, p. 4; no. 136, p. 2; no. 157, p. 2; no. 215, p. 1; no. 236, p. 3; no. 271, p. 2; Ṭahṭāwī, *Takhlīṣ*, pp. 138, 142, 203, 262; idem, *Qalā'id*, pt. 1, pp. 29, 30, 32; idem, *Kanz*, p. 26.

15. Indeed, in classical dictionaries, such as *Lisān al-ᶜArab* and the *Qāmūs*, the term appears under the root q-ṣ-r. Cf. also Khwārizmī, pp. 113–14; Jawāliqī, p. 271; ᶜAsqalānī, p. 49a; Dahsha, p. 100a; Golius, Meninski and Richardson (1771), s.v. For examples of its use in classical texts see: Levi Della Vida, pp. 268ff. (discussing a ninth-century Arabic translation of Paulus Orosius's chronicle of Roman history); Ibn Khuradadhbih, p. 43; Masᶜūdi, *Tanbīh*, pp. 106ff.; idem, *Murūj*, vol. 2, pp. 33ff.; Ibn al-ᶜIbrī, pp. 65–92; ᶜUmarī, *Taᶜrīf*, pp. 52, 60, 62; Qalqashandī, vol. 5, pp. 384ff.; vol. 8, pp. 35, 44; Ibn Khaldūn, pp. 232–33, 480.

16. E.g. Ibn Saᶜīd, p. 182; Amari, pp. 322–26, 339, 418–22, 509–22, and appendix, p. 61 (where it appears as *al-bādūr* and *al-inbāradūr*); ᶜUmarī, *Kalām*, pp. 89, 96; Ibn Khaldūn, p. 234 (*inbaradhūr*). For further references see Gottschalk, "*Al-anbaratūr*."

17. Meninski, s.v.

18. For the use of *qayṣar* and *imbarāṭūr* during the first third of the century see e.g. Jabartī, *Maẓhar*, p. 285; Turk, pp. 4, 5, 47, 217; Shihābī, pp. 219, 320, 430, 432, 440, 448, 450, 451, 452, 460, 471, 475, 476, 477, 480, 489, 505; *al-Waqā'iᶜ al-Miṣriyya*, 1829–1830, no. 130, p. 2; no. 157, p. 1; no. 164, p. 4; Ṭahṭāwī, *Qalā'id*, pt. 1, pp. 2, 28, 29, 32, 73; idem, *Kanz*, pp. 30, 31.

19. *Pādishāh* was originally a Parthian title denoting a subordinate king, and

later came to mean a supreme sovereign. See further Bianchi and Kieffer, *Dictionnaire*, and Barbier de Meynard, *Dictionnaire*, s.v.; *al-Hilāl*, Nov 1893, p. 165.
20. See Ḥasan al-Bāshā, *Alqāb*, pp. 271–73, 274.
21. For instances in which French kings were called *pādishāh* see *Mucāhedāt*, vol. 1, pp. 4–14, 34–35; Ferīdūn, vol. 2, pp. 248, 490ff. In the late eighteenth century Ottoman rulers began to confer this title upon heads of other states; see e.g. Cevdet, vol. 1, p. 285; vol. 8, p. 281 (references to Russia); vol. 1, pp. 269–75, 277–81 (references to England). This change was a clear symptom of the decline in the empire's international standing.
22. E.g. Ferīdūn, vol. 2, p. 398; *Mucāhedāt*, vol. 3, pp. 209–52 (pp. 249ff.—treaty of Belgrade, which provided for the change); Cevdet, vol. 5, p. 273.
23. E.g. Ferīdūn, vol. 1, p. 12; vol. 2, pp. 97, 412–15, 419–22, 425–28; *Muacāhedāt*, vol. 3, pp. 88, 102–12, 156–63, 172ff.
24. E.g. Cevdet, vol. 8, p. 45f.; *Mucāhedāt*, vol. 1, pp. 41–51; vol. 4, p. 242.
25. See Ferīdūn, vol. 2, and *Mucāhedāt*, vols. 2 and 3, passim.
26. Ṭahṭāwī, *Qalā'id*, pt. 1, pp. 10–11.
27. See examples in notes 6, 7, 12, 14, and 18 above.
28. For some of the last occurrences in which *malik* was still applied to the Russian czar and Roman emperors, during the 1840s and 1850s, see: Bayyāc, pp. 15, 22, 23, 24, 35, 36; Ṭahṭāwī, *Tacrībāt*, p. 81; Aḥmad Ṭahṭāwī, *Rawḍ*, pp. 5, 37, 48, 49 (cf. Voltaire, *Pierre*, vol. 1, pp. 4, 61, 81, 82); *Acmāl al-jamciyya al-Sūriyya*, p. 61; Bustrus, p. 84.
29. Ṭahṭāwī, *Qalā'id*, pt. 2, p. 104 (cf. Depping, p. 233).
30. Ṭahṭāwī, *Tacrībāt*, appendix, p. 92. See also pt. 1, pp. 77, 81, 272, and appendix, p. 64; *al-Waqā'ic al-Miṣriyya*, 1842, no. 623, quoted by Ḥamza, vol. 1, p. 118.
31. E.g. Bayyāc, pp. 23, 35; Maḥmūd, vol. 1, p. 46 (cf. Robertson, vol. 1, p. 78); Aḥmad Ṭahṭāwī, *Rawḍ*, p. 5 (cf. Voltaire, *Pierre*, vol. 1, p. 4); Bustrus, p. 98; *cUṭārid*, 9 Oct 1858, p. 1; 16 Oct 1858, p. 3; 13 Nov 1858, pp. 2, 3; 7 July 1859, p. 4; *Ḥadīqat al-akhbār*, 26 June 1858, p. 3; 3 July 1858, p. 4; 11 Sep 1858, p. 1; 13 Sep 1858, p. 1; 16 Oct 1858, p. 1; *al-Jawā'ib*, 20 Nov 1870, p. 1, 27 Nov 1870, p. 3, and 6 Dec 1870, p. 3 (text of the 1856 Treaty of Paris—references to "*sulṭān* of all the Russians" and "*sulṭān* of the French"); Abū al-Sucūd, *Dars*, p. 15 (the Roman empire—*al-salṭana al-Rūmāniyya*); Ḥunayn Khūrī, *Tuḥfa*, pp. 62, 64, 79, 80, 81, 222; *al-Naḥla*, 15 June 1877, pp. 8, 10, and 1 July 1877, p. 34; *al-Muqaṭṭam*, 6 Apr 1889, p. 1 (references to the "*malika* of the English and *sulṭāna* of India"); Kancān, p. 118.
32. Ṭahṭāwī, *Takhlīṣ*, p. 253, and *Qalā'id*, pt. 1, p. 72.
33. See Ḥasan al-Bāshā, *Alqāb*, p. 336; Ferīdūn, vol. 2, pp. 76, 78, 96, 396, 419, 504; Jabartī, *Mudda*, p. 85; Sharqāwī, p. 81.
34. S.v. in *Lisān al-cArab*, the *Qāmūs*, Bustānī's *Muḥīṭ* and Lane. Cf. *rex magnus* in Golius.
35. E.g. *Birjīs Bārīs*, 24 June 1859, p. 2; 7 July 1859, pp. 1, 3; 21 July 1859, pp. 1, 2, 4; 1 Sep 1859, pp. 1, 2; 9 Nov 1859, pp. 2, 4; 7 Dec 1859, p. 4; 4 Jan 1860, p. 4; 8 May 1862, p. 1; 11 Mar 1863, p. 1; 6 Jan 1864, p. 1; 16 Mar 1864, p. 2; 13 Apr 1864, p. 1; Ḥarā'irī, pp. 3, 4. The term continued to appear occasionally in later years as well; e.g. cAbd al-Sayyid, *Silwān*, p. 109; *al-Ṣadā*, 5 Mar 1876, p. 2; *Al-Naḥla*, 15 Aug 1877, p. 71; 1 Sep 1877, p. 96; 1 Oct 1877, p. 115; 1 Mar 1878, p. 278.

36. For the use of *qayṣar* and *imbarāṭūr* prior to the birth of the Arabic press, see e.g. Zarābī, *Bidāya*, p. 181; idem, *Qurra*, vol. 1, pp. 3, 4, 9, 39, 40; Bayyāᶜ, pp. 18, 27, 30, 37, 39, 42, 71, 82, 96, 98, 106; Abū al-Suᶜūd, *Naẓm*, pp. 42, 44, 161–62, 166–67, 176, 199, 200, 202, 204; Maḥmūd, vol. 1, pp. 21, 46, 133, 162, 163 (cf. Robertson, vol. 1, pp. 12, 78, 289, 359, 360, 361); Qāsim, pp. 137, 138, 140, 142; Aḥmad Ṭahṭāwī, *Rawḍ*, pp. 37, 39, 40, 48 (cf. Voltaire, *Pierre*, vol. 1, pp. 61, 64, 66, 81); Bustrus, pp. 65, 69, 71, 73, 84, 94, 114, 118, 121, 122, 123. 37. E.g. Ṭahṭāwī, *Takhlīṣ*, p. 261; idem, *Kanz*, pp. 53, 54; idem, *Taᶜrībāt*, pt. 1, pp. 122, 123; pt. 2, p. 64; Zarābī, *Qurra*, vol. 1, p. 81 (cf. Desmichels, vol. 1, p. 145); Abū al-Suᶜūd, *Naẓm*, p. 202; Bayyāᶜ, pp. 15, 16, 69; Maḥmūd, vol. 1, pp. 121, 162, 171–72 (cf. Robertson, vol. 1, pp. 259, 359, 381); Qāsim, pp. 217, 218, 222, 230, 231; Aḥmad Ṭahṭāwī, *Rawḍ*, pp. 249, 314 (cf. Voltaire, *Pierre*, vol. 2, pp. 145, 260).

38. For these examples see, respectively, *al-Qāhira*, 29 July 1886, p. 3; *al-Muqaṭṭam*, 9 Mar 1894, p. 1. In addition to these two newspapers, such differentiation normally appeared in *Kawkab al-mashriq*, *al-Qāhira al-ḥurra*, *al-Hilāl*, *al-Manār*, *al-Jāmiᶜa al-ᶜUthmāniyya* and Ṣannūᶜ's *al-Badā'iᶜ*.

39. E.g. Abū al-Suᶜūd, *Naẓm*, p. 42; Maḥmūd, vol. 1, pp. 21, 162, 163 (cf. Robertson, vol. 1, pp. 12, 359, 361); *al-Arghūl*, rabīᶜ al-thānī 1315 (1897), p. 167; *al-Mawsūᶜāt*, 26 Feb 1899, p. 251.

40. In one instance even a verb was devised from the noun *qayṣar:* the French marshal MacMahon was reported to have "called upon the people *an yumallikuhu wa-yuqayṣiruhu*"; see *al-Jawā'ib*, 5 Dec 1877, p. 1.

41. Bayyāᶜ, p. 7.

42. Abū al-Suᶜūd, *Naẓm*, pp. 71–72.

43. E.g. *Ḥadīqat al-akhbār*, 22 May 1858, p. 1; 5 June 1858, p. 3; 3 July 1858, p. 4; 17 July 1858, p. 1; 24 July 1858, p. 3; 31 July 1858, pp. 1, 3; 14 Aug 1858, p. 1; 25 Jan 1866, p. 1; *al-Nashra al-usbūᶜiyya*, 13 June 1871, p. 6; 21 May 1872, p. 167; 16 Mar 1888, p. 88; *Thamarāt al-funūn*, 25 May 1875, p. 1; *al-Ahrām*, 5 Aug 1876, p. 1; *al-Ṣadā*, 5 Mar 1876, p. 2; 20 June 1876, p. 1; 15 Nov 1876, p. 1; 5 May 1877, p. 2; *al-Baṣṣīr*, 21 May 1881, p. 1; *Kawkab al-mashriq*, 17 May 1883, p. 1.

44. *al-Arghūl*, rabīᶜ al-thānī 1315 (1897), p. 165.

Chapter 3

1. Jean Jacques Rousseau, *Du Contrat Social*, ed. Ronald Grimsley (Oxford, 1972), esp. pp. 188ff.

2. Cf. *Grande Encyclopédie* (Paris, 1887–1902), vol. 13, pp. 1073–1075; Duguit, pp. 1–3, 62–65, 73–74, and s.v. *citoyen* in the index.

3. Ra'īf Khūrī, p. 39.

4. Lane, s.v.; Mottahedeh, *Loyalty*, pp. 120–21; Gibb and Bowen, pt. 1, p. 273f., and s.v. in index. In Ottoman usage the term (Turkish *raᶜiyyet*, pl. *reᶜāyā*) was applied more specifically to the peasants in the empire, who formed the great bulk of the population. A related Ottoman term was *tebāᶜa*, from the Arabic *tabīᶜa*, subjugation. This was an old Turkish (as well as Persian) word for a subject, which was also used in international treaties and correspondence to desig-

nate subjects and citizens of foreign states; see e.g. *Muᶜāhedāt*, passim. The word
was included with that sense in the 1876 Ottoman constitution.

5. For these examples see *al-Dīwān al-khuṣūṣī*, p. 3; *al-Hilāl*, May 1898, p.
660. For more examples see below.

6. For these examples see, respectively, Ṭahṭāwī, *Kanz*, p. 28; *Muntakhabāt
al-jawā'ib*, vol. 5, p. 85; *al-Jinān*, 1872, p. 183. For similar instances see:
al-Waqā'iᶜ al-Miṣriyya, 1830, no. 243, p. 2; Zarābī, *Qurra*, vol. 1, pp. 12, 103 (cf.
Desmichels, vol. 1, pp. 18, 186); Bayyāᶜ, passim; Aḥmad Ṭahṭāwī, *Rawḍ*, p. 328
(cf. Voltaire, *Pierre*, vol. 2, p. 295); *al-Jawā'ib*, 18 Feb 1868, pp. 1, 2; 8 Jan 1871,
p. 2; 10 Jan 1877, p. 1; 24 Jan 1877, p. 1; 11 July 1877 p. 4; 16 Mar 1881, p. 4;
al-Naḥla, 11 May 1870, p. 11; *al-Jinān*, 1872, p. 185; *Thamarāt al-funūn*, 11 May
1875, p. 1; Ṭarābulusī, p. 473; Khūrī-Shiḥāda, *Āthār* (history), introduction, p. k;
al-Iᶜlām, 19 Jan 1885; Qalfāẓ, *Ta'rīkh Buṭrus*, p. 49; *al-Hilāl*, Nov 1892, p. 74;
Dec 1892, p. 107.

7. For these examples see, respectively, ᶜUṭārid, 2 July 1859, p. 2, and *Birjīs
Bārīs*, 4 Jan 1860, p. 4. For similar instances see *al-Waqā'iᶜ al-Miṣriyya*, 1829–
1830, no. 139, p. 1; no. 240, p. 1; Ṭahṭāwī, *Takhlīṣ*, pp. 138ff.; idem, *Qalā'id*, pt.
1, p. 94; pt. 2, p. 104; ᶜUṭārid, 2 July 1859, p. 2; *Birjīs Bārīs*, 7 July 1859, pp. 1, 2;
26 Oct 1859, p. 2; 7 Dec 1859, p. 1; 4 Jan 1860, p. 4; 2 Jan 1862, p. 1; 13 Feb
1862, p. 1; 15 Feb 1865, p. 1; 8 Nov 1865, p. 1; *Ḥadīqat al-akhbār*, 18 Jan 1866, p.
1; *al-Nashra al-usbūᶜiyya*, 13 Aug 1872, p. 261; Jubaylī, pt. 1, p. 7; *al-Jawā'ib*, 4
Apr 1878, p. 7; *Muntakhabāt al-jawā'ib*, vol. 2, p. 236; *al-Jinān*, 1872, p. 329;
1874, p. 587; Fāris al-Shidyāq, *Kashf*, p. 352; *al-Laṭā'if*, 15 Mar 1890, p. 511;
Thamarāt al-funūn, 1 Feb 1892, p. 3; *al-Hilāl*, Jan 1894, p. 318; Oct 1897, p. 146;
Feb 1899, pp. 270, 279; *al-Ra'y al-ᶜāmm*, 19 June 1897; *al-Mawsūᶜāt*, 9 July 1899,
p. 160; Kanᶜān, p. 33.

8. With regard to the United States, see e.g. Ṭahṭāwī, *Kanz*, p. 116; *Birjīs
Bārīs*, 18 Jan 1860, p. 3; *al-Jawā'ib*, 26 Dec 1882, p. 4; *al-Qāhira al-ḥurra*, 17 Apr
1887, p. 3; *Thamarāt al-funūn*, 2 Apr 1894, p. 4; *al-Muqaṭṭam*, 13 Mar 1896, p. 1;
al-Hilāl, May 1898, p. 659; *al-Mawsūᶜāt*, 21 Sep 1899, p. 328; *al-Ra'īs*, Oct 1900,
p. 422. With regard to France, see *Birjīs Bārīs*, 4 Jan 1860, p. 4; *al-Jawā'ib*, 8 Aug
1877, p. 3; *Ḍiyā' al-khāfiqayn*, Feb 1892, p. 4; *al-Mawsūᶜāt*, 21 Sep 1899, p. 328.

9. E.g. Ṭahṭāwī, *Takhlīṣ*, pp. 144, 153, 253, 254, 263; idem, *Qalā'id*, pt. 1,
p. 94; Maḥmūd, vol. 1, p. 46 (cf. Robertson, vol. 1, p. 77); ᶜUṭārid, 2 July 1859,
p. 2; *Birjīs Bārīs*, 4 Jan 1860, p. 4; 8 Nov 1865, p. 1. Terms for "deputies" and
"representatives" are discussed in chapter 5.

10. Qur'ān, IV:59.

11. Rāfiᶜī, ᶜAṣr Ismāᶜīl, vol. 2, pp. 85–88.

12. *Al-Jawā'ib*, 24 Jan 1877, p. 1. For similar examples see *al-Waqā'iᶜ al-
Miṣriyya*, 1829–1830, no. 27, p. 1; no. 36, p. 1; *Nafīr Sūriya*, 8 Oct 1860 and 22
Feb 1861; *al-Jawā'ib*, 10 Jan 1877, p. 1; 17 Jan 1877, p. 2; 1 July 1877, p. 1; 27
Sep 1877, p. 3; Rāfiᶜī, ᶜAṣr Ismāᶜīl, vol. 2, p. 214; *Ḍiyā' al-khāfiqayn*, 2 Apr 1892,
p. 43; *al-Fayyūm*, 9 Feb 1895, p. 103; *al-Ahrām*, 10 July 1896, p. 2.

13. See *Birjīs Bārīs*, 7 July 1859, p. 2; 4 Jan 1860, p. 4; 2 Jan 1862, p. 1; 15
Feb 1865, p. 1; *al-Bashīr*, 4 Feb 1871, p. 179; *al-Jawā'ib*, 15 Nov 1876, p. 4; 11
July 1877, p. 4; *Dā'irat al-maᶜārif*, vol. 4, p. 560; Kanᶜān, p. 33.

14. Ṭahṭāwī, *Manāhij*, pp. 360–61.

15. See e.g. *al-Jawā'ib*, 10 Jan 1877, p. 1.

16. Rāfiᶜī, ᶜAṣr Ismāᶜīl, vol. 2, pp. 160–61.

17. E.g. *al-Jawā'ib,* 18 Feb 1868, p. 2; 20 Dec 1870, p. 2; 9 June 1875, p. 3; 15 Nov 1876, p. 4; 1 July 1877, p. 3; 8 Aug 1877, p. 3; 26 Dec 1882, p. 4; *Muntakhabāt al-jawā'ib,* vol. 6, p. 28; *al-Jinān,* 1874, p. 585; *al-Janna,* 29 July 1881, p. 2; *al-Qāhira al-ḥurra,* 17 Apr 1877, p. 3; 29 Sep 1888, p. 1; 14 Oct 1888, p. 1; 15 Oct 1888, p. 3; *Thamarāt al-funūn,* 13 Apr 1891, p. 4; 11 Mar 1895, p. 4; *Ḍiyā' al-khāfiqayn,* Feb 1892, p. 4; *al-Muqaṭṭam,* 13 Mar 1896, p. 1; *al-Hilāl,* Mar 1896, p. 523; June 1897, p. 758; *al-Manār,* vol. 1 (1897–1898), p. 605; *al-Mawsūʿāt,* 21 Sep 1899, p. 328; *al-Mu'ayyad,* 7 Feb 1900, p. 5.

18. *Ḥadīqat al-akhbār,* 12 Mar 1863, p. 1; 23 Nov 1865, p. 1; Khayr al-Dīn, pp. 75, 85; *al-Jawā'ib,* 25 Feb 1868, p. 4; Lāz, p. 45 (cf. Crevier, p. 36); *Muntakhabāt al-jawā'ib,* vol. 5, p. 168 (cf. Duguit, p. 284), 338; *al-Janna,* 2 Sep 1881, p. 1; *al-Muqaṭṭam,* 10 Jan 1894, p. 1; *al-Hilāl,* Jan 1896, p. 394; Fikrī, p. 498. See also references in Zolondek, "Ash-Shaʿb."

19. See Lane, s.v.; also Mottahedeh, "Shuʿūbiyah," esp. pp. 161–68.

20. Turk, pp. 2, 3, 4, 5, 98; cf. Shihābī, pp. 51, 214, 215, 218, 219, 320.

21. Turk, pp. 2–5, 11–12, 195–96; Shihābī, pp. 214–15, 218–19, 320, 430, 602

22. E.g. *Ḥadīqat al-akhbār,* 22 May 1858, p. 2; 19 May 1858, p. 1; 19 June, p. 1; 15 Jan 1863, p. 2; ʿUṭārid, 9 Oct 1858, p. 1; 30 Oct 1858, p. 2; *al-Jinān,* 1870, p. 103; 1871, pp. 417, 419, 420, 453; 1874, p. 118; *al-Jawā'ib,* 17 Sep 1870, p. 23; 10 Oct 1870, p. 56; 11 Mar 1871, pp. 227, 232; 5 Mar 1876, p. 1; 5 June 1876, p. 1; *Dā'irat al-maʿārif,* vol. 1, p. 272; vol. 2, pp. 509–11; vol. 6, p. 534; vol. 8, p. 232; Ṣāliḥ, pp. 79, 93, 98; *al-Waṭanī al-Miṣrī,* 29 Sep 1883, p. 6; Isḥaq, *Durar,* p. 49; Khilāṭ, pp. 78, 99; *Thamarāt al-funūn,* 12 June 1893, p. 3; *al-Muqtaṭaf,* 1 Dec 1896, p. 888; *al-Arghūl,* rabīʿ al-thānī 1315 (1897), p. 165; *al-Hilāl,* Aug 1897, p. 901; *al-Muqaṭṭam,* 5 Jan 1897, p. 1; 1 Apr 1898, p. 1; 5 Feb 1897, p. 1; *al-Mushīr,* 17 July 1897, p. 1183. For more examples see Zolondek, "Ash-Shaʿb" and "Language."

23. E.g. *Ḥadīqat al-akhbār,* 29 May 1858, p. 1; *al-Jawā'ib,* 3 May 1870, p. 4; *al-Bashīr,* 10 Oct 1870, p. 56; 11 Mar 1871, p. 227; *al-Jinān,* 1870, p. 103 (cf. *New York Times,* 7 Dec 1869, p. 1); 1871, pp. 417, 419; *al-Ṣadā,* 5 Mar 1876, p. 1; 30 Aug 1876, p. 1; 30 Sep 1876, p. 1; *Dā'irat al-maʿārif,* vol. 1, p. 272; *al-Muqaṭṭam,* 5 Feb 1897, p. 1.

24. *Al-Mushīr,* 2 May 1896; 1 Aug 1896. See also Zolondek, "Ash-Shaʿb".

25. Kāmil, pp. 288–91.

26. *Al-Manār,* vol. 1 (1897–1898), p. 109. For similar examples see *al-Jinān,* 1874, p. 259; 1879, p. 378; 1885, p. 26; Jubaylī, vol. 1, p. 6; Isḥaq, *Kitābāt,* pp. 146, 281; Ṭarābulusī, p. 426; *al-Janna,* 2 Sep 1881, p. 1; *al-ʿUrwa al-wuthqā,* 3 Apr 1884, p. 102; Tawfīq, *Rasā'il,* p. 47; *al-Laṭā'if,* 1892–1893, p. 423; *al-Arghūl,* rabīʿ al-thānī 1315 (1897), p. 165; *al-Muqaṭṭam,* 15 Jan 1897, p. 1; 5 Feb 1897, p. 1; 17 Mar 1900, p. 1.

27. Quoted by Zolondek, "Ash-Shaʿb," p. 9, note 2.

28. Isḥaq, *Kitābāt,* pp. 147, 281.

29. Kāmil, pp. 44, 236–37.

30. For these examples see *Muntakhabāt al-mu'ayyad,* 1890, p. 138; *al-Muqaṭṭam,* 17 Feb 1900, p. 1. See also *Ḥadīqat al-akhbār,* 26 June 1858, p. 2; 8 Jan 1859, p. 1; 3 May 1860, p. 1; *al-ʿAṣr al-Jadīd,* 1 Aug 1881, p. 2; *Dalīl Miṣr,* 1889–1890, p. 114; Sometimes the expressions *ibn al-balad* and *baladī,* respectively synonymous with *ibn al-waṭan* and *waṭanī,* were used; see e.g. Jabartī, *ʿAjā'ib,* vol. 3, p. 154; *Ḥadīqat al-akhbār,* 28 Aug 1858, p. 2.

144   *Notes*

31. *Nafīr Sūriya*, 25 Oct 1860.
32. Isḥaq, *Durar*, pp. 246–47; Riḍā, *Ta'rīkh al-ustādh*, vol. 2, p. 194. Cf.
Haim, "Islam and the theory," pp. 288–89.
33. See Don Raphael, p. 55 (cf. Machiavelli, p. 82—*gli cittadini* rendered as
abnā' al-balad); *Muntakhabāt al-jawā'ib*, vol. 2, p. 236; Isḥaq, *Kitābāt*, p. 288;
Dā'irat al-maᶜārif, vol. 5, p. 547; *Kawkab al-mashriq*, 4 Jan 1883, p. 1. Cf. also
Rāfiᶜī, *ᶜAṣr Ismāᶜīl*, vol. 2, p. 314.
34. Isḥaq, *Durar*, pp. 246–47.
35. Wakīl, pp. 60–61.

Chapter 4

1. M. A. J. Beg, "al-Khāṣṣa wal-ᶜāmma," *EI²;* Mottahedeh, *Loyalty*, pp.
115–16.
2. See ᶜAsqalānī, pp. 24b–27b; Qalqashandī, s.v. *arbāb* and *aṣḥāb* in the
term index; Ḥasan al-Bāshā, *Alqāb*, pp. 293–300, 367–76; *Dā'irat al-maᶜārif*, vol.
7, p. 132; vol. 8, pp. 404–18; vol. 9, p. 146; Raymond, vol. 2, pp. 380–81, 430,
505–6, 521, 528, 582, 701, 754, 757, 791; Nawwār, p. 382.
3. Jabartī, *ᶜAjā'ib*, vol. 3, pp. 51, 76, 78, 82, 145, 147, 153, 159, 161, 164,
190. Cf. idem, *Mudda*, s.v. *arbāb* and *aṣḥāb* in the index; *al-Waqā'iᶜ al-Miṣriyya*,
1830, no. 158, p. 1.
4. *Dā'irat al-maᶜārif*, vol. 7, p. 132.
5. E.g. *Ḥadīqat al-akhbār*, 11 Sep 1858, p. 1; 12 Feb 1859, p. 1; 23 Feb
1860, p. 1; *al-Jawā'ib*, 25 Feb 1868, p. 3; 8 Mar 1869, p. 1; 1 Dec 1875, p. 4; 24
Jan 1878, p. 1; *al-Bashīr*, 4 Feb 1871, p. 179; 15 Feb 1878, p. 3; *Thamarāt
al-funūn*, 26 Nov 1875, p. 1; 20 Apr 1891, p. 4; *al-Naḥla*, 1 Nov 1877, pp. 148–49;
1 Aug 1878, p. 49; Isḥaq, *Durar*, p. 155; *al-Jinān*, 1885, p. 578; *al-Qāhira
al-ḥurra*, 13 Sep 1888, p. 1; *Ḍiyāᶜ al-khāfiqayn*, Mar 1892, p. 21; *al-Rajā'*, 29 Mar
1895, p. 2.
6. E.g. Jabartī, *Maẓhar*, p. 193; Turk, pp., 3, 4, 71; Qāsim, p. 368; *Ḥadīqat
al-akhbār*, 23 Oct 1858, p. 1; *ᶜUṭārid*, 6 Nov 1858, p. 2; 2 July 1859, p. 4;
al-Jawā'ib, 8 Mar 1871, p. 3.
7. E.g. *Wādī al-nīl*, 4 June 1869, p. 206.
8. E.g. Ṭahṭāwī, *Takhlīṣ*, p. 153; Lāz, pp. 7, 8, 44, 45 (cf. Crevier, pp. 34,
37, 44, 61); *al-Bashīr*, 3 June 1871, p. 349 (cf. Goubard, vol. 1, p. 287.)
9. E.g. Shihābī, pp. 214, 319, 320; Don Raphael, p. 44 (cf. Machiavelli, p.
66); *al-Waqā'iᶜ al-Miṣriyya*, 1829–1830, no. 117, p. 1; no. 125, p. 2; no. 132, pp.
3, 4; no. 236, p. 4; Ṭahṭāwī, *Takhlīṣ*, p. 140; Zarābī, *Bidāya*, pp. 75, 76, 96; idem,
Qurra, vol. 1, pp. 10ff. (cf. Desmichels, vol. 1, pp. 14ff.); Bayyāᶜ, pp. 28, 47, 48,
56 (cf. Voltaire, *Charles*, pp. 34, 53, 70, 77); Abū al-Suᶜūd, *Naẓm*, p. 182;
Maḥmūd, vol. 1, pp. 47, 354–55; vol. 2, p. 42 (cf. Robertson, vol. 1, p. 80; vol. 2,
p. 407; vol. 3, p. 92); Qāsim, pp. 150, 222, 223, 226, 242, 244, 245, 247, 344;
Aḥmad Ṭahṭāwī, *Rawḍ*, pp. 42, 251, 285, 323 (cf. Voltaire, *Pierre*, vol. 1, p. 69;
vol. 2, pp. 149, 208, 270); *Ḥadīqat al-akhbār*, 24 July 1858, p. 2; 4 June 1859, p. 4;
22 Mar 1860, p. 1; Lāz, pp. 2, 5, 6 (cf. Crevier, p. 56); *al-Jawā'ib*, 12 Apr 1870, p.
7; 5 Mar 1871, p. 3; *Wādī al-nīl*, 18 June 1869, p. 265; Jubaylī, vol. 1, pp. 57, 60,
61, 63; *al-Naḥla*, 15 Oct 1877, p. 140; al-Ṭarābulusī, p. 145; *al-Bashīr*, 7 Sep 1882,
p. 1; Mubārak, vol. 3, p. 1051.

10. E.g. *Ḥadīqat al-akhbār*, 2 July 1859, p. 2; 16 Feb 1860, p. 1; *al-Jawā'ib*, 9 Mar 1869, p. 1.

11. S.v. in C. T. Onions et al., *The Oxford Dictionary of English Etymology*. The Latin *membrum* had existed with a similar meaning since the second century B.C.; s.v. in C. T. Lewis and C. Short, *A New Latin Dictionary* (New York, 1895).

12. Al-Farābī, *Ārā'*, pp. 55ff.

13. S.v. ᶜ-ḍ-w in: *Lisān al-ᶜArab*, Richardson (1777), Johnson, Biberstein-Kazimirski (1846 and 1860); s.v. *member* in Richardson (1780), Ruphy, Marcel (1837); s.v. *sénateur* in Handjèri. Elious Bocthor, in his *Dictionnaire* (1828–1829), mentions *ᶜuḍw* as the equivalent of *membre—partie du corps politique*, and defines *sénateur* as *ᶜuḍw min aᶜḍā' al-dīwān*.

14. For the use of the term in the early years of the century see e.g. Jabartī, *ᶜAjā'ib*, vol. 3, pp. 160, 186; Naᶜām, p. 79 (cf. Marquam, p. 134); Qāsim, pp. 256, 272, 275, 276; *Aᶜmāl al-jamᶜiyya al-Sūriyya*, 1852, introduction; *Ḥadīqat al-akhbār*, 5 June 1858, pp. 2, 3; 10 July 1858, p. 1; 14 Aug 1858, p. 1; 11 Sep 1858, p. 1; 8 Jan 1859, p. 1; 19 Feb 1859, p. 1; 10 Nov 1859, p. 1; 2 Feb 1865, p. 2; *ᶜUṭārid*, 30 Oct 1858, p. 2; 6 Nov 1858, pp. 1, 2; 2 July 1859, p. 2; Lāz, pp. 3ff. (cf. Crevier, pp. 43ff.). As the usage of this word in a political sense struck roots, Buṭrus al-Bustānī noted in his *Muḥīṭ* (1870) that "it is sometimes applied to an individual [member] of a group and assembly" (*fard min jamāᶜa wa-jamᶜiyya*).

15. E.g. Sāmī, pt. 3, vol. 1, p. 168; vol. 2, pp. 550, 672–80, 804; *Ḥadīqat al-akhbār*, 5 Jan 1860, p. 2; 16 Jan 1862, p. 2; 6 Mar 1862, p. 1; 3 Apr 1862, p. 2; 2 Feb 1865, p. 2; *Nafīr Sūriya*, 14 Jan 1861; *Thamarāt al-funūn*, 10 Nov 1875, p. 2; *al-Jawā'ib*, 21 Dec 1876, p. 2; 6 Jan 1877, pp. 2, 3; 21 Nov 1878, p. 5; *al-Jinān*, 1878, p. 11; Rāfiᶜī, *ᶜAṣr Ismāᶜīl*, vol. 2, pp. 85, 90, 291.

16. See Māwardī, pp. 5ff.; Riḍā, *Khilāfa*, pp. 17, 41, 57–61; Gardet, especially pp. 123, 165, 170, 177; E. I. J. Rosenthal, *Political Thought*, under this term in the index.

17. E.g. *al-Dīwān al-khuṣūṣī*, p. 1, and cf. Jabartī, *ᶜAjā'ib*, vol. 3, p. 185.

18. Khayr al-Dīn, p. 75.

19. See e.g. Abū al-Suᶜūd, *Dars*, p. 13; Jubaylī, vol. 1, pp. 32, 35, 57, 58; *al-Ṣadā'*, 20 Mar 1876, p. 1; Ṭarābulusī, p. 145; Mubārak, vol. 3, p. 1047; *al-Hilāl*, Feb 1894, p. 349.

20. Aḥmad Ṭahṭāwī, *Rawḍ*, p. 232 (cf. Voltaire, *Pierre*, vol. 2, p. 116); Bayyāᶜ, p. 94 (cf. Voltaire, *Charles*, p. 110). See also other examples in Khayr al-Dīn, p. 83; *al-Jawā'ib*, 27 Feb 1883, p. 4; Fāris al-Shidyāq, *Kashf*, p. 113.

21. See Ḥasan al-Bāshā, *Alqāb*, pp. 364–67; idem, *Funūn*, vol. 2, pp. 627–51; s.v. *shaykh* and *mashā'ikh* in the term index to Qalqashandī, and in the index to Jabartī, *Mudda*; s.v. *cheikh, cheikh de corporation* and *šaiḫ* in the index to Raymond; Baer, ch. 3; Shaw, *Financial and Administrative Organization*, pp. 6, 54, 185; *al-Waqā'iᶜ al-Miṣriyya*, 1829–1830, no. 49, pp. 1ff.; no. 52, pp. 1ff.; Mishāqa, *Mashhad*, pp. 29–31; *Dā'irat al-maᶜārif*, vol. 10, pp. 644–46.

22. E.g. Shihābī, p. 214; Ṭahṭāwī, *Takhlīṣ*, p. 252.

23. *Al-Rajā'*, 29 Mar 1895, p. 2.

24. Ṭahṭāwī, *Takhlīṣ*, p. 286.

25. See Beeston, p. 112.

26. *Al-Waqā'iᶜ al-Miṣriyya*, 1829, no. 49, pp. 1–2; no. 52, p. 1; Ṭahṭāwī, *Takhlīṣ*, 258; idem, *Qalā'id*, pt. 2, p. 104; idem, *Kanz*, p. 6; Qāsim, pp. 246–47; *Ḥadīqat al-akhbār*, 13 Feb 1862, p. 1; 16 Oct 1862, p. 3; *Birjīs Bārīs*, 22 Nov 1865,

p. 1; 11 Apr 1866, p. 1; Lāz, pp. 2ff. (cf. Crevier, pp. 42–43); Khayr al-Dīn, pp. 154, 304; *al-Ṣadā'*, 30 Sep 1876, pp. 1, 2; 15 Oct 1876, p. 1; *al-Nūr al-tawfīqī*, 15 Nov 1888, p. 16; *Muntakhabāt al-mu'ayyad*, 1890, p. 439; Khalīl Sarkīs, *Riḥla*, pt. 2, p. 92; Zakī, *Safar*, pp. 221, 370.

27. In Don Raphael's translation of Machiavelli's *Il Principe*, prepared in 1824–25, *senatori* was curiously rendered as *arbāb al-ʿakākīz*, *shuyūkh al-mashyakha* (p. 44—cf. Machiavelli, p. 66). This however, was an isolated occurrence at the time. Another half century passed before the word *shaykh* acquired broad acceptance in this sense.

28. For the use of *shaykh* to denote senator see e.g. *al-Jinān*, 1875, pp. 61, 151, 439, 841; 1876, pp. 6, 13, 48, 114, 153, 155; *Dā'irat al-maʿārif*, vol. 2, pp. 525, 684; vol. 3, p. 333; vol. 9, p. 146; *al-ʿAṣr al-jadīd*, 1 Aug 1881, p. 2; 24 Aug 1881, p. 1; 12 Oct 1881, p. 2; 30 Nov 1881, p. 1; *Thamarāt al-funūn*, 1 Aug 1881, p. 1; 6 Jan 1890, p. 2; *al-Bashīr*, 26 Jan 1882, p. 1; 11 June 1890, p. 2; Isḥaq, *Durar*, pp. 102–3; idem, *Kitābāt*, pp. 276–79; *al-Qāhira al-ḥurra*, 22 Apr 1888, p. 3; Tawfīq, *Riḥla*, vol. 7, p. 6; *al-Muqaṭṭam*, 14 Feb 1889, p. 1; 2 July 1892; p. 3; 14 Oct 1893, p. 3; 18 Jan 1894, p. 3; 20 Dec 1895, p. 3; 27 Jan 1896, p. 1; 7 Feb 1896, p. 1; 17 Mar 1897, p. 3; 1 Apr 1898, p. 1; 10 Jan 1900, p. 1; Zakī, *Safar*, p. 264; *al-Rajā'*, 10 Apr 1895, p. 1; *al-Muqtaṭaf*, vol. 20 (1896), pp. 881, 889; *al-Manār*, vol. 1 (1897–1898), p. 159; *al-Hilāl*, May 1898, pp. 659, 661; *al-Jāmiʿa al-ʿUthmāniyya*, 1899, pp. 14, 68; *al-Mu'ayyad*, 17 Mar 1900, p. 6.

29. E.g. *al-Jinān*, 1875, pp. 61, 151; 1876, pp. 6, 13; *Dā'irat al-maʿārif*, vol. 2, p. 525; vol. 3, p. 333; Isḥaq, *Kitābāt*, p. 276; *al-Qāhira al-ḥurra*, 22 Apr 1883, p. 3; *al-Muqaṭṭam*, 14 Feb 1889, p. 1; *Thamarāt al-funūn*, 6 Jan 1890, p. 2; Zakī, *Safar*, p. 264; *al-Mu'ayyad*, 17 Mar, 1900, p. 6.

30. S.v. ʿ-y-n in Lane; Mottahedeh, *Loyalty*, pp. 123–29.

31. See e.g. Jabartī, *Mudda*, pp. 42, 43, 45, 49, 58, 59, 66, 95; Sāmī, pt. 3, vol. 1, pp. 118, 141, 147; vol. 2, p. 715; Qusṭanṭīn al-Bāshā, *Mudhakkirāt*, p. 56.

32. Hourani, "Ottoman reform"; Karpat, "Land regime"; idem, "Transformation"; Davison, "Ádvent"; Ṭannūs al-Shidyāq, passim. See also H. Bowen, "Aʿyān," *EI²*.

33. Abū al-Suʿūd, *Dars*, pp. 12–13.

34. E.g. Turk, p. 4; Shihābī, p. 551; *al-Waqā'iʿ al-Miṣriyya*, 1829–1830, no. 132, pp. 2, 3; Ṭahṭāwī, *Qalā'id*, pt. 1, p. 79; idem, *Kanz*, pp. 27, 34; Bayyāʿ, p. 73 (cf. Voltaire, *Charles*, p. 91); Zarābī, *Bidāya*, p. 74; Maḥmūd, pp. 29, 46 (cf. Robertson, vol. 1, pp. 31, 79); *Ḥadīqat al-akhbār*, 16 Oct 1858, p. 1; 23 Jan 1862, p. 4; *al-Bashīr*, 3 June 1871, p. 349; *al-Jinān*, 1874, p. 259; 1875, p. 39; Jubaylī, vol. 1, pp. 7, 59; *Thamarāt al-funūn*, 30 Mar 1880, p. 2; *al-Jawā'ib*, 16 Mar 1881, p. 4; 25 Oct 1881, p. 4; 23 Jan 1884, p. 4; Mubārak, vol. 3, pp. 1046, 1051; Fāris al-Shidyāq, *Kashf*, p. 112; *al-Iʿlām*, 17 Jan 1885, p. 1; 28 June 1888, p. 1; *Dā'irat al-maʿārif*, vol. 10, p. 96; Bājūrī, p. 52; *al-Ustādh*, 29 Nov 1892, p. 351; Khalīl Sarkīs, *Riḥla*, pt. 2, p. 17; *al-Hilāl*, Oct 1893, p. 66; Feb 1894, p. 371; Kanʿān, p. 32.

35. For an Arabic text of the constitution see *al-Jawā'ib*, 4–6 Jan 1877. The section dealing with *hey'et-i aʿyān* is to be found ibid, 6 Jan 1877, pp. 2–3. See also Devereux, pp. 227–34.

36. Some of the early nineteenth-century lexicographers defined the term with this meaning. Bocthor, in his 1828–29 *Dictionnaire*, offered the expression *dīwān aʿyān al-mamlaka* as a translation for *sénat*, which he somewhat vaguely

described as "assemblée de personnes considérables dans laquelle réside une partie de l'autorité suprême". Confusingly, he also offered *dīwān aʿyān al-dawla* as the equivalent of *parlement*, in the sense of "assemblée des grandes de l'état pour juger une affaire considérable". Handjèri, in 1841, similarly translated *sénat* as *dīwān al-wujūh wal-aʿyān*. The term was occasionally used in that sense already before the 1870s—see e.g. *Ḥadīqat al akhbār*, 2 July 1859, p. 2; Ḥarāʾirī, p. 32. But it was only during the last quarter of the century that its usage with that meaning became widespread.

37. For some examples of its use with this meaning see: *al-Naḥla*, 15 June 1877, p. 10; 15 Oct 1877, p. 141; 1 Mar 1878, pp. 275–76; 15 Dec 1878, p. 205; 15 Apr 1879, p. 232; *al-Jawāʾib*, 5 Dec 1878, p. 8; 6 Feb 1878, p. 4; 23 Feb 1880, p. 4; 19 Dec 1882, p. 1; 13 Feb 1883, p. 4; *al-Bashīr*, 4 Jan 1872, p. 2; 5 Jan 1882, p. 2; 7 Sep 1882, p. 1; 2 May 1888, p. 2; *al-Jinān*, 1878, p. 40; 1879, pp. 97, 103; 1885, pp. 100, 102; *Thamarāt al-funūn*, 13 Jan 1879, p. 3; 14 Feb 1881, p. 2; 11 Feb 1892, p. 4; 9 Jan 1893, p. 3; 19 Feb 1894, p. 3; 26 Aug 1895, p. 4; 17 Aug 1896, p. 4; *al-Janna*, 27 July 1880, p. 7; *al-Baṣṣīr*, 21 Apr 1881, p. 1; 25 Aug 1881, p. 2; *Dāʾirat al-maʿārif*, vol. 5, p. 386; vol. 10, p. 96; Fāris al-Shidyāq, *Kashf*, pp. 313, 314; *al-Iʿlām*, 28 Jan 1885, p. 1; 4 Nov 1886, p. 1; 28 June 1888, p. 1; *al-Qāhira*, 4 Jan 1886, p. 3; *al-Qāhira al-ḥurra*, 16 Apr 1887, p. 1; 10 Mar 1888, p. 3; *al-Muqaṭṭam*, 4 Mar 1889, p. 2; 25 June 1892, p. 3; 2 Aug 1893, p. 3; 3 Feb 1894, p. 3; 17 Feb 1900, p. 3; Khilāṭ, p. 244; Fikrī, pp. 496–98; Khalīl Sarkīs, *Riḥla*, pt. 2, p. 43; *al-Hilāl*, Apr 1893, p. 287; Oct 1893, pp. 93–94; *al-Mushīr*, 10 July 1897, p. 1180.

38. Ḥasan al-Bāshā, *Alqāb*, pp. 179–86, 188–90; Defrémery; Sourdel, vol. 2, pp. 493–94; Tyan, *Institutions*, vol. 1, pp. 531ff.; see also Qalqashandī, vol. 4, pp. 423–26; vol. 7, pp. 262–63, 302. In the Ottoman army *amīr* and *amīr al-umarāʾ* as rank names were modified to *mīr* and *mīrmīrān*, respectively; their Turkish equivalents were *bey* and *beylerbey*.

39. Cahen, *L'Évolution;* idem, "Iḳṭāʿ," *EI²;* idem, "Djaysh," *EI²*.

40. For Egypt, see s.v. *amīr* and *umarāʾ* in the term index to Qalqashandī; Shaw, *Financial and Administrative Organization*, esp. pp. 3, 199–200, 239–51; Raymond, s.v. *émirs* in the index; Jabartī, *Mudda*, pp. 11, 18, 20, 21, 22, 25, 32, 34, 42, 45, 54, 73, 76, 90; Sharqāwī, p. 76; Sāmī, pt. 3, vol. 1, pp. 116, 126; vol. 2, p. 795.

For Mount Lebanon, see Shihābī, passim; Ṭannūs al-Shidyāq, passim; Mishāqa, *Mashhad*, p. 29f.

41. *Al-Jinān*, 1871, pp. 417–20.

42. *Al-Jinān*, 1875, p. 584.

43. *Al-Jinān*, 1874, p. 169; *Dāʾirat al-maʿārif*, vol. 1, p. 274.

44. *Al-Jinān*, 1874, p. 118. For more examples see Turk, p. 3; Naʿām, p. 85 (cf. Marquam, p. 144); Maḥmūd, vol. 1, p. 29 (cf. Robertson, vol. 1, p. 31); Qāsim, pp. 140, 144, 247; *al-Jinān*, 1870, pp. 101, 429, 430; 1871, p. 218; 1872, pp. 328, 582; 1874, pp. 119, 513, 587–88, 626; 1875, pp. 149, 150; 1876, pp. 76, 149; 1878, pp. 183, 385; 1879, p. 11; *al-Janna*, 23 July 1880, p. 2; 27 July 1880, p. 7; 17 Aug 1880, p. 7; 25 Jan 1881, p. 1; 28 Jan 1881, p. 1; *Dāʾirat al-maʿārif*, vol. 1, pp. 281, 302; Khūrī-Shiḥāda, *Āthār* (geography), p. 44; idem, *Āthār* (history), introduction, p. ṭ; Isḥaq, *Kitābāt*, p. 279; Qalfāẓ, *Taʾrīkh Buṭrus*, pp. 88, 91.

45. For the use of *amīr* and *amīr al-umarāʾ* in this sense see e.g. Jabartī, *Mudda*, pp. 83, 86; Shihābī, p. 442; Ṭahṭāwī, *Kanz*, p. 56; idem, *Manāhij*, p. 218;

148   *Notes*

Bayyāᶜ, p. 50 (cf. Voltaire, *Charles*, p. 72); *al-Jinān*, 1870, pp. 429, 658; 1885, p. 205; Naqqāsh, vol. 5, p. 6; *Thamarāt al-funūn*, 4 July 1881, p. 1.
46. E.g. Turk, pp. 3, 4; Maḥmūd, vol. 1, p. 121 (cf. Robertson, vol. 1, p. 259); Aḥmad Ṭahṭāwī, *Rawḍ*, p. 40 (cf. Voltaire, *Pierre*, vol. 1, p. 66); *al-Jinān*, 1872, pp. 38, 225; 1879, p. 387; 1885, p. 205; *al-Janna*, 25 July 1879, p. 1; 27 July 1880, p. 7; *Dā'irat al-maᶜārif*, vol. 5, p. 386; *al-Nashra al-usbūᶜiyya*, 29 June 1885, p. 205; 12 Oct 1885, p. 328; Tawfīq, *Riḥla*, pt. 7, p. 2; Qalfāẓ, *Ta'rīkh mulūk*, pp. 180–81; *al-Ustādh*, 25 Oct 1892, p. 220; *al-Hilāl*, Nov 1892, p. 74; Dec 1895, p. 283; May 1896, p. 675; Khalīl Sarkīs, *Riḥla*, pt. 2, p. 44.
47. C. Van Arendonk, "Sharīf," *EI¹*; Bodman, pp. 79ff.; Shaw, *Ottoman Egypt*, pp. 103–4; Raymond, vol. 2, pp. 420–21, 755–56; Hourani, "Changing face," pp. 97–99; Fāris, pp. 92ff.; Ḥasan al-Bāshā, *Alqāb*, pp. 357–59; *Dā'irat al-maᶜārif*, vol. 10, p. 437.
48. Lane, s.v.; Ḥasan al-Bāshā, *Alqāb*, p. 359.
49. *Al-Waqā'iᶜ al-Miṣriyya*, 1842, no. 623, quoted by Ḥamza, vol. 1, p. 118.
50. *Ḥadīqat al-akhbār*, 22 Jan 1859, p. 1; 9 Apr 1859, p. 2.
51. Khūrī-Shiḥāda, *Āthār* (geography), p. 44; *al-Nashra al-usbūᶜiyya*, 29 June 1885, p. 208. For similar examples see Turk, pp. 3–4; Shihābī, p. 464; Ṭahṭāwī, *Takhlīṣ*, p. 147; idem *Qalā'id*, pt. 2, p. 99; Zarābī, *Qurra*, vol. 1, pp. 5, 12 (cf. Desmichels, vol. 1, pp. 6, 18); Abū al-Suᶜūd, *Naẓm*, p. 182; idem, *Dars*, p. 13; Maḥmūd, vol. 1, pp. 29, 145 (cf. Robertson, vol. 1, pp. 31, 320); Bayyāᶜ, p. 49 (cf. Voltaire, *Charles*, p. 71); Qāsim, pp. 244ff.; Aḥmad Ṭahṭāwī, *Rawḍ*, p. 287 (cf. Voltaire, *Pierre*, vol. 2, p. 211); Bustrus, p. 68; *Ḥadīqat al-akhbār*, 26 June 1858, p. 2; *Nafīr Sūriya*, 22 Apr 1861; *al-Jinān*, 1871, pp. 417–20; Khūrī-Shiḥāda, *Āthār* (geography), p. 27; Ḥunayn Khūrī, *Tuḥfa*, pp. 81, 89, 111, 112, 249, 250; Jubaylī, vol. 1, pp. 11, 57, 59; Ṭarābulusī, pp. 144–45, 474; *Dā'irat al-maᶜārif*, vol. 5, p. 386; vol. 10, pp. 94–95; Isḥaq, *Durar*, p. 74; *al-Laṭā'if*, 15 Aug 1889, p. 152; Khalīl Sarkīs, *Riḥla*, pt. 2, p. 17; *al-Hilāl*, Oct 1893, pp. 66–67; Feb 1894, p. 371; May 1898, p. 661; Mar 1899, p. 345; *al-Mawsūᶜāt*, 15 Nov 1898, p. 6; 23 Aug 1899, p. 241.
52. E.g. ᶜUṭārid, 13 Nov 1858, p. 2; Birjīs Bārīs, 7 July 1859, pp. 1–2; 24 Sep 1859, p. 4; 15 Feb 1865, p. 1; *Thamarāt al-funūn*, 11 May 1875, p. 1; 14 Sep 1876, p. 3; *al-Naḥla*, 15 June 1877, p. 8; 1 Sep 1877, p. 82; 15 May 1878, p. 347; *al-Ahrām*, 13 Dec 1878, p. 1; Ṭarābulusī, p. 463; *al-Bashīr*, 30 Mar 1882, p. 3; *al-Laṭā'if*, vol. 4 (1889–1890), p. 153; vol. 7 (1892–1893), p. 424; Kanᶜān, p. 34.
53. E.g. *Ḥadīqat al-akhbār*, 17 May 1858, p. 1; 29 May 1858, p. 1; 13 July 1858, p. 4; 14 Aug 1858, p. 1; 28 Aug 1858, pp. 1, 2; 19 Feb 1859, p. 1; 19 Mar 1859, p. 1; 30 May 1861, p. 1; 15 Aug 1861, p. 1; 27 Mar 1862, p. 1; 17 Apr 1862, p. 1; 8 Apr 1863, p. 1; *al-Ahrām*, 13 Dec 1878, p. 1; Ṭarābulusī, p. 463.
54. E.g. *Ḥadīqat al-akhbār*, 30 Aug 1858, p. 2; 11 Sep 1858, p. 2; 2 July 1859, p. 2; 6 Mar 1862, p. 2; 6 Mar 1865, p. 3; Birjīs Bārīs, 15 Feb 1865, p. 1; *al-Jinān*, 1874, p. 587; 1875, pp. 149, 150; *al-Naḥla*, 15 June 1877, pp. 8, 10; 1 Sep 1877, p. 82.
55. S.v. n-b-l in *Lisān al-ᶜArab;* the *Qāmūs;* Golius; Richardson (1777); Freytag; Dozy. See also Qalqashandī, vol. 6, p. 159, where the term appears as an honorific for ᶜulamā'.
56. E.g. *al-Jawā'ib*, 5 Mar 1871, p. 3; 4 Sep 1883, p. 4; Isḥaq, *Durar*, pp. 23, 74; idem, *Kitābāt*, pp. 146, 151, 279; Fāris al-Shidyāq, *Kashf*, p. 112; *Thamarāt al-funūn*, 2 Sep 1889, p. 2; Zakī, *Safar*, p. 264.
57. See e.g. for Britain: *Thamarāt al-funūn*, 5 Aug 1878, p. 4; 30 Mar 1880,

p. 1; 2 Sep 1889, p. 2; 16 June 1890, p. 3; 12 Oct 1891, p. 3; 13 Feb 1893, p. 2;
al-Janna, 1 Mar 1881, p. 1; *al-ʿAṣr al-jadīd*, 22 June 1881, p. 1; 16 July 1881, p. 2;
1 Aug 1881, p. 2; *al-Bashīr*, 1 Mar 1882, p. 1; 10 Aug 1882, p. 1; 17 Aug 1882, p.
2; 28 Mar 1888, p. 3; 25 July 1888, p. 3; *al-Nashra al-usbūʿiyya*, 16 Mar 1885, p.
88; 25 May 1885, p. 167; 20 July 1885, p. 232; 17 Aug 1885, p. 264; 2 Mar 1888, p.
72; for France: Isḥaq, *Durar*, p. 100; *al-Jinān*, 1885, p. 72; for the United States:
al-Bashīr, 12 Apr 1885, p. 4; 16 Apr 1885, p. 2; for Brazil: *al-Hilāl*, Feb 1894, p.
349; for Hungary: *al-Rajā'*, 29 Mar 1895, p. 3.
    58. *Dā'irat al-maʿārif*, vol. 10, pp. 94–95.
    59. *Muqaddam*—a title used in Mount Lebanon for a tribal head. In the
definition of Buṭrus al-Bustānī it indicates "the third rank [in the hierarchy] of
tribal leaders" (*akābir al-ʿashā'ir*); see *Muḥīṭ*, s.v. q-d-m.
    60. *Al-Hilāl*, Feb 1894, p. 371.
    61. E.g. Shihābī, p. 431; *Ḥadīqat al-akhbār*, 19 June 1858, p. 2; *Birjīs Bārīs*,
7 Dec 1859, p. 2; Khayr al-Dīn, pp. 186, 204, 211; Sāmī, pt. 3, vol. 2, pp. 713,
794; *al-Jinān*, 1874, pp. 114–15, 513, 585; *Thamarāt al-funūn*, 11 May 1875, p. 1;
al-Jawā'ib, 6 Feb 1878, p. 4; *al-Naḥla*, 15 Dec 1878, p. 205; *Dā'irat al-Maʿārif*,
vol. 4, p. 550; *al-Janna*, 23 July 1880, p. 7; *al-Baṣṣīr*, 18 Aug 1881, p. 2; *al-Bashīr*,
16 Mar 1882, p. 1; Isḥaq, *Kitābāt*, pp. 260–61; Naqqash, vol. 5, p. 1; *al-ʿUrwa
al-wuthqā*, 13 Mar 1884, pp. 45, 77; *al-Nashra al-usbūʿiyya*, 16 Mar 1885, p. 88;
al-Qāhira, 3 Aug 1886, p. 3; *al-Iʿlām*, 12 Aug 1886, p. 2; *al-Qāhira al-ḥurra*, 10
Mar 1888, p. 3; *al-Muqaṭṭam*, 7 July 1892, p. 1; Khalīl Sarkīs, *Riḥla*, pt. 2, pp. 17,
43; Fikrī, pp. 495, 498; *al-Hilāl*, Feb 1894, p. 371; *al-Mushīr*, 26 Jan 1896, p. 575;
al-Mawsūʿāt, 26 Apr 1899, p. 392; *al-Mu'ayyad*, 4 Feb 1900, p. 5.
    62. E.g. *Ḥadīqat al-akhbār*, 12 Jan 1860, p. 1; Sāmī, pt. 3, vol. 2, p. 713;
al-Jawā'ib, 29 Mar 1870, pp. 5, 6; *al-Jinān*, 1875, pp. 4, 11, 12, 13, 39, 77, 78, 83;
al-Janna, 25 July 1879, p. 1; *al-ʿUrwa al-wuthqā*, 5 June 1884, p. 3; *al-Nashra
al-usbūʿiyya*, 8 June 1885, p. 184; Tawfīq, *Riḥla*, vol. 7, pp. 1, 2, 4; *Muntakhabāt
al-mu'ayyad*, 1890, p. 437; *al-Ustādh*, 25 Oct 1892, p. 220; *al-Hilāl*, Nov 1892, p.
75; Khalīl Sarkīs, *Riḥla*, pt. 2, p. 28; *al-Arghūl*, 15 jumāda al-thāniya 1314 (1896),
p. 46; *al-Mushīr*, 26 Mar 1897, p. 1061; *al-Ra'y al-ʿāmm*, 19 Sep 1897, p. 242;
al-Manār, Vol. 1 (1897–1898), pp. 296–97; *al-Mawsūʿāt*, 24 July 1899, p. 188.
    63. Zarābī, *Qurra*, vol. 1, p. 11 (cf. Desmichels, vol. 1, p. 16); *Birjīs Bārīs*,
12 Oct 1864, p. 1; *Muntakhabāt al-jawā'ib*, vol. 5, p. 168; *al-Nashra al-usbūʿiyya*,
23 July 1872, p. 238.
    64. Ṭahṭāwī, *Takhlīṣ*, pp. 138ff., 265ff.
    65. Khilāṭ, p. 243; Khalīl Sarkīs, *Riḥla*, pt. 2, p. 54.

Chapter 5

    1. Jabartī, *Maẓhar*, pp. 187, 223; Mishāqa, *Mashhad*, p. 59.
    2. E.g. Jabartī, *ʿAjā'ib*, vol. 3, pp. 43, 152; *al-Waqā'iʿ al-Miṣriyya*, 1829–
1830, no. 111, pp. 3, 4; no. 113, p. 2; no. 120, p. 2; Ṭahṭāwī, *Takhlīṣ*, p. 254;
Bayyāʿ, p. 192 (cf. Voltaire, *Charles*, p. 195); *al-Bashīr*, 5 Nov 1870, p. 80;
al-Ahrām, 14 Dec 1896, p. 1; *al-Mushīr*, 25 Apr 1896, pp. 667–70. Cf. also
Korkut, pt. 1, p. 76.
    3. Ṭahṭāwī, *Takhlīṣ*, pp. 138ff., 254–55, 264ff. (cf. text of the French consti-
tution in Duverger, pp. 80ff.).

4. Ṭahṭāwī, *Takhlīṣ*, pp. 144, 151, 254.

5. In the Qur'ān *wakīl* appears as one of the ninety-nine names of God, denoting guardian, protector and witness. The verb occurs several times (in the fifth form), in the sense of "relying upon" or "trusting in" Allāh.

6. Otto Spies, "Wakāla," *EI¹;* Tyan, *Organisation Judicaire,* pp. 262–75.

7. See e.g. Raymond, vol. 1, pp. 172, 201, 294, 297–98; vol. 2, p. 579; Lapidus, pp. 137, 149; Rivlin, pp. 29–30, 78, 192–93. Bianchi and Kieffer (*Dictionnaire,* s.v.,) define *tucār vekīlī* as "facteur, commis de marchands, et député du commerce."

8. Qalqashandī, vol. 4, pp. 44, 45, 63, 198, 234, 238; vol. 14, p. 377; Lapidus, p. 122.

9. Jabartī, *Maẓhar,* p. 260. See also pp. 129, 136, 137, 138, 146, 148, 259, 264, 265, 274, 277, 278, 282, 301 303, 344.

10. Ibid, pp. 188–97.

11. E.g. Sāmī, pt. 3, vol. 1, pp. 109, 120, 146, 147, 150, 154, 155, 159, 174, 179, 185, 391; vol. 2, pp. 500, 515; *Dalīl Miṣr,* 1889–1890, pp. 118ff.; 1890–1891, pp. 15ff.

12. Şānīzāde, vol. 1, pp. 66, 69; Gibb and Bowen, pt. 1, pp. 108–109; Kekule, pp. 25–6; Lewis, "Başvekil," *EI²;* idem, *Emergence,* pp. 98, 376–78; Shaw, *History,* vol. 2, pp. 36–7; idem, *Financial and Administrative Organization* pp. 148, 272–73. For the relevant section in the Ottoman constitution see *al-Jawā'ib,* 4 Jan 1877, p. 3, and Devereux, pp. 67–69.

13. Bianchi, *Vocabulaire,* s.v. *commissaire* and *ministre;* idem, *Dictionnaire,* s.v. *chargé, commissaire, ministère* and *ministre;* Marcel (1837), s.v. *commissaire;* Humbert, pp. 207, 209; Handjèri, s.v. *ministère, ministre,* and *représentant;* Berggren, s.v. *charger;* Biberstein-Kazimirski (1846 and 1860), s.v. *wakīl.* See also Bianchi and Kieffer s.v. *vekīl.*

14. Turk, p. 68; Shihābī, p. 458 (cf. *Correspondance de Napoleon Iᵉʳ* [Paris, 1856], vol. 11, p. 68); *al-Waqā'iʿ al-Miṣriyya,* 1829–1830, no. 125, p. 2; no. 157, pp. 1, 2; no. 182, p. 1; Ṭahṭāwī, *Takhlīṣ,* p. 138; Bayyāʿ, p. 53 (cf. Voltaire, *Charles,* p. 75); Zarābī, *Bidāya,* p. 88; Qusṭanṭīn al-Bāshā, *Mudhakkirāt,* p. 119; Maḥmūd, vol. 1, p. 143; vol. 2, pp. 42, 43 (cf. Robertson, vol. 1, p. 316; vol. 2, pp. 91, 96); Naʿām, pp. 68, 86 (cf. Marquam, pp. 115, 146); Aḥmad Ṭahṭāwī, *Rawḍ,* p. 285 (cf. Voltaire, *Pierre,* vol. 2, p. 209); *Ḥadīqat al-akhbār,* 10 May 1858, p. 1; 17 May 1858, p. 1; 16 Oct 1858, p. 1; 20 Feb 1862, p. 1; 27 Mar 1862, p. 1; *al-Bashīr,* 8 July 1871, p. 400; *al-Jinān,* 1874, no. 587; *al-Ahrām,* 12 Aug 1876, p. 2; *al-Janna,* 25 Jan 1881, p. 1; *al-ʿUrwa al-wuthqā,* 24 Apr 1884, p. 152; Naqqāsh, vol. 5, pp. 4, 7; Qalfāẓ, *Ta'rīkh Buṭrus,* p. 86; *al-Manār,* vol. 1 (1897–1898), p. 275; *al-Jāmiʿa al-ʿUthmāniyya,* 1899, p. 30; *al-Mawsūʿāt,* Feb 1899, pp. 248–49; 24 July 1899, p. 168.

15. Şānīzāde, vol. 4, p. 3. The description appears under the year 1230/1815. See also Lewis, *Emergence,* pp. 73, 85–86, and idem, "Ḥurriyya," *EI².*

16. Bocthor (1828–1829), s.v. *parlement* and *états généraux.*

17. Ṭahṭāwī, *Takhlīṣ,* pp. 140, 141, 144, 151–53, 253–54, 263. Cf. idem, *Kanz,* pp. 22, 56–57, 115–16; *Qalā'id,* pt. 1, p. 94; *Taʿrībāt,* p. 286; *Muqaddima waṭaniyya,* p. 7; *al-Waqā'iʿ al-Miṣriya,* 1842, no. 623, quoted by Ḥamza, vol. 1, p. 116 (the journal at that time was edited by Ṭahṭāwī).

18. Ṭahṭāwī, *Takhlīṣ,* pp. 138, 140.

19. E.g. Bayyāʿ, p. 6 (cf. Voltaire, *Charles,* p. 34); Abū al-Suʿūd, *Naẓm,* p.

182; Maḥmūd, vol. 1, p. 46 (cf. Robertson, vol. 1, p. 77); Naʿām, p. 86 (cf. Marquam, pp. 146–47); Qāsim, pp. 245, 247, 252; Aḥmad Ṭahṭāwī, *Rawḍ*, p. 265 (cf. Voltaire, *Pierre*, vol. 2, p. 174).

20. *Ḥadīqat al-akhbār*, 11 Sep 1858, p. 1; *Birjīs Bārīs*, 18 Jan 1860, p. 3; *al-Jinān*, 1871, p. 419.

21. For a discussion of *dīwān* and *majlis* see chapter 8. For the use of *wukalāʾ* in this sense, and of *majlis al-wukalāʾ*, see e.g. *Ḥadīqat al-akhbār*, 29 May 1858, p. 1; 5 June 1858, p. 2; 7 July 1858, p. 1; 2 Jan 1862, p. 2; 20 Feb 1862, p. 1; 19 June 1862, p. 1; *Birjīs Bārīs*, 26 Oct 1859, p. 3; Khayr al-Dīn, pp. 75, 137, 186, 204, 206, 249, 340; Calligaris, ed. Paris, p. 8; ed. Beirut, p. 7; *Wādī al-nīl*, 23 Apr 1869, p. 16; 30 Apr 1869, pp. 45, 46; 14 May 1869, p. 205; 16 June 1869, p. 360; *al-Jinān*, 1870, p. 103 (cf. *New York Times*, 7 Dec 1869, p. 1); 1871, pp. 417, 420; 1872, p. 26; 1876, p. 191; *al-Bashīr*, 10 Oct 1870, p. 56; 11 Mar 1871, p. 232; 27 May 1871, p. 338; *Dāʾirat al-maʿārif*, vol. 1, p. 272; Isḥaq, *Kitābāt*, pp. 146, 270f.; *Thamarāt al-funūn*, 14 Nov 1881, p. 2; 5 Oct 1891, p. 3; *al-Baṣṣīr*, 18 Aug 1881, p. 2; *al-Nashra al-usbūʿiyya*, 29 June 1885, p. 208; Kanʿān, p. 35.

22. Qalqashandī, vol. 4, pp. 16–18, 21, 24ff., 63ff., 108ff., 215ff., 233ff.; vol. 5, pp. 453–54; vol. 8, pp. 217ff., and s.v. *nāʾib* and *nuwwāb* in the term index; D. Ayalon, *Studies*, I, pp. 57–58, 60–61; idem, *Mamluk*, V, p. 47; Shoshan, pp. 96–97.

23. Gibb and Bowen, pt. 2, pp. 121–33; Shaw, *Financial and Administrative Organization*, pp. 59–60; Tyan, *Organisation judicaire*, pp. 101ff.; Bianchi and Kieffer, s.v.

24. Jabartī, *Maẓhar*, pp. 188–89.

25. Don Raphael, p. 2.

26. For these examples see, respectively: Zarābī, *Qurra*, vol. 1, p. 10 (cf. Desmichels, vol. 1, p. 14); *al-Jinān*, 1870, p. 429; Ṭahṭāwī, *Taʿrībāt*, pt. 2, p. 93; *al-Bashīr*, 25 Nov 1871, p. 596; 24 Dec 1870, pp. 131–32. For similar examples see: Turk, p. 67; Ṭahṭāwī, *Qalāʾid*, pt. 1, p. 26; Naʿām, p. 59 (cf. Marquam, p. 101); Aḥmad Ṭahṭāwī, *Rawḍ*, pp. 237, 285 (cf. Voltaire, *Pierre*, vol. 2, pp. 124, 209); *Ḥadīqat al-akhbār*, 5 Jan 1860, p. 1; 12 Jan 1860, p. 1; *Birjīs Bārīs*, 1 Feb 1860, p. 2; 6 July 1864, p. 2; 31 Aug 1864, p. 2; 15 Mar 1865, p. 1; *al-Jinān*, 1872, pp. 131, 225 (cf. *The Spectator* (London), 24 Feb 1872, p. 234); 1875, p. 583; 1885, p. 72; *al-Nashra al-usbūʿiyya*, 9 June 1872, p. 1; *Muntakhabāt al-jawāʾib*, vol. 6, pp. 245; vol. 7, p. 184; *al-Laṭāʾif*, 15 Feb 1896, p. 83; *al-Mawsūʿāt*, 15 Nov 1898, p. 9; *al-Jāmiʿa al-ʿUthmāniyya*, 1899, p. 68.

27. Bustānī, *Muḥīṭ*, s.v.

28. Ṭahṭāwī, *Takhlīṣ*, p. 141; idem, *Kanz*, pp. 22, 57. See also Qāsim, p. 223.

29. Baer, p. 57, note 154; cf. ibid, p. 32.

30. Rāfiʿī, *ʿAṣr Ismāʿīl*, vol. 2, pp. 81–82. See further details on pp. 78ff.

31. E.g. *al-Jawāʾib*, 18 Feb 1868, p. 4; 22 Mar 1870, p. 6; 16 Nov 1870, p. 3; 15 Feb 1877, p. 2; *Wādī al-nīl*, 16 June 1869, p. 360; 15 Feb 1870, p. 1270; Abū al-Suʿūd, *Dars*, pp. 12–13.

32. For the use of *nuwwāb* and *majlis al-nuwwāb* until mid-1870s (thereafter these terms became highly common), see e.g. *Ḥadīqat al-akhbār*, 8 Feb 1866, p. 1; *al-Jawāʾib*, 18 Feb 1868, p. 4; 22 Mar 1870, p. 6; 29 Mar 1870, p. 5; 21 Apr 1870, pp. 4–6; 19 Mar 1871, p. 3; 16 June 1875, p. 4; *Muntakhabāt al-jawāʾib*, vol. 2, pp. 95, 124–25; *Wādī al-nīl*, 30 Apr 1869, p. 44; *al-Jinān*, 1870, p. 334;

1872, pp. 149, 225, 441 (cf. *The Spectator* (London), 24 Feb 1872, p. 234); 1874, pp. 76, 77, 78, 225, 363, 478–80, 626; 1875, pp. 150–52, 257–58, 584; *al-Bashīr*, 25 Feb 1871, p. 212; 11 Mar 1871, pp. 227, 232; 9 Sep 1871, p. 402; Abū al-Su'ūd, *Dars*, p. 13.

33. For a few exceptional occurrences see: Na'ām, p. 86 (describing the British Parliament as *majlis mab'ūthī al-milla;* cf. Marquam, p. 146); Bayyā', p. 73 (translating *ambassadeurs* as *mab'ūthīn;* cf. Voltaire, *Charles*, p. 91); Qāsim, pp. 344, 345.

34. *Al-Jawā'ib*, 6 Jan 1877, p. 3; Devereux, chapters 6–8 and appendixes B and C.

35. E.g. *al-Ṣadā*, 15 Nov 1876, p. 1; 1 Dec 1876, p. 1; 5 Feb 1877, p. 1; *Thamarāt al-funūn*, 16 Dec 1878, p. 3; 23 Dec 1878, p. 4; 5 Feb 1880, p. 3; 23 Feb 1880, p. 2; 9 Mar 1880, p. 3; 14 Feb 1881, p. 3; 28 Mar 1881, p. 2; *al-Naḥla*, 1 Feb 1878, pp. 250, 251, 254; *al-Jinān*, 1879, pp. 8, 10, 168; 1885, pp. 5, 26, 132; *al-Janna*, 25 Jan 1881, p. 2; 1 Feb 1881, p. 1; 2 Sep 1881, p. 1; Isḥaq, *Kitābāt*, p. 272; *Dā'irat al-ma'ārif*, vol. 4, pp. 301, 307–8; vol. 5, pp. 386, 547; vol. 7, p. 133; *al-Baṣṣīr*, 21 Apr 1881, p. 1; 4 Aug 1881, p. 1; 11 Aug 1881, p. 1; 18 Aug 1881, p. 1; 25 Aug 1881, p. 2; *al-Bashīr*, 7 Sep 1882, p. 1; 21 Jan 1885, p. 3; *Kawkab al-mashriq*, 6 July 1882, p. 4; 10 Aug 1882, p. 1; 28 Dec 1882, p. 2; 11 Jan 1883, p. 2; 3 May 1883, pp. 1, 2; *al-Nashra al-usbū'iyya*, 30 Mar 1885, p. 103; *al-Rajā'*, 29 Mar 1895, p. 2; 31 May 1895 p. 1.

36. *Meb'ūsān*, however, has remained current in Turkish.

37. Isḥaq, *Kitābāt*, p. 272. The Italian in parentheses reflects Turkish influence.

Chapter 6

1. Bagehot, p. 101.

2. F. Rosenthal, "Dawla," *EI²;* Lewis, "Hukumet," pp. 418–21; Mottahedeh, *Loyalty*, pp. 94, 185ff.

3. It is often difficult to identify the precise intent of an author referring to a foreign *dawla*. In many cases the writer himself chose this loose term to express the imprecise notion of a country's political leadership. For instances in which *dawla* clearly means royal or imperial dynasty, see: Shihābī, p. 440; Ṭahṭāwī, *Takhlīṣ*, p. 260; idem, *Ta'rībāt*, p. 58; Abū al-Su'ūd, *Naẓm*, p. 162; *Ḥadīqat al-akhbār*, 25 Oct 1862, p. 1; *al-Bashīr*, 27 May 1871, p. 338 (quoting *al-Janna*); Ṣāliḥ, pp. 19, 52, 53, 96, 97; Jubaylī, passim; Qalfāẓ, *Ta'rīkh Buṭrus*, p. 63.

For other instances see: Jabartī, *Mudda*, pp. 7, 10, 11, 50, 60; Turk, pp. 1, 2, 3, 4, 107; Shihābī, pp. 219, 239, 297, 431, 440, 441, 459, 476; *al-Waqā'i' al-Miṣriyya*, 1829–1830, no. 125, pp. 3, 4; no. 126, p. 4; no. 139, p. 1; no. 182, p. 1; no. 194, p. 2; Ṭahṭāwī, *Takhlīṣ*, pp. 72, 140; idem, *Ta'rībāt*, pp. 37, 58, 85, 96, and appendix, p. 62; Qusṭanṭīn al-Bāshā, *Mudhakkirāt*, p. 77; Abū al-Su'ūd, *Naẓm*, p. 162; *Birjīs Bārīs*, 13 Oct 1859, p. 3; *Ḥadīqat al-akhbār*, 20 Feb 1862, p. 1; 27 Mar 1862, p. 1; *al-Jawā'ib*, 6 June 1870, p. 7; 20 Dec 1870, p. 4; *Muntakhabāt al-jawā'ib*, vol. 5, p. 338; vol. 6, p. 115; *al-Janna*, 29 July 1881, p. 1; Tawfīq, *Riḥla*, vol. 5, p. 7; *al-I'lām*, 17 Feb 1887, p. 2; 28 June 1888, p. 1. See also *Dā'irat al-ma'ārif*, vol. 8, pp. 153–59.

4. S.v. in T. C. Onions et al. *The Oxford Dictionary of English Etymology;*

H. C. Dowdall, "The word 'state'," *Law Quarterly Review*, 39, 153 (Jan 1923), pp. 98–125; cf. A. P. d'Entreves, "State," in Wiener, vol. 4, pp. 314–15.

5. Bagehot, p. 101.

6. See Hourani, "*Ottoman reform*"; idem, "*Changing face*"; Lewis, "Dustūr, ii" *EI²*, pp. 640–41.

7. E.g. Ṭahṭāwī, *Takhlīṣ*, p. 252; idem *Kanz*, pp. 49, 74; idem *Qalā'id*, pt. 2, p. 104 (cf. Depping, p. 223); idem *Taʿrībāt*, pp. 46, 52, 85, 167, and appendix, p. 51; idem, *Murshid*, p. 461; Zarābī, *Qurra*, vol. 1, p. 105; Bustrus, p. 18; Khayr al-Dīn, pp. 87, 88; *al-Jinān*, 1871, p. 493; 1875, p. 582; *al-Bashīr*, 27 May 1871, p. 339; Abū al-Suʿūd, *Dars*, p. 12; Isḥaq, *Durar*, pp. 50, 70; *Dā'irat al-maʿārif*, vol. 9, p. 12; *al-Laṭā'if*, vol. 7 (1892–1893), p. 423; *al-Hilāl*, June 1897, pp. 744, 783.

8. Ṭahṭāwī, *Taʿrībāt*, appendix, p. 51. Ṭahṭāwī also offered this explanation in *al-Waqā'iʿ al-Miṣriyya*, 1842, no. 623, quoted by Ḥamza, vol. 1, p. 118. Cf. Jean Jacques Rousseau, *Du contrat social*, ed. Ronald Grimsley (Oxford, 1972), pp. 161–74.

9. Ṭahṭāwī, *Takhlīṣ*, pp. 140, 252; idem, *Qalā'id*, pt. 2, p. 104 (cf. Depping, p. 223); idem, *Taʿrībāt*, pp. 37, 48, 58, 96, 290, and appendix, p. 51. See also Zarābī, *Qurra*, vol. 1, p. 105 (cf. Desmichels, vol. 1, p. 192).

10. E.g. *al-Jinān*, 1872, p. 225 (translating an article from the London *Spectator*, 24 Feb 1872, p. 234, which discussed "constitutional monarchy"); 1876, p. 219; *Dā'irat al-maʿārif*, vol. 4, p. 550.

11. *Al-Jinān*, 1871, pp. 492–93 (cf. *Correspondance de Napoleon Iᵉʳ* (Paris, 1856), vol. 3, p. 457).

12. *Al-Ra'y al-ʿāmm*, 19 June 1897, p. 163.

13. *Al-Ustādh*, 29 Nov 1892, pp. 350–51. For more examples see: Khayr al-Dīn, p. 58; *al-Bashīr*, 15 Apr 1871, p. 280; *al-Jinān*, 1876, p. 77; Ṣāliḥ, pp. 117, 126, 128; *Dā'irat al-maʿārif*, vol. 3, p. 332; vol. 5, pp. 386, 547; *al-Baṣṣīr*, 18 Aug 1881, p. 2; *al-Hilāl*, 1898, p. 661.

14. Lane, s.v. An analogous case is that of the Hebrew word *halakha*, denoting Jewish legal tradition, which is derived from the root h-l-kh, to walk or go.

15. Y. Linant de Bellefonds et al., "Ḳānūn," *EI²*; Schacht, *Introduction*, pp. 89–92; Lewis, "Turkey: Westernization," pp. 324–25; idem, in *BSOAS*, 1954, p. 599; Ebul'üla Mardin, pp. 280–84.

16. Sharqāwī, p. 75.

17. Ṭahṭāwī, *Takhlīṣ*, p. 140.

18. Turk, p. 3.

19. Ṭahṭāwī, *Takhlīṣ*, pp. 138, 140, 141 (cf. Duverger, p. 81), 148, 253. See also pp. 147–48, where article 68, referring to "le Code civil et les lois" is rendered as *qawānīn al-siyāsāt*—while in article 73, "des lois et des réglements" is translated as *qawānīn wa-siyāsāt*.

20. For these examples see respectively: *al-Bashīr*, 3 June 1871, p. 349 (cf. Goubard, vol. 1, p. 287); Khūrī-Shiḥāda, *Āthār* (geography), pt. 3, pp. 623–24; Kanʿān, p. 35; *al-Baṣṣīr*, 25 Aug 1881, p. 2; *al-Jawā'ib*, 21 Apr 1870, p. 6, and 3 May 1870, p. 5; Qāsim, pp. 251, 276; Tawfīq, *Riḥla*, vol. 7, p. 5. For more examples see: Turk, pp. 3, 34, 35; Shihābī, p. 214; Zarābī, *Bidāya*, p. 75; Qāsim, pp. 248, 250, 276; *Ḥadīqat al-akhbār*, 22 May 1858, p. 2; *ʿUṭārid*, 9 Oct 1858, p. 2; Marrāsh, *Riḥla*, p. 42; Calligaris, ed. Beirut, p. 7; *al-Jawā'ib*, 21 Apr 1870, p. 6; 29 July 1877, p. 3; *al-Jinān*, 1872, p. 655; *al-Nashra al-usbūʿiyya*, 7 Oct 1873, p. 320. For similar occurrences in later years, see e.g. Ḥunayn Khūrī, *Tuḥfa*, pp. 67,

68, 69, 70; *Dā'irat al-maᶜārif*, vol. 2, p. 446 (*ᶜulamā' al-sharīᶜa*) in Germany; vol. 5, p. 548; Isḥaq, *Durar*, p. 14.

21. Neither *Lisān al-ᶜArab* nor the *Qāmūs* mention a plural form for the word *sharīᶜa*.

22. E.g. Shihābī, p. 551 (referring to *Code Napoleon*); Zarābī, *Bidāya*, p. 74 (laws in ancient Athens); Khūrī-Shiḥāda, *Āthār* (geography), pt. 3, pp. 623–24; Jubaylī, pt. 1, p. 23; Ḥunayn Khūrī, *Tuḥfa*, pp. 69, 70; *al-Baṣṣīr*, 11 Aug 1881, p. 2 (international law—*al-sharā'iᶜ al-dawliyya*); *Kawkab al-mashriq*, 11 Jan 1883, pp. 3–4; *al-Jinān*, 1885, p. 100; *Dā'irat al-maᶜārif*, vol. 8, p. 233; Khilāṭ, p. 164; *al-Hilāl*, Nov 1892, p. 75; May 1898, p. 659; *al-Manār*, vol. 1 (1897–1898), p. 109.

23. E.g. Qāsim, p. 239; *al-Jawā'ib*, 21 Apr 1870, p. 6; *al-Jinān*, 1872, p. 493 (cf. *Correspondance de Napoleon Iᵉʳ*, Paris, 1856, vol. 3, p. 457); 1885, p. 100; *al-Nashra al-usbūᶜiyya*, 7 Oct 1873, p. 320; Khūrī-Shiḥāda, *Āthār* (geography), vol. 1, p. 40; Jubaylī, pt. 1, pp. 23, 66; *Kawkab al-mashriq*, 11 Jan 1883, pp. 3–4; *al-Hilāl*, Nov 1892, p. 75; May 1898, pp. 659, 661; *al-Mawsūᶜāt*, 26 Feb 1899, p. 251.

24. Ṭahṭāwī, *Takhlīṣ*, pp. 140, 253; *al-Waqīᶜ al-Miṣriyya*, 1842, no. 623, quoted by Ḥamza, vol. 1, pp. 115–17 (the paper at that time was edited by Ṭahṭāwī, who expounded that "*sharṭa* is a translation of Cart, meaning the pledge (*ᶜahd*) which the people obtain from the king.") See also Qāsim, p. 369; *al-Bashīr*, 15 July 1871, p. 407; Ḥunayn Khūrī, *Tuḥfa*, p. 232. The Tunisian Khayr al-Dīn likewise borrowed the term *kūnstītūsyūn*—see Khayr al-Dīn, pp. 77, 137.

25. *Al-Bashīr*, 3 June 1871, p. 348 (cf. Goubard, vol. 7, p. 260).

26. *Qāmūs* and Lane, s.v.

27. For such instances, in which *sharraᶜa* may be understood to denote "establishment of rules" see Jabartī, *ᶜAjā'ib*, vol. 3, pp. 144, 145.

28. *Al-Waqā'iᶜ al-Miṣriyya*, 1842, no. 623, quoted by Ḥamza, vol. 1, p. 118.

29. Turk, p. 3; *al-Waqā'iᶜ al-Miṣriyya*, 1829–1830, no. 125, p. 2; 1842, no. 623, quoted by Ḥamza, vol. 1, p. 116; Ṭahṭāwī, *Kanz*, p. 22; Zarābī, *Qurra*, vol. 1, pp. 17, 67 (cf. Desmichels, vol. 1, pp. 27, 120); Abū al-Suᶜūd, *Naẓm*, p. 184f. (*al-jamᶜiyya al-murattiba* in France; the 1791 constitution is called *tartīb*); Maḥmud, vol. 1, pp. 45, 46, 145 (cf. Robertson, vol. 1, pp. 76, 78, 320); Qāsim, p. 276; Calligaris, Beirut ed., pp. 77, 185, 188, 202 (cf. Paris ed., pp. 94, 216, 220, 235: the original *kunstītūsyūn* was changed in the Beirut ed. into *tartīb umūr al-dawla* or *tartīb*); Jabaylī, pt. 1, p. 66; Ṭarābulusī, p. 463.

30. Ṭahṭāwī, *Takhlīṣ*, pp. 140, 142 (cf. Duverger, p. 82).

31. *Al-Waqā'iᶜ al-Miṣriyya*, 1842, no. 623, quoted by Ḥamza, vol. 1, p. 118.

32. Abū al-Suᶜūd, *Dars*, p. 12.

33. *Al-Waqā'iᶜ al-Miṣriyya*, 1842, no. 623, quoted by Ḥamza, vol. 1, p. 116. See also Ṭahṭāwī, *Takhlīṣ*, p. 143 (cf. Duverger, p. 82); Zarābī, *Bidāya*, p. 74; Abū al-Suᶜūd, *Dars*, pp. 186, 188; Qāsim, pp. 239, 251, 253.

34. See e.g. *Wādī al-nīl*, 15 Feb 1870, p. 1270; Ḥunayn Khūrī, *Tuḥfa*, p. 70; Isḥaq, *Durar*, p. 103; idem, *Kitābāt*, p. 279; *Muntakhabāt al-mu'ayyad*, p. 409; *Dā'irat al-maᶜārif*, vol. 10, p. 96; *al-Hilāl*, May 1898, p. 661; Ṣannūᶜ, *Badā'iᶜ;* Kanᶜān, p. 196.

35. S.v. in Lane. For the use of *sanna* in the late nineteenth century, see e.g. *al-Jinān*, 1872, p. 655; *al-Nashra al-usbūᶜiyya*, 29 Apr 1873, p. 135; *Dā'irat al-maᶜārif*, vol. 2, p. 684; vol. 3, p. 333; Khilāṭ, pp. 91, 164; *al-Hilāl*, Nov 1892,

pp. 75, 101; Aug 1897, p. 901; May 1898, pp. 659, 661; *al-Muqaṭṭam*, 11 Dec 1896, p. 1; Kanʿān, p. 32.

36. See Aḥmad ibn Abī al-Ḍiyāf, *Itḥāf ahl al-zamān bi-akhbār mulūk Tūnis wa-ʿahd al-amān* (Tunis, 1964), vol. 5, pp. 32–33, 50–55; Muḥammad Bayram, Ṣafwat al-Iʿtibār bi-mustawdaʿ al-amṣār wal-aqṭār (Cairo, 1884–1886), vol. 2, p. 17.

37. Quoted by Lewis, *Emergence*, pp. 157–58.

38. Lewis, "Dustūr-ii," *EI²;* Devereux, pp. 60–79. An Arabic translation of the constitution appears in *al-Jawā'ib*, 4 Jan 1877, pp. 2–3; 6 Jan 1877, pp. 2–4; 10 Jan 1877, p. 3.

39. E.g. Abū al-Suʿūd, *Dars*, p. 12; *al-Jawā'ib*, 11 July 1877, p. 3 (reference to the French constitution of 1875); *Dā'irat al-maʿārif*, vol. 4, p. 307; vol. 7, p. 133; *al-Baṣṣīr*, 11 Aug 1881, p. 1; 25 Aug 1881, p. 1; Fikrī, p. 496; *al-Muqaṭṭam*, 11 Dec 1896, p. 1; *al-Hilāl*, May 1898, p. 661. The term was occasionally used in later years as well. In 1925 it became the name of the constitution of Iraq, and in 1928 of that of Trans-Jordan.

40. E.g. *Dā'irat al-maʿārif*, vol. 4, p. 554; *al-Hilāl*, Nov 1893, p. 184 (*al-lā'iḥa al-ʿuẓma*).

41. See text in Rāfiʿī, *ʿAṣr Ismāʿīl*, vol. 2, pp. 287–90. The decree was followed by an "organisational act"—*lā'iḥa niẓāmiyya*, providing rules for the functioning of the council. See text, ibid, pp. 290–98.

42. For texts of both the original drafts and the amended document see Rāfiʿī, *ʿAṣr Ismāʿīl*, pp. 195–206.

43. See text in Rāfiʿī, *Miṣr wal-Sūdān*, pp. 217–38.

44. Khayr al-Dīn, p. 77. See also *Ḥadīqat al-akhbār*, 8 Feb 1866, p. 2; *al-Jawā'ib*, 21 Apr 1870, p. 6; 17 Jan 1878, p. 8; *Muntakhabāt al-jawā'ib*, vol. 5, p. 245 (cf. Duverger, p. 112); *al-Jinān*, 1872, pp. 492–93 (cf. *Correspondance de Napoleon Iᵉʳ*, Paris, 1856, vol. 3, pp. 465–67); 1874, p. 256; *Dā'irat al-maʿārif*, vol. 2, p. 684; vol. 3, p. 333; Kanʿān, p. 32.

45. E.g. *Muntakhabāt al-jawā'ib*, vol. 5, pp. 144, 194, 196; *Ḥadīqat al-akhbār*, 26 Jan 1865, p. 2.

46. Lane, s.v.; "Dustūr," *EI²;* Qalqashandī, vol. 6, p. 53; vol. 10, pp. 152, 154; Ḥasan al-Bāshā, *Alqāb*, p. 288; Gardet, p. 261 (discussing its use in the professional guilds); *Aʿmāl al-jamʿiyya al-Sūriyya*, 1852, introduction.

47. *Dā'irat al-maʿārif*, vol. 4, p. 300. For similar examples, see *al-Naḥla*, 20 Sep 1877, pp. 98, 100; *Muntakhabāt al-jawā'ib*, vol. 7, p. 68; *al-Iʿlām*, 28 Jan 1885.

48. *Ḥadīqat al-akhbār*, 14 Aug 1858, p. 1 (cf. *The Times* (London), 27 July 1858, pp. 4ff.).

49. *Al-Ṣadā*, 5 June 1876, p. 2.

50. *Al-Jawā'ib*, 4 Jan 1877, pp. 2–3.

51. *Dā'irat al-maʿārif*, vol. 2, p. 684.

52. Isḥaq, *Durar*, p. 74.

53. E.g. *al-Jinān*, 1879, p. 387; *al-Bashīr*, 16 Feb 1882, p. 2; 24 Oct 1888, p. 2; 23 Feb 1889, p. 1; *al-Muqaṭṭam*, 9 Apr 1889, p. 2.

54. For these examples see *al-Muqtaṭaf*, 1896, p. 890; *al-Rajā'*, 9 Nov 1898, p. 2. For more examples see *Thamarāt al-funūn*, 5 Aug 1878, p. 4; Isḥaq, *Kitābāt*, p. 279; *al-Bashīr*, 16 Feb 1882, p. 2; 11 Apr 1888, p. 1; 2 May 1888; p. 2;

al-Laṭā'if, 15 July 1888, p. 131; *al-Qāhira al-ḥurra,* 21 Apr 1888, p. 3; *al-Muqaṭṭam,* 9 Mar 1889, p. 2; Khilāṭ, pp. 91–92; Zakī, *Safar,* p. 266; *al-Ahrām,* 9 July 1896, p. 1; *al-Ra'y al-ʿāmm,* 19 June 1897, pp. 163, 164; *al-Mawsūʿāt,* 26 Feb 1889, p. 251; *al-Jāmiʿa al-ʿUthmāniyya,* 1899, p. 68; Jirjāwī, pp. 110, 111. 55. E.g. *al-Muqaṭṭam,* 8 Apr 1889, pp. 1–2; Khilāṭ, p. 124; *al-Ahrām,* 9 July 1896, p. 2; Kanʿān, p. 32; Jirjāwī, p. 109.

Chapter 7

1. E.g. Lewis, "The concept of an Islamic republic," *WI,* 4 (1955), p. 4, where he quotes a contemporary Turkish reference to the second caliph ʿUmar as "the second President of the Islamic Republic," and mentions other similar references; Şerif Mardin, pp. 296–97; Riḍā, *Khilāfa,* p. 5.

2. See e.g. John Adams, *A Defence of the Constitution of Government of the United States of America* (Boston, 1788), passim. Adams discusses democratic, aristocratic and monarchical republics.

3. Al-Farābī, *Ārā',* esp. pp. 53ff.; Ibn Bājja, pp. 8–12; Ibn Khaldūn, p. 303. See also E. I. J. Rosenthal, *Political Thought,* pp. 93ff., 120, 124ff., 160, 175ff.; Najjar, *Democracy.*

4. Ibn Saʿīd, p. 182; Abū al-Fidā', pp. 199–200, 211; Qalqashandī, vol. 5, pp. 404, 405, 411; vol. 8, pp. 46–48. One fourteenth-century writer adopted the Italian *comune* (*kumūn*), which he explained in similar terms, but his usage of this term remained an isolated occurrence; see ʿUmarī, *Kalām,* pp. 96–98.

5. See e.g. Korkut, vol. 1, pp. 50, 58, 72, 74; vol. 2, pp. 124, 128, 130, 132, 134.

6. Paine, p. 369.

7. In Muslim Spain the word carried a third meaning: a municipal council, composed of local elders and notables and running the affairs of a city. It was also sometimes used for similar councils in the professional guilds there. See Mu'nis, pp. 595–96, and cf. Dozy, s.v.

8. For the usage of *mashyakha* in French documents see e.g. al-Ṣāwī, plates 43, 48, 49, 70, 79, 87a, 90–97; Boustani, passim. A parallel case is provided by the occasional Ottoman practice of referring to the government of Venice as *Venedik Beyleri,* the Signoria.

9. E.g. Ferīdūn, vol. 1, p. 13; vol. 2, pp. 479–81; *Muʿāhedāt,* vol. 2, pp. 130–214, passim. Cf. Lewis, "Djumhūriyya," *EI².*

10. E.g. Cevdet, vol. 4, pp. 150, 156, 157, 160, 162, 165, 236, 240; *Muʿāhedāt,* vol. 1, pp. 35–38; vol. 3, pp. 37–60. See also Lewis, "Djumhūriyya," *EI²,* for more examples.

11. See Jabartī, *Mudda,* plate 13, for a reproduction of the original proclamation, and page 11 for a discussion of the notion by Jabartī. For the use of the term in other French proclamations, see e.g. plates 14, 15a, 15b; al-Ṣāwī, plates 6a, 37, 45, 46, 49, 51, 52, 53, 55, 57a, 58, 60, 62, 69; Boustani, passim. It is noteworthy that the two chief translators of the expedition, Venture de Paradis and Amédée Jaubert, received their linguistic training in Istanbul, and that the former also served as an official dragoman at the Ottoman court; see al-Shayyāl, *Ta'rīkh al-tarjama . . . fī ʿahd al-ḥamla al-Faransāwiyya,* pp. 46–47; Lewis, "Im-

pact," p. 42. Interestingly, Richardson's Persian-Arabic-English dictionaries of 1777 and 1780 offer the term *jumhūr* as the Arabic equivalent of "republick" [sic].
12. Jabartī, *Mudda*, pp. 11, 46–50; idem, *Mazhar*, p. 60.
13. Sharqāwī, p. 75.
14. Turk, pp. 1–5, 78, 97–98, 112, 146. For similar instances see Shihābī, pp. 214, 218, 319–20, 439.
15. Ṭahṭāwī, *Qalā'id*, pt. 2, p. 104 (cf. Depping, p. 223); Abū al-Suʿūd, *Naẓm*, p. 184.
16. E.g. Ṭahṭāwī, *Qalā'id*, pt. 1, pp. 52, 57; idem, *Taʿrībāt*, pp. 69, 77; *Ḥadīqat al-akhbār*, 24 May 1858, p. 1; 5 June 1858, p. 1; 26 June 1858, pp. 1, 2; 17 July 1858, p. 1; 6 Sep 1858, p. 1; 18 Sep 1858, p. 1; 8 Jan 1859, p. 1; 5 Feb 1859, p. 3; 5 Apr 1860, p. 1; 16 May 1861, p. 1; 9 Jan 1862, p. 1; 15 Jan 1863, p. 2; ʿUṭārid, 9 Oct 1858, pp. 2, 3; 16 Oct 1858, p. 4; 23 Nov 1858, p. 4; *Birjīs Bārīs*, 28 Aug 1862, p. 1; 31 Aug 1864, p. 2; 11 Apr 1866, p. 1; *al-Jawā'ib*, 26 Apr 1870, p. 5; 17 Jan 1878, p. 8; *al-Bashīr*, 17 Sep 1870, pp. 21, 23; 22 Oct 1870, pp. 60, 61; 26 Nov 1870, p. 104; 18 Mar 1871, p. 239; 6 May 1871, p. 310; *al-Nashra al-usbūʿiyya*, 11 Mar 1873, p. 80; Khūrī-Shiḥāda, *Āthār* (geography), pt. 3, pp. 539, 638; *Kawkab al-mashriq*, 4 Jan 1883, p. 3; 11 Jan 1883, pp. 2, 3; *al-Hilāl*, Feb 1894, p. 373.
17. Khayr al-Dīn, p. 301 (an electoral region in Prussia); Qāsim, p. 257, and Lāz, passim (*al-mashyakha al-baladiyya*—the Paris city council); Qāsim, p. 272 (the Paris provincial council—*mashyakhat nāḥiyat Bārīs*); *al-Bashīr*, 6 May 1871, p. 3 (the Paris Commune—*ḥizb mashyakhat Bārīz*); *al-Jinān*, 1875, p. 584 (rural local government in Russia); *Dā'irat al-maʿārif*, vol. 1, p. 282 (knighthood; the title "Sir"—*sār*—is identified as *shaykh wa-amīr*); *al-Nashra al-usbūʿiyya*, 26 Oct 1885, p. 341 (*mashyakhat al-kanā'is al-Injlīziyya*); Zakī, *Safar*, p. 221 (the mayor of London—*shaykh al-mashyakha*); ibid., p. 264, and idem, *Dunyā*, p. 47 (the *Directoire*); *al-Hilāl*, Sep 1894, pp. 46–47 (the Mamluks in Egypt taking hold of *mashyakhat al-bilād*).
18. For early occurrences of *cumhūriyet* with the meaning of republic, see e.g. ʿAbd Allāh ʿAzīz and Ḥasan Efendi, *Italiyā ta'rīḫi* (a translation of Carlo Botta's *Storia d'Italia;* Cairo, 1834), pp. 18–19; Cevdet, vol. 6, pp. 152, 157, 158, 160, 236. On the other hand, cf. *Muʿāhedāt*, vol. 5, pp. 141ff., 157ff., where the French republic is still called *cumhūr* in treaties from 1879 and 1881. In mid-nineteenth-century Turkish dictionaries, the equivalent of republic still appears as *cumhūr;* see Handjèri, Bianchi, s.v. *république;* Bianchi and Kieffer, s.v. *cumhūr*. As late as 1891 Redhouse offered *cumhūr* as the only Turkish word for the notion.
19. For a few instances in which *jumhūr* was used after the French evacuation of Egypt see Turk, p. 5; Shihābī, pp. 188, 215, 320, 458. For the use of *jumhūriyya* by Ṭahṭāwī see his *Takhlīṣ*, pp. 252–53; idem, *Kanz*, pp. 4, 6; idem, *Qalā'id*, pt. 1, pp. 11, 14, 27, 52, 57; pt. 2, p. 101; The dictionaries, however, continued to monitor *jumhūr* along with *mashyakha* as the equivalents of republic; s.v. *république* in Bocthor (1828–1829 and 1869), Marcel, Humbert, Berggren; and s.v. *jumhūr* in Biberstein-Kazimirski and Johnson. Zenker's *Handwörterbuch* seems to have been the first to include *jumhūriyya* (along with *jumhūr*) as equivalent of republic, after the word had been in use in that sense for several decades.
20. Ṭahṭāwī, *Takhlīṣ*, p. 252. See also a similar but somewhat more vague definition, in idem, *Taʿrībāt*, appendix, pp. 72–73.

21. Zarābī, *Qurra*, vol. 1, p. 81 (cf. Desmichels, vol. 1, p. 145); Mahmūd, vol. 1, p. 28 (cf. Robertson, vol. 1, p. 30.)

22. E.g. *al-Jawā'ib*, 26 Apr 1870, p. 5; *al-Nashra al-usbūʿiyya*, 11 Mar 1873, p. 80; *Dā'irat al-maʿārif*, vol. 9, p. 416.

23. For instances in which the two terms appear together, see Tahtāwī, *Qalā'id*, pt. 1, pp. 52, 57; idem, *Taʿrībāt*, pp. 69, 77; Abū al-Suʿūd, *Nazm*, p. 188. For other occurrences of *jumhūriyya* during the pre-press period, see e.g. Zarābī, *Bidāya*, pp. 75, 76, 78; idem, *Qurra*, vol. 1, p. 10 (cf. Desmichels, vol. 1, p. 14); Abū al-Suʿūd, *Nazm*, p. 194; Naʿām, pp. 24, 64, 79 (cf. Marquam, pp. 38, 109, 134); Bayyāʿ, pp. 18, 46 (cf. Voltaire, *Charles*, pp. 44, 69); Mahmūd, vol. 1, p. 48 (cf. Robertson, vol. 1, p. 84); Qāsim, pp. 5, 140, 215, 219, 243, 254; Ahmad Tahtāwī, *Rawd*, p. 39 (cf. Voltaire, *Pierre*, p. 64).

24. E.g. *Birjīs Bārīs*, 24 June 1859, p. 2; 26 Oct 1859, pp. 3, 4; 9 Nov 1859, p. 4; 23 Nov 1859, p. 4; 18 Jan 1860, p. 3. Occasionally the paper used *mufāwada* instead of *fawdā*, with the very same meaning.

25. An illuminating contrast is offered by the case of modern Japanese, in which the word *kyowa*, chosen to denote "republic," initially meant "harmony." I owe this remark to Professor Marius Jansen of Princeton University.

26. For the use of the term during the early years of the press, see e.g. *Hadīqat al-akhbār*, 25 Sep 1858, p. 3; 29 Jan 1859, p. 2; 9 Mar 1865, p. 1; 11 Jan 1866, p. 1; *al-Jawā'ib*, 9 Feb 1869, p. 4; 26 Apr 1870, p. 5; 20 Dec 1870, p. 2; *Muntakhabāt al-jawā'ib*, vol. 2, pp. 191, 203, 229; vol. 5, pp. 107, 245; *al-Bashīr*, 10 Oct 1870, p. 50; 18 Jan 1871, p. 1; 25 Feb 1871, p. 212; *al-Jinān*, 1872, pp. 26, 38, 114, 457, 660, 688; 1874, p. 225; *al-Nashra al-usbūʿiyya*, 11 Mar 1873, p. 80; *Thamarāt al-funūn*, 22 Jan 1875, p. 1.

27. Abū al-Suʿūd, *Dars*, p. 13. For similar distinctions see Jubaylī, pt. 1, p. 57; Hunayn Khūrī, *Tuhfa*, pp. 81–85; *Dā'irat al-maʿārif*, vol. 6, p. 534.

28. Ishaq, *Durar*, p. 49.

29. *Dā'irat al-maʿārif*, vol. 6, p. 534. See also *al-Bashīr*, 13 May 1871, p. 318, and 10 June 1871, pp. 360–62, where the International Workingmen's Association is described as *al-jumhūriyya al-ʿāmma*.

30. For a discussion of Islam and democracy see: Kramers, "L'Islam"; Lewis, "Democracy"; Gardet, pp. 331–43; Tyan, *Institutions*, vol. 1, pp. 70–71; vol. 2, pp. 319ff.; Najjar, "Democracy" (where further references are given on p. 107, note 1).

31. Al-Farābī, *al-Siyāsa*, p. 69. See also idem, *Ārā'*, p. 62; Ibn Bājja, p. 54; F. Rosenthal, *Muslim Concept*, pp. 100–1; Najjar, "Democracy." In one instance, in a ninth- or tenth-century Arabic translation of Aristotle's *Rhetoric*, the foreign word *dimuqrātiyya* was used; see ʿAbd al-Rahmān Badawī, *Arīstūtālīs*, p. 37.

32. Tahtāwī, *Taʿrībāt*, appendix, pp. 51, 76; idem in *al-Waqāʾiʿ al-Misriyya*, 1842, no. 642, quoted by Hamza, vol. 1, p. 118; Zarābī, *Bidāya*, p. 74; Mahmūd, vol. 1, p. 131 (cf. Robertson, vol. 1, p. 284).

33. *Dā'irat al-maʿārif*, vol. 6, p. 534.

34. *Thamarāt al-funūn*, 8 Aug 1878, p. 4; Fāris al-Shidyāq, *Bakūra*, p. 290; *al-Nūr al-tawfīqī*, 1 Jan 1889, p. 88.

35. See Richardson (1780), s.v. democracy and republick [sic]; Bocthor (1828–1829 and 1869), Marcel (1837), Handjèri and Belot, *Dictionnaire*, s.v. *démocratie* and *république;* Cameron, s.v. *jumhūriyya*. Other dictionaries, such as

Ruphy, Biberstein-Kazimirski (1846 and 1860), Belot (*Vocabulaire*) and Salmoné provided no definition at all for "democracy."

36. *Al-Bashīr*, 10 June 1871, p. 356; 8 July 1871, p. 401; 2 Sep 1871, pp. 478, 480.

37. *Al-Bashīr*, 3 June 1871, p. 348 (cf. Goubard, vol. 1, p. 260), where the term is given as a translation of *démagogie*.

38. *Al-Muqtaṭaf*, 1 Dec 1896, p. 888.

Chapter 8

1. On the controversy regarding the origin of *dīwān* see Lane, s.v. and further references in "Dīwān," *EI²*, p. 223.

2. Dūrī, *Nuẓum*, pp. 186–209; Sourdel, vol. 2, pp. 586–605; Klausner, pp. 15–19; Shaw, *History*, vol. 1, pp. 25ff., 118ff., 280ff.; idem, *Financial and Administrative Organization*, s.v. *dīvān* in index; Rivlin, pp. 314–15; Duri and Gottschalk, "Dīwān—i,ii," *EI²*.

3. Jabartī, *Mudda*, esp. pp. 27ff., 63ff.; also Rāfiʿī, *Taʾrīkh al-ḥaraka*, vol. 1, pp. 95–117; vol. 2, pp. 9–20.

4. *Correspondance de Napoleon Iᵉʳ* (Paris, 1856), vol. 5, p. 32.

5. Rāfiʿī, *ʿAṣr Muhammad ʿAlī*, pp. 227–28, 465ff.; Qusṭanṭīn al-Bāshā, *Mudhakkirāt*, p. 56; Shihābī, p. 856; Sāmī, pt. 3, vol. 1, pp. 83, 95, 110, 115, 324; Deny, pp. 104ff.; Rivlin, p. 77ff.

6. For these examples see Ṭahṭāwī, *Takhlīṣ*, pp. 138, 139, 142–43 (cf. Duverger, p. 83); Bayyāʿ, p. 17 (cf. Voltaire, *Charles*, p. 43); *Ḥadīqat al-akhbār*, 26 June 1858, p. 2; 19 Jan 1860, p. 1. For similar examples see Don Raphael, p. 97 (cf. Machiavelli, pp. 140, 142, referring to the ancient Roman senate); Ṭahṭāwī, *Qalāʾid*, pt. 2, p. 101 (cf. Depping, p. 256); Zarābī, *Bidāya*, pp. 75, 104 (*dīwān al-sināt* in ancient Athens—apparently the *areopagus*, or council of notables); Bayyāʿ, pp. 17, 75 (cf. Voltaire, *Charles*, pp. 43, 93); Naʿām, p. 13 (cf. Marquam, p. 18); Qāsim, p. 247; Aḥmad Ṭahṭāwī, *Rawḍ*, pp. 235, 241, 249, 310, 314 (cf. Voltaire, *Pierre*, vol. 2, pp. 121, 132, 145, 252, 259); *Ḥadīqat al-akhbār*, 21 Aug 1858, p. 1; 8 Jan 1859, p. 1; 15 Jan 1859, p. 1; 3 May 1860; p. 1; 15 Mar 1866, p. 1; *ʿUṭārid*, 6 Nov 1858, p. 4; *al-Jawāʾib*, 5 June 1875, p. 3; 16 June 1875, p. 4.

7. Shihābī, p. 437 (*dīwān al-ʿālī* [sic]; *al-Waqāʾiʿ al-Miṣriyya*, 1829–1830, no. 240, p. 1 (*dīwān al-mashwara*); *ʿUṭārid*, 6 Nov 1858, p. 2; 13 Nov 1858, p. 3 (*al-dīwān al-ʿumūmī al-Inklīzī*); *Ḥadīqat al-akhbār*, 10 May 1858, p. 1 (*dīwān Lundrā*); 30 Apr 1863, p. 1 (*dīwān Inkiltirā*); *al-Jinān*, 1870, pp. 3, 331; *al-Naḥla*, 15 May 1878, pp. 347–48.

8. Maḥmūd, vol. 1, p. 46 (cf. Robertson, vol. 1, p. 77—the *États Généraux* referred to as *al-dīwān*); Ṭahṭāwī, *Takhlīṣ*, pp. 138ff. (cf. Duverger, pp. 82–84—references to the *Chambre des Députés*), and p. 147 (cf. Duverger, p. 85—*l'États* is translated as *al-dīwān*); Bustrus, p. 68 (the *Convention—al-dīwān*); Calligaris, Beirut ed., p. 217 (reference to the *Corps Législatif* during Napoleon's Consulate as *dīwān Faransā al-kabīr*).

9. *Ḥadīqat al-akhbār*, 28 Aug 1858, p. 1.

10. *ʿUṭārid*, 13 Nov 1858, p. 4 (*dīwān al-mashyakha*); *Ḥadīqat al-akhbār*, 23 Feb 1865, p. 1 (*dīwān al-wilāyāt al-muttahida*); *Birjīs Bārīs*, 18 Jan 1860, p. 3; *al-Jinān*, 1870, p. 103 (cf. *New York Times*, 7 Dec 1869—the Senate called *dīwān*

al-jumhūriyya). See also Ṭahṭāwī, *Taʿrībāt*, p. 286, where the assembly of the Colombian republic is described as *dīwān ʿumūmī*).

11. E.g. Ṭahṭāwī, *Takhlīṣ*, pp. 138ff. (cf. Duverger, pp. 82–84), 253, 263; *Ḥadīqat al-akhbār*, 24 May 1858, p. 2; 5 June 1858, p. 2; *al-Jinān*, 1870, pp. 331, 334, 335; *al-Naḥla*, 15 Oct 1877, p. 141; *al-Laṭā'if*, vol. 7 (1892–1893), p. 424.

12. *Lisān al-ʿArab*, s.v. A further extension was its use as an honorific, along with other terms denoting place, such as *maqām* and *maqarr;* see Qalqashandī, vol. 5, pp. 455, 496ff., and s.v. in the term index; Ḥasan al-Bāshā, *Alqāb*, pp. 455–59.

13. Raymond, vol. 2, pp. 559–60.

14. E.g. *ʿAjā'ib*, vol. 3, pp. 76, 144–45, 151, 153, 154, 156; vol. 4, p. 254; *Mudda*, pp. 27, 45, 46, 55, 59.

15. *Al-Waqā'iʿ al-Miṣriyya*, 1829–1830, no. 32ff.; no. 54ff., no. 258, pp. 1ff.; Deny, pp. 107–11, 120–21, 123–24; Rāfiʿī, *ʿAṣr Muḥammad ʿAlī*, pp. 465ff.; Rivlin, p. 77f.

16. Shaw, "Central legislative councils," pp. 57–84; Davison, "Advent," pp. 97ff.; Rustum, pp. 36ff.

17. *Al-Waqā'iʿ al-Miṣriyya*, 1829–1830, no. 273, p. 3 ("*majlis Faransā*, known as *shāmbrūpūtā*"); Ṭahṭāwī, *Takhlīṣ*, pp. 143, 146, 254–55, 264–65 (in France, *majlis rusul al-ʿamālāt*); Zarābī, *Bidāya*, p. 64; idem, *Qurra*, vol. 1, pp. 17, 79 (cf. Desmichels, vol. 1, pp. 27, 142–43); Bayyāʿ, p. 15 (cf. Voltaire, *Charles*, p. 41—reference to the Polish Royal Court); Abū al-Suʿūd, *Naẓm*, p. 182 (*majlis min al-ashrāf* in prerevolutionary France); Maḥmūd, vol. 1, p. 354 (cf. Robertson, vol. 2, p. 405—reference to the Imperial Court of the Holy Roman Empire); Naʿām, pp. 84–85 (cf. Marquam, p. 114); Qāsim, pp. 152, 223, 242ff.

18. *Birjīs Bārīs*, 24 June 1859, p. 4.

19. *Birjīs Bārīs*, 7 July 1859, pp. 1–2; 21 July 1859, p. 3; 29 Sep 1859, p. 4; 4 Jan 1860, p. 4; 18 Jan 1860, pp. 3, 4; 2 Jan 1862, p. 1; 27 Feb 1862, p. 1; 8 May 1862, p. 1; 13 Apr 1864, p. 1; 25 May 1864, p. 1; 8 June 1864, p. 1.

20. *Al-Naḥla*, 15 Jan 1877, p. 8; 1 Oct 1877, p. 118; 15 Apr 1878, p. 314; 15 Dec 1878, p. 205; 1 Jan 1879, p. 214; Mar 1880, p. 121; Khilāṭ, pp. 163, 188; *Thamarāt al-funūn*, 15 Apr 1895, p. 4; 22 July 1895, p. 4; 12 Aug 1895, p. 4; 25 Jan 1897, p. 2; Ṣannūʿ, *Ḥusn al-ishāra*, p. 25.

21. Zaydān, *Ta'rīkh ādāb*, vol. 4, pp. 67–93; Hourani, "Djamʿiyya," *EI²*, pp. 428–29; Davison, *Reform*, pp. 180–82.

22. Jabartī, *ʿAjā'ib*, vol. 3, p. 190.

23. E.g. Qāsim, pp. 244, 245, 251, 252, 276; *Ḥadīqat al-akhbār*, 17 May 1858, p. 1; 8 Jan 1859, p. 1; 8 Feb 1866, p. 2; *Lāz*, pp. 6, 44f. (cf. Crevier, pp. 36f., 58); *al-Jinān*, 1870, p. 330; 1871, pp. 453–54, 468–71; 1872, pp. 25–28, 149; Jubaylī, pt. 1, p. 11.

24. E.g. *al-Jawā'ib*, 12 Mar 1871, p. 3 (*jamāʿat al-shūrā*—the French *Assemblée*); 5 June 1875, p. 3; 3 Aug 1875, p. 4; 8 Dec 1875, p. 3.

25. E.g. *Ḥadīqat al-akhbār*, 10 May 1858, p. 1; 24 May 1858, p. 1; 5 June 1858, p. 3; 3 July 1858, p. 4; 10 July 1858, p. 1; 17 July 1858, p. 1; 31 July 1858, p. 1; 14 Aug 1858, p. 1 (*al-qāʿa al-ʿāmma* in Britain); 9 Feb 1860, p. 1; 8 Feb 1866, p. 2 (*qāʿat al-nuwwāb* in the U.S.); *ʿUṭārid*, 30 Oct 1858, p. 2 (*al-qāʿa al-ʿumūmiyya* in Britain); 3 Nov 1858, p. 2; 6 Nov 1858, p. 2; 13 Nov 1858, p. 2 (*qāʿat al-shurafā'* in Britain); *al-Jinān*, 1871, p. 431; *al-Ahrām*, 16 Aug 1878, p. 2 (*qāʿat al-ʿumūm* in France); Khayr al-Dīn, pp. 137, 203, 204, 206, 211, 311 (refer-

ences to the British Parliament and each of its houses, the French *Chambre des Députés* and the Prussian Upper House, as *qamira*); *al-Bashīr*, 25 Feb 1871, p. 212, and 15 Apr 1871, p. 280 (*al-awḍa al-Faransāwiyya*); 14 Oct 1871, p. 541 (*awḍat al-nuwwāb* in France).

26. *Ḥadīqat al-akhbār*, 1 Feb 1866, p. 1; 8 Feb 1866, p. 2.

27. For the three examples quoted here see respectively: *Muntakhabāt al-jawā'ib*, vol. 5, p. 88; *Ḥadīqat al-akhbār*, 18 Sep 1858, p. 2; *Birjīs Bārīs*, 1 Feb 1860, p. 2.

For more examples of the use of *jamᶜiyya* with this meaning see: *Ḥadīqat al-akhbār*, 17 July 1858, p. 1; 24 July 1858, p. 1; 7 Aug 1858, p. 1; 21 Aug 1858, p. 1; 16 Oct 1858, p. 1; 1 Sep 1859, p. 1; 5 Jan 1860, p. 1; 8 Mar 1866, p. 1; 22 Mar 1866, pp. 1, 2; ᶜ*Uṭārid*, 9 Oct 1858, p. 2; *al-Jinān*, 1871, p. 110; 1872, p. 23; 1874, pp. 513–14; 1875, p. 419; *Muntakhabāt al-mu'ayyad*, 1890, p. 215.

For the use of *majlis* with this meaning, see e.g. *Ḥadīqat al-akhbār*, 10 May 1858, p. 1; 10 July 1858, p. 1; 30 Oct 1858, p. 2; *Birjīs Bārīs*, 26 Sep 1862, p. 1; 8 June 1864, p. 1; 31 Aug 1864, p. 2; 15 Mar 1865, p. 1; *al-Jawā'ib*, 19 Jan 1869, pp. 1–2; 20 Nov 1870, p. 4; 27 Nov 1870, p. 3; 12 Dec 1870, p. 1; *Muntakhabāt al-jawā'ib*, vol. 5, pp. 90–92; *al-Jinān*, 1874, p. 169; *al-Iᶜlām*, 17 Jan 1885, p. 2; Tawfīq, *Riḥla*, pt. 7, p. 9.

In the early 1860s international conferences were sometimes designated by other names. See e.g. *Ḥadīqat al-akhbār*, 10 May 1858, p. 1; *Birjīs Bārīs*, 31 Aug 1864, p. 2. The word *mu'tamar*, at present the accepted name for this notion, was introduced in the late 1870s. For its early occurrences see e.g. *Muntakhabāt al-jawā'ib*, vol. 6, p. 246; vol. 7, pp. 106, 178, 194; Isḥaq, *Kitābāt*, pp. 122, 150–51; *al-Naḥla*, 1 July 1878, pp. 18–19; *Dā'irat al-maᶜārif*, vol. 3, p. 563; *al-Janna*, 23 July 1880, p. 2; 27 July 1880, p. 1; 3 Aug 1880, p. 1.

28. Qur'ān, III:59; XLII:38. For some exceptional Islamic views that were critical of the idea, see e.g. Lewis, "Meşveret," p. 777.

29. For medieval North Africa and Spain see Ibn Khaldūn, p. 27; Ibn al-Khaṭīb, pp. 49ff.; Mu'nis, pp. 647–48; ᶜInān, *Dawlat al-Islām*, vol. 2, p. 685; Levi-Provencal, pp. 127–28, 130, 131, 146, 230, 494; Tyan, *Organization judi-caire*, pp. 214–19, 230–36, and cf. Dozy, s.v. For the Qarmaṭian *shūrā*, see Ibn Ḥawqal, pp. 25–26. For Mamluk Egypt, see Qalqashandī, vol. 6, pp. 28, 70; vol. 11, pp. 153–56; D. Ayalon, *Studies*, I, p. 69. Cf. also Ḥilmī, pp. 153–57.

30. See Berkes, pp. 232–33, 238–39, and cf. review by Lewis in *BSOAS*, 1966, p. 387; Lewis, "Meşveret," pp. 779–81; Findley, "Madjlis al-shūrā," *EI²*, and references therein.

31. E.g. *al-Waqā'iᶜ al-Miṣriyya*, 1829–1830, no. 113, p. 3; no. 114, p. 2; no. 125, p. 2; no. 127; p. 2; no. 132, pp. 2, 3, 4; no. 138, p. 3; no. 236; p. 4; no. 240, pp. 1, 3.

32. Ṭahṭāwī, *Takhlīṣ*, pp. 81, 139 (the French *Chambre des Pairs*), 225, 263; idem, *Qalā'id*, pt. 1, pp. 44 (the ancient Roman senate), 90 (the assembly in Mexico—*dīwān mashwara ᶜumūmiyya*), 94; idem, *Kanz*, p. 22; idem, *Taᶜrībāt*, pp. 77 (reference to Switzerland), 277 (the United States Congress); *al-Waqā'iᶜ al-Miṣriyya*, 1842, no. 623, quoted by Ḥamza, vol. 1, p. 116 (reference to Portugal).

33. E.g. Zarābī, *Bidāya*, pp. 64, 68, 75, 111 (references to ancient Greece and Persia); idem, *Qurra*, vol. 1, pp. 4, 10, 11, 79 (cf. Desmichels, vol. 1, pp. 4, 14, 15, 16, 142–43); Abū al-Suᶜūd, *Naẓm*, p. 182 (the 1789 French *États Généraux*—*al-mashwara al-ᶜumūmiyya*); Bayyāᶜ, pp. 10, 14, 30, 48, 49, 53, 56 (cf.

Voltaire, *Charles*, pp. 37, 41, 55, 70, 71, 74, 77); Maḥmūd, vol. 1, pp. 46, 124, 140, 143, 169, 333, 339, 352; vol. 2, pp. 42, 44 (cf. Robertson, vol. 1, pp. 77, 265, 306, 316–17, 374–75; vol. 2, pp. 352, 371, 402; vol. 3, pp. 91–92, 96); Qāsim, pp. 142, 150, 152, 222, 226, 245, 246; Aḥmad Ṭahṭāwī, *Rawḍ*, pp. 42, 59 (cf. Voltaire, *Pierre*, vol. 1, pp. 69, 101).

34. E.g. *al-Jawā'ib*, 8 Aug 1877, p. 3; 7 Nov 1877, p. 6; *Dā'irat al-maᶜārif*, vol. 3, p. 559; vol. 9, p. 12; Ṭarābulusī, p. 474; *al-Baṣṣīr*, 11 Aug 1881, p. 1; Qalfāẓ, *Ta'rīkh Buṭrus*, pp. 60, 215; *Thamarāt al-funūn*, 9 Sep 1889, p. 2.

35. E.g. *Birjīs Bārīs*, 18 Jan 1860, p. 3; *al-Jawā'ib*, 25 Feb 1868, p. 3; 2 Mar 1868, p. 4; 26 May 1868, p. 4; 5 Apr 1870, p. 4; 20 Dec 1870, p. 2; 15 Dec 1875, p. 3; *Muntakhabāt al-jawā'ib*, vol. 2, p. 123.

36. E.g. *Ḥadīqat al-akhbār*, 28 Aug 1858, p. 1; 11 Sep 1858, p. 1; *Birjīs Bārīs*, 8 June 1864, p. 1 (the Parliament—*majlis shūrā al-mamlaka*); *al-Jawā'ib*, 8 Mar 1869, p. 1; 22 Mar 1870, p. 7; 20 June 1870, p. 5; 5 Mar 1871, p. 3 (*arbāb al-shūrā fī Lundrā*); 12 Mar 1871, p. 3 (*majlis al-mashwara al-aᶜlā*—the House of Lords?); 15 Mar 1871, p. 3; 3 Aug 1875, p. 4; 8 Aug 1877, p. 3; 28 Aug 1883, p. 3; *al-Ahrām*, 5 Aug 1876, p. 3; *al-Naḥla*, 15 Apr 1877, p. 8; 1 Sep 1877, p. 72; Isḥaq, *Kitābāt*, p. 272; *al-Baṣṣīr*, 28 Apr 1881, p. 1; Fāris al-Shidyāq, *Kashf*, p. 313; *al-Iᶜlām*, 28 June 1888, p. 1; Kanᶜān, p. 37.

37. E.g. *Wādī al-nīl*, 30 Apr 1869, p. 46; 15 Feb 1870, p. 1270; *al-Jinān*, 1870, p. 2; *al-Bashīr*, 15 Apr 1871, pp. 280, 282; 13 May 1871, p. 321; 27 May 1871, p. 340 (translates *l'Assemblée Législative* of Paris, 1792, as *al-shūrā*; cf. Goubard, vol. 2, p. 303); 9 Sep 1871, p. 492; *al-Jawā'ib*, 5 Mar 1871, p. 3; 12 Mar 1871, p. 3; 8 Dec 1875, p. 3; 21 June 1876, p. 3; 24 Oct 1877, p. 4; 7 Nov 1877, p. 4; *Muntakhabāt al-jawā'ib*, vol. 2, pp. 93–95, 153f., 196; *al-Ṣadā*, 5 Mar 1876, p. 1; Khūri-Shiḥāda, *Āthār* (geography), pt. 3, p. 639; *al-Ahrām*, 19 Aug 1876, p. 1; *al-Baṣṣīr*, 21 Apr 1881, p. 1; 28 Apr 1881, p. 1; *Kawkab al-mashriq*, 4 Jan 1883, p. 1; 11 Jan 1883, p. 2; Khilāṭ, p. 180.

38. *Birjīs Bārīs*, 26 Oct 1859, p. 3. See also Khilāṭ, p. 92, where the legislative power of cantonal assemblies in Switzerland is described as *quwwa shūrawiyya*.

39. For the Egyptian institutions see sources quoted in note 15 above; also ᶜAbd al-Karīm, pp. 93ff., 675–77; Heyworth-Dunne, *Introduction*, pp. 181, 191, 193, 205, 206, 207; Rāfiᶜī, *ᶜAṣr Ismāᶜīl*, vol. 2, p. 78ff.; idem, *Miṣr wal-Sūdān*, p. 41f.; Naqqāsh, vol. 4, pp. 149ff. For the Ottoman bodies see Davison, *Reform*, pp. 239–44, and the review by Lewis, *MES*, Jan 1965, pp. 290–91; Shaw, "Central legislative councils," pp. 53–57, 73f.; Findley, *Bureaucratic Reform*, pp. 172, 174–76, 247–50, 307–9.

40. Şerif Mardin, *Genesis*, pp. 133–34, 308ff., 376, 390; Berkes, pp. 232–33, 239, 307–8, 340–42; Hourani, *Arabic Thought*, pp. 144–45, 234; Safran, pp. 47, 80–83.

41. E.g. Tawfīq, *Riḥla*, pt. 3, p. 4; pt. 7, p. 7; idem, *Rasā'il*, p. 49; *Thamarāt al-funūn*, 9 Dec 1889, p. 2; *al-Ahrām*, 6 Mar 1890, p. 2.

42. MacDonald, "Ḥizb," *EI²*; see also Blochet.

43. Qur'ān, V:56 and LVIII:22.

44. Khayr al-Dīn, p. 264; *al-Jinān*, 1870, p. 435; *al-Jawā'ib*, 5 Apr 1870, p. 1. See also *al-Bashīr*, 3 Sep 1870, p. 2; 4 Mar 1871, p. 220.

45. Turk, p. 4

46. *Muntakhabāt al-jawā'ib*, vol. 2, p. 123. The report is from January 1870.

47. Jubaylī, pt. 1, p. 23. For similar examples see: Abū al-Suʿūd, *Naẓm*, p. 162; Naʿām, p. 104 (cf. Marquam, p. 180); *Ḥadīqat al-akhbār*, 15 Mar 1866, p. 1; *al-Bashīr*, 4 Nov 1871, p. 571; Ṣāliḥ, p. 76; Jubaylī, pt. 1, pp. 46, 48, 59; Ṭarābulusī, pp. 144–45.

48. Ṭahṭāwī, *Murshid*, p. 460; *Ḥadīqat al-akhbār*, 2 May 1861, p. 1; *al-Bashīr*, 13 May 1871, p. 318. For more examples see *Muntakhabāt al-jawāʾib*, vol. 2, p. 190; *al-Jinān*, 1872, p. 187; Qalfāẓ, *Taʾrīkh Buṭrus*, p. 51. Nineteenth-century dictionaries confirmed this general usage. Biberstein-Kazimirski defined *ḥizb* as *troupe d'hommes*, and Bustānī's *Muḥīṭ* offered *ṭāʾifa* as a synonym. See also Steingass, s.v.

49. In fact the term was sometimes used with this more precise intent in the early years of the century. At that stage, however, it could convey no more than a vague notion. References to the French monarchists of revolutionary times as *ḥizb al-sulṭān*, to the republicanists as *ḥizb al-mashyakha*, to the Montagnards as *ḥizb al-jabal*, and so forth, although technically accurate, must have been largely meaningless and indistinguishable from "groups" loosely understood. See e.g. Turk, p. 4; Shihābī, p. 218; Abū al-Suʿūd, *Naẓm*, p. 187; Qāsim, p. 253.

50. E.g. *ʿUṭārid*, 6 Nov 1858, p. 2; *Ḥadīqat al-akhbār*, 28 Dec 1865, pp. 1, 2; *al-Jinān*, 1870, p. 332; 1885, p. 646; *Muntakhabāt al-jawāʾib*, vol. 5, p. 130; *al-Ahrām*, 7 Apr 1877, p. 2; *al-Jawāʾib*, 22 Nov 1877, p. 4; *al-Naḥla*, 20 Sep 1877, pp. 98–101; *al-Bashīr*, 18 Jan 1878, p. 1; *al-Baṣṣīr*, 18 Aug 1881, p. 1; *al-ʿUrwa al-wuthqā*, 20 Mar 1884, p. 46; *al-Laṭāʾif*, 1887–1888, p. 137; *al-Muqaṭṭam*, 9 Apr 1889, pp. 1–2.

51. E.g. *ʿUṭārid*, 6 Nov 1858, p. 2; *Ḥadīqat al-akhbār*, 22 Jan 1859, p. 1; 11 June 1859, p. 2; 21 July 1859, p. 2; *al-Jawāʾib*, 17 May 1870, pp. 5, 6; *al-Bashīr*, 18 Mar 1871, p. 239; 15 Apr 1871, p. 280; 8 July 1871, p. 401; 4 Nov 1871, p. 571; 18 Jan 1878, p. 1; 1 Mar 1882, p. 1; *Muntakhabāt al-jawāʾib*, vol. 2, p. 191; vol. 5, p. 130; *al-Jinān*, 1872, p. 28; 1874, pp. 481–84, 688–89, 836–39; 1879, pp. 97, 161; 1885, pp. 198, 417, 641; Khūrī-Shiḥāda (geography), pt. 1, pp. 2, 43; *al-Ahrām*, 9 Aug 1878, p. 1; 13 Dec 1878, p. 1; 20 Dec 1878, p. 1; *al-Janna*, 6 Aug 1880, p. 2; 2 Sep 1881, p. 1; *al-Baṣṣīr*, 21 Apr 1881, p. 1; Isḥaq, *Durar*, p. 81; *al-ʿUrwa al-wuthqā*, 20 Mar 1884, pp. 46, 47; 3 Apr 1884, p. 103; *al-Iʿlām*, 17 Jan 1885, p. 1; *al-Laṭāʾif*, 1887–1888, pp. 137, 197–99; *al-Ustādh*, 4 Jan 1893, p. 459.

52. Ṭahṭāwī, *Takhlīṣ*, p. 252; Abū al-Suʿūd, *Naẓm*, p. 186; Isḥaq, *Durar*, p. 161; *al-Jinān*, 1885, pp. 26, 27, 100; Abū naẓẓāra, 24 July 1886. See also *al-Hilāl*, Oct 1893, p. 66, where the author explains that "the [British] Conservative [Party] is their *jamāʿa* of *ashrāf* and *aʿyān*."

53. Schölch, pp. 120–27.

54. Naqqāsh, vol. 7, pp 44–45. Also quoted by Elie Kedourie, *Arabic Political Memoirs and Other Studies* (London, 1974), p. 28.

55. *Al-Hilāl*, Apr 1899, p. 397.

Conclusion

1. Lozano, p. 62.

2. Ṭahṭāwī, *Qalāʾid*, pt. 1, p. 27; Maḥmūd, vol. 3, pp. 37ff. (cf. Robertson, vol. 4, pp. 247ff.)

3. Ṭahṭāwī, *Manāhij*, p. 350; idem, *Taʿrībāt*, appendix, p. 69. For similar occurrences of this loan-word, see for example idem, *Takhlīṣ*, p. 259; idem in

al-Waqā'i *al-Miṣriyya*, 1842, no. 623, quoted by Ḥamza, vol. 1, pp. 117–18; Zarābī, *Bidāya*, p. 90; *ʿUṭārid*, 9 Oct 1858, pp. 1, 2; 16 Oct 1858, p. 1; 30 Oct 1858, p. 2; 6 Nov 1858, p. 1; *al-Jarīda al-ʿaskariyya al-Miṣriyya*, 1865, pt. 1, p. 32; *al-Naḥla*, 1 Dec 1877, pp. 189–91; *al-Bashīr*, 16 Apr 1885, p. 4; Nawwār, p. 363 (and see Nawwār's remarks on p. 362).

4. Stetkevych, p. 37.

Sources

Dictionaries, Lexicons and Glossaries

al-ᶜAsqalānī, Shihāb al-Dīn. *Nuzhat al-albāb fī al-alqāb*. N.p., 912/1506. British Library MS. no. Add.7351.

Badawī, A. Zakī. *A Dictionary of the Social Sciences*. Beirut, 1978.

Badger, George Percy. *An English Arabic Lexicon*. London, 1881.

Barbier de Meynard, A. C. *Dictionnaire turc-français*. 2 vols. Paris, 1886.

Belot, Jean Baptiste. *Dictionnaire français-arabe*. Beirut, 1890.

————. *Petit dictionnaire français-arabe*. Beirut, 1892.

————. *Vocabulaire arabe-français*. 2nd ed. Beirut, 1888.

Berggren, J. *Guide français-arabe vulgaire*. Upsala, Sweden 1844.

Bianchi, T. X. *Dictionnaire français-turc*. 2nd ed. 2 vols. Paris, 1843–1846.

————. *Vocabulaire français-turc*. Paris, 1831.

———— and J. D. Kieffer. *Dictionnaire turc-français*. 2 vols. Paris, 1850.

Biberstein-Kazimirski, A[lbert] de. *Dictionnaire arabe-français*. 4 vols. Paris, 1846. Revised ed., Paris, 1860.

Bocthor, Ellious. *Dictionnaire français-arabe*. 2 vols. Paris, 1828–1829. 2nd ed., Paris, 1849; 4th ed., Paris, 1869.

al-Bustānī, Buṭrus. *Muḥīṭ al-muḥīṭ*. 2 vols. Beirut, 1870.

Cameron, Donald. *An Arabic-English Vocabulary*. London, 1892.

al-Dahsha, Nūr al-Dīn. *Tuḥfat dhawī al-arab fī mushkil al-asimā' walnasab*. N.p., 908/1502. British Library MS. no. Add.7351.

165

Dozy, R. *Supplément aux dictionnaires arabes.* 2 vols. Leiden, 1881.

al-Fīrūzābādī, Majd al-Dīn. *al-Qāmūs al-muḥīṭ.* 2 vols. Cairo, 1855.

Freytag, Georg Wilhelm Friedrich. *Lexicon Arabico-Latinum.* 4 vols. Halis, Saxony, 1830–1837.

Golius, Jacobus. *Lexicon Arabico-Latinum Contextum ex Probatioribus Orientis Lexicographis.* Amsterdam, 1653.

Habeiche, Joseph J. *Dictionnaire français-arabe.* 2 vols. Cairo, 1890.

Handjèri, Alexandre. *Dictionnaire français-arabe-persan et turc.* Moscow, 1840–1841.

Hindoglu, Artin. *Dictionnaire abrégé français-turc.* Vienna, 1831.

——— *Dictionnaire abrégé turc-français.* Vienna, 1838.

Humbert, Jean. *Guide de la conversation arabe ou vocabulaire français-arabe.* Paris and Geneva, 1838.

Ibn Manẓūr, Muḥammad ibn al-Mukarram. *Lisān al-ᶜArab.* 20 vols. Cairo, 1300–1307/1883–1890.

al-Jawāliqī, Mawhūb ibn Aḥmad. *Al-muᶜarrab min al-kalam al-aᶜjamī ᶜalā ḥurūf al-muᶜajjam.* Leipzig, 1867.

Johnson, Francis. *Dictionary, Persian, Arabic and English.* London, 1852.

Lane, Edward William. *An Arabic English Lexicon.* 8 vols. London, 1863–1893.

[*Lisān al-ᶜArab*—see Ibn Manẓūr].

Marcel, Jean Jacques. *Vocabulaire français-arabe des dialects vulgaires africaines; d'Alger, de Tunis, de Maroc et d'Egypt.* Paris, 1837. 2nd ed., Paris, 1869. 5th ed., Paris, 1885.

Meninski, Franciszek. *Lexicon Arabico-Persico-Turcicum.* Vienna, 1680. Revised ed., 1780.

Onions, Charles Talbut, G. W. S. Friedrichsen and R. W. Burchfield. *The Oxford Dictionary of English Etymology.* New York and Oxford, 1966.

Pakalin, M. Z. *Osmanli Tarih Deyimleri ve Terimleri Sözlüğü.* 3 vols. Istanbul, 1946–1956.

[*al-Qāmūs al-muḥīṭ*—see al-Fīrūzābādī].

Redhouse, James W. *A Turkish and English Lexicon.* Istanbul, 1891.

Richardson, John. *A Dictionary, English, Persian and Arabic.* Oxford, 1780. Revised ed., 1810.

———. *A Dictionary, Persian, Arabic and English.* 2 vols. Oxford, 1771–1780; Oxford, 1777. Revised eds., London, 1806 and 1829.

Ruphy, Jean Francois. *Dictionnaire abrégé français-arabe.* Paris, 1802.

Salmoné, H. Anthony. *Arabic-English Dictionary on a New System.* 2 vols. London, 1890.

Schiaparelli, C. *Vocabulista in Arabico.* Florence, 1871.

Steingass, Francis Joseph. *Arabic-English Dictionary.* London, 1884.

al-Tahānawī, Muḥammad Aʿlā ibn ʿAlī. *Kashshāf iṣṭilāḥāt al-funūn.* 2 vols. Calcutta, 1862.

Zenker, Julius Theodore. *Turkisch-Arabisch-Persisches Handwörterbuch.* 2 vols. Leipzig, 1886–1876.

Pre-Nineteenth-Century Arabic and Turkish Sources

Abū al-Fidā'. *Taqwīm al-buldān.* Ed. M. Reinard and Mac Gukin de Slane. Paris, 1840.

Amari, Michele, ed. *Biblioteca Arabo-Sicula.* Leipzig, 1856.

Badawī, ʿAbd al-Raḥmān, ed. *Arīsṭūṭālis: al-khiṭāba; al-tarjama al-ʿArabiyya al-qadīma.* Cairo, 1959.

————, ed. *Al-Uṣūl al-Yūnāniyya lil-naẓariyyāt al-siyāsiyya fī al-Islām.* Cairo, 1954.

De Castries, Henri. *Les sources inédites de l'histoire de Maroc de 1530 à 1845.* 21 vols. Paris, 1905–1960.

al-Farābī, Abū Nāṣir. *Ārā' ahl al-madīna al-fāḍila.* Ed. Friedrich Dietrici. Leiden, 1895.

————. *Al-Siyāsa al-madaniyya.* Hyderabad, 1931.

Ferīdūn, Aḥmed. *Münşe'āt-i Selāṭīn.* 2 vols. Istanbul, 1857–1858.

Ibn Bājja, Abū Bakr ibn al-Ṣā'igh. *Tadbīr al-mutawaḥḥid.* Ed. Don Miguel Asin Palacios. Madrid, 1946.

Ibn Ḥawqal, Abū al-Qāsim al-Nusaybī. *Kitāb ṣūrat al-arḍ.* In *Bibliotheca Geographicorum Arabicorum.* Leiden, 1938.

Ibn al-ʿIbrī, Ghrighūryūs bin Ahrūn. *Ta'rīkh mukhtaṣar al-duwal.* Beirut, 1958.

Ibn Khaldūn, ʿAbd al-Raḥmān. *Muqaddima.* 3rd print. Beirut, 1900.

Ibn Khuradadhbih, ʿUbayd Allāh ibn ʿAbd Allāh. *Al-Masālik walmamālik.* Ed. C. Barbier de Meynard. Paris, 1865.

Ibn Saʿīd, ʿAlī ibn Mūsā. *Kitāb al-jughrāfiyya.* Ed. Ismāʿīl al-ʿArabī. Beirut, 1970.

al-Khwārizmī, Abū ʿAbd Allāh Muḥammad. *Mafātīḥ al-ʿulūm.* Ed. G. Van Vloten. Leiden, 1895.

Korkut, Besim, ed. *Al-Wuthā'iq al-ʿArabiyya fī dār al-maḥfūẓāt bimadīnat Dubrūwnik.* 3 vols. Sarajevo, 1960, 1961, 1969.

al-Masʿūdi, Abū al-Ḥasan. *Murūj al-dhahab wa-maʿādin al-jawhar.* Ed. Ch. Pellat. Beirut, 1966. Vol. 3.

————. *al-Tanbīh wal-ishrāf.* Cairo, 1938.

al-Māwardī, ʿAlī ibn Muḥammad. *Al-Aḥkām al-sulṭāniyya.* Cairo, 1298/1880.

al-Qalqashandī, Abū al-ʿAbbās Aḥmad. *Ṣubḥ al-aʿshā.* Cairo, 1915. 14 vols. Index by Muḥammad Qindīl al-Baqlī, Cairo, 1973.

Ṣāʿid ibn Aḥmad al-Andalusī. *Ṭabaqāt al-umam.* Cairo, n.d.

al-Shahrastāni, Muḥammad ʿAbd al-Karīm. *Al-Milal wal-niḥal.* Ed. ʿAbd al-ʿAzīz Muḥammad al-Wakīl. Cairo, 1968.

al-Ṭabarī. *Taʾrīkh al-rusul wal-mulūk.* Ed. M. J. de Goeje. 15 vols. Leiden, 1901.

al-Tawḥīdī, Abū al-Ḥayyān. *Al-Imtāʿ wal-muʾānasa.* Ed. Aḥmad Amīn and Aḥmad Zayn. Cairo, 1939.

al-ʿUmarī, Shihāb al-Dīn. *Kalām jumalī fī amr mashāhir mamālik ʿubbād al-ṣalīb.* Published in: *Atti della R. Accademia dei Lincei 1882– 1883.* 3rd series. Rome, 1883, pp. 67–103.

———. *Al-Taʿrīf bil-muṣṭalaḥ al-sharīf.* Cairo, 1312/1894.

Arabic and Turkish Works from the Nineteenth Century

This section lists the main body of sources explored in this study, with brief annotations. For Arabic translations, the original versions (whenever identifiable) are given, with indications of the editions used here.

Books

ʿAbd al-Sayyid, Mikhāʾīl. *Silwān al-Shajī fī al-radd ʿalā Ibrāhīm al-Yāzijī.* Istanbul, 1872. A part of a controversy between Fāris al-Shidyāq and Ibrāhīm al-Yāzijī, on tasks of Arabic in modern times. Apparently written by Shidyāq himself.

Abū al-Suʿūd, ʿAbd Allāh. *Al-Dars al-tām fī al-taʾrīkh al-ʿāmm.* Cairo, 1879. A history of ancient civilisations, compiled from various European sources.

—————— *Naẓm al-laʾālī' fī al-sulūk fī man ḥakam Faransā min al-mulūk.* Cairo, 1841. A translation of, or accumulation from, unidentified sources on the history of the French monarchy, including one of the earliest Arabic accounts of the French Revolution.

al-ʿAqīqī, Anṭūn Ḍāhir. *Thawra wa-fitna fī Lubnān.* ed. Yūsuf Ibrāhīm Yazbak. Beirut, 194–?. A contemporary account of events in Mount Lebanon from 1841 to 1873.

ʿAṭāullāh Mehmed (known as Şānīzāde.) *Tarīkh-i Şānīzāde.* Istanbul, 1290–1292?/1873–1875? Ottoman history written during the early nineteenth century, by the official imperial historiographer.

Badīr, Muḥammad. *Taʾrīkh ḥiṣār al-Ifranj li-ʿAkkā al-maḥrūsa wa-ḥuṣūl al-naṣr ʿalayhim.* N.p., n.d. Princeton, Garrett Collection, MS. no 623(96H). A poem commemorating al-Jazzār's victory over Bonaparte in Acre.

al-Bājūrī, Maḥmūd ʿUmar. *Al-Durar al-bahiyya fī al-riḥla al-Urubā-wiyya.* Cairo, 1891. The author's impressions from Europe, which he visited en route to the eighth Orientalists' Congress in Stockholm.

al-Bāshā, Qusṭanṭīn. ed. *Mudhakkirāt ta'rīkhiyya.* Beirut, 1926. A chronicle of events in Syria and Palestine during the stormy 1830s and 1840s by an anonymous contemporary observer.

Bayyāᶜ, Muḥammad Muṣṭafā. *Maṭāliᶜ shumūs al-siyar fī waqā'iᶜ Karlūs al-thānī ᶜashar.* Cairo, 1841. A translation of F. M. A. Voltaire's *Histoire de Charles XII, Roi de Suede* (the edition examined: *Histoire; extraits,* Paris, 1911).

al-Bustānī, Buṭrus et al. *Dā'irat al-maᶜārif.* 11 vols. Beirut. Vol. 1, 1876; vol. 2, 1877; vol. 3, 1878; vol. 4, 1880; vol. 5, 1881; vol. 6, 1882; vol. 7, 1883; vol. 8, 1884; vol. 9, 1887; vol. 10, 1890; vol. 11, 1900. A universal encyclopedia begun by Buṭrus al-Bustānī and continued, after his death in 1883, by his relatives Sulaymān, Najīb and Naṣīb. It was never completed; the last volume ends with the letter ᶜayn. Many entries deal with Western history, politics and culture.

Bustrus, Salīm. *Al-Nuzha al-shahiyya fī al-riḥla al-Salīmiyya.* Beirut, 1856. One of the earliest published accounts of a trip to Europe, including visits to Italy, France, England, Belgium, Prussia and other countries.

Calligaris, Louis. *Sīrat Nabulyūn al-awwal.* Paris, 1856. Revised ed., Beirut, 1868. A biography of Napoleon by a French colonel in Tunis. The revision of the book in Beirut included many illuminating changes in language.

Cevdet, Aḥmed. *Ta'rīkh.* 8 vols. Istanbul, 1885. A detailed history of the Ottoman Empire from 1774 to 1826 by the official imperial historiographer.

[*Dā'irat al-Maᶜārif*—see Bustānī, Buṭrus et al.]

al-Dīwān al-khuṣūṣī. Traduction litterale de la lettre écrit en arabe, et adressée par les membres du Divan du Caire au général Bonaparte. Paris, 1801. Arabic and French texts.

Don Raphael (Rafā'īl Anṭūn Zakhkhūr Rāhib). *Kitāb al-amīr.* Cairo, 1824–1825(?). MS. in Dār al-Kutub (Cairo). A translation by an Italian priest of Niccolo Machiavelli's *Il Principe* (used here: a bilingual Italian-English edition by Mark Musa, New York, 1964).

Fikrī, Amīn. *Irshād al-alibbā' ilā maḥāsin Urubā.* Cairo, 1893. A report on a trip in Europe.

al-Ḥarā'irī, Sulaymān. ᶜArḍ al-badā'iᶜ al-ᶜāmm. Paris, 1867. An account of the author's trip to the international trade fair in Paris, in 1866.

Isḥaq, Adīb. *Al-Durar.* Alexandria, 1866. This and the next work are posthumous collections of articles published by one of the more lucid spokesmen of Arab society. Many of them deal with political matters and European–Middle Eastern relations.

——. *Al-Kitābāt al-siyāsiyya wal-ijtimāᶜiyya.* Ed. Nājī ᶜAlūsh. Beirut, 1978. (See above.)

al-Jabartī, ᶜAbd al-Raḥmān. *ᶜAjā'ib al-āthār fī al-tarājim wal-akhbār.* Cairo, 1297/1880. 4 vols. On this and other works by Jabartī, see Introduction.

——. *Maẓhar al-taqdīs bi-dhihāb dawlat al-Fransīs.* Ed. Hasan Muḥammad Jawhar and ᶜUmar al-Dasūqī. Cairo, 1969.

——. *Ta'rīkh muddat al-Fransīs bi-Miṣr, muḥarram-rajab 1213h; 15 June–December 1978m.* Ed. Shmuel Moreh. Leiden, 1975.

al-Jirjāwī, ᶜAlī Aḥmad. *Al-Riḥla al-Yabāniyya.* N.p., 1907. An account of a trip taken to Japan around the turn of the century, by the editor of *al-Irshād.* Includes illuminating remarks on various aspects of Indian and Japanese civilizations.

al-Jubaylī, Ḥasan. *Burhān al-bayān wa-bayān al-burhān fī istikmāl wa-ikhtilāl dawlat al-Rūmān.* Cairo, 1877. A translation of Montesquieu's *Considérations sur les causes de la grandeur des Romaines et de leur décadence,* Paris, 1734.

Kāmil, Muṣṭafā. *Muṣṭafā Kāmil fī 34 rabīᶜan.* Ed. ᶜAlī Fahmī Kāmil. Cairo, 1910. A collection of writings and speeches by the Egyptian nationalist leader around the end of the nineteenth century.

Kanᶜān, Bishāra. *Al-ᶜAlam al-Inklīzī.* Cairo, n.d. (1899 or 1900.) Vol. 1 (out of 2) was studied. A modern history of England.

Khayr al-Dīn al-Tūnisī. *Aqwam al-masālik fī maᶜrifat aḥwāl al-mamālik.* Tunis, 1867. A lucid account of political life in Europe by a leading nineteenth-century Tunisian statesman. The precise source of the detailed intelligence in the book still remains to be identified. The book's introduction was translated into French under Khayr al-Dīn's own supervision; its title, *Réformes nécessaires aux états musulmans,* hints at the author's motives in writing his treatise.

Khilāṭ, Dimitrī. *Sifr al-safar ilā maᶜraḍ al-ḥaḍar.* Cairo, 1891. A report on travels in Europe, with many comments on political institutions and practices.

Khūrī, Ḥunayn Niᶜmat Allāh. *Al-Tuḥfa al-adabiyya fī ta'rīkh tamaddun al-mamālik al-Urubāwiyya.* Alexandria, 1877. A translation of M. F. Guizot's *Histoire de la civilisation en Europe,* Paris, 1846.

al-Khūrī, Salīm Jibrā'īl, and Salīm Mikhā'īl Shiḥāda. *Āthār al-adhār* [herein referred to as: *Āthār (geography)*]. 3 vols. Beirut, 1875. The first three volumes of a projected universal geographical and historical encyclopedia. The project seems to have been cut short at an early stage. See also below.

——. *Āthār al-adhār.* [herein referred to as: *Āthār (history)*]. Beirut,

1877. A volume dealing with historical subjects in the above series.

Lammens, Henri. *Al-Riḥla al-Sūriyya fī Amīrikā al-mutawassiṭa waljanūbiyya*. Translated into Arabic by Rashīd al-Khūrī al-Shartūnī. Beirut, 1894. The original version could not be traced; it was probably never published. The book contains a geographical and historical survey of central and south American countries.

Lāz, Muḥammad. *Qānūn yataʿallaq bi-tartīb wa-niẓām al-mashyakha albaladiyya*. Cairo, 1867. A translation of the Paris municipal code. Parts of the original text are included in: H. Crevier, *Recueil des actes des corps administratifs*, Paris, 1843, vol. 3.

Maḥmūd, Khalīfa. *Itḥāf al-mulūk al-alibā' bi-taqaddum al-jamʿiyyāt bibilād Urubā*. Cairo, 1841. A translation of William Robertson's history of Emperor Charles V. The Arabic rendition was made from the French translation: *L'Histoire du règne de l'Empereur Charles Quint*, 6 volumes, Amsterdam, 1771. The first volume of the Arabic version appeared under the above title; the other three were published nine years later under the name:

———. *Itḥāf mulūk al-zamān bi-ta'rīkh al-imbarāṭūr Shārlikān*. Cairo, 1850.

al-Mardīnī, ʿAbd al-Salām. *Umm al-ʿibar fī dhikr man maḍā wa-marra*. A survey of Islamic history by an early nineteenth-century ʿālim, including an account of the French occupation of Egypt. The chapter on this last subject was reproduced with annotations by Muḥammad Kafāfī, "al-Ḥamla al-faransiyya ʿalā Miṣr fī riwāyāt aḥad al-muʿāṣirīn," in ʿAbd al-Raḥmān al-Badawī, ed., *Ilā Ṭaha Ḥusayn*, Cairo, 1962, pp. 369–96.

Marrāsh, Fransīs. *Ghābat al-ḥaqq*. Aleppo, 1865. An allegory discussing modern ideas such as freedom and equality and their application to Middle Eastern society.

———. *Riḥlat Bārīs*. Beirut, 1867. A short account of the author's impressions from a trip to France.

al-Marṣafī, Ḥusayn. *Risālat al-kalim al-thamān*. Cairo, 1881. A tract on the meaning of eight words: *umma, waṭan, ḥukūma, ʿadl, ẓulm, siyāsa, ḥurriyya* and *tarbiyya*. Despite some surprisingly modern observations, which one would not expect from a prominent ʿālim at the time, the book was little more than an isolated curiosity.

Mishāqa, Mikhā'īl. *Mashhad al-ʿiyān bi-ḥawādith Sūriya wa-Lubnān*. Cairo, 1900. A brief history of Syria and Lebanon by a Greek Catholic Lebanese. The book was completed in 1873.

———. *Muntakhabāt min "al-jawāb ʿalā iqtirāḥ al-aḥbāb"*. Ed. Asad Rustum and Subḥī Abū Shaqrā. Beirut, 1955. Mishāqa's memoires, relating the story of his youth and education in Lebanon and Egypt in the first half of the nineteenth century. He met with and learned from numerous Europeans, about whose civilization he made interesting remarks. The book was completed in the early 1870s.

Mucāhedāt Mecmūcası. 5 vols. Istanbul, 1294–1298/1877–1880. Collected Ottoman documents, mainly international treaties, from the seventeenth, eighteenth and (mainly) nineteenth centuries.

Mubārak, cAlī. *cAlam al-dīn.* 4 vols. Alexandria, 1882. An allegorical dialogue between an Azhari shaykh and a British orientalist, on religio-philosophical and social questions. Written by a leading Egyptian intellectual who was both a product and a shaper of modernization in nineteenth-century Egypt.

Nacām, Sacd. *Siyāḥat Amirīkā.* Cairo, 1845. A translation of M. H. Marquam's *Promenade en Amérique,* Paris, 1838. The book was written for youth.

al-Nadīm, cAbd Allāh. *Sulāfat al-Nadīm.* 2 vols. Cairo, 1901, 1914. A collection of articles by an eloquent spokesman of the cUrābī movement, compiled from his newspapers and manuscripts.

al-Naqqāsh, Salīm Khalīl. *Miṣr lil-Miṣriyīn.* Alexandria, 1884. Vols. 4–9. A detailed account of events in Egypt during the cUrābī revolt and the beginning of British occupation. Includes texts of many documents and speeches.

al-Qalcāwī, Muṣṭafā al-Ṣafawī. *Ṣafwat al-zamān fiman tawallā calā Miṣr min amīr wa-sulṭān.* N.p., ca. 1805. Princeton, Garrett Collection, MS. no. 615(183H). A history of Egyptian government from the Muslim conquest to Muhammad Ali, including brief remarks on the French administration of the country.

Qalfāẓ, Nakhla. *Ta'rīkh Buṭrus al-kabīr* Beirut, 1886. A history of Russia under Peter the Great. It is the first of a four-volume work on modern Russia (*Ta'rīkh Rūsiyā*), apparently an independent compilation of information from various sources.

———. *Ta'rīkh mulūk al-Muslimīn.* Beirut, 1891.

Qāsim, Ḥasan. *Ta'rīkh mulūk Faransā.* Cairo, 1847. A translation of a French book on the history of France, including a remarkably detailed discussion of the French Revolution. The original author (identified by the translator as "Mūnīqūrus") could not be traced.

Riḍā, Muḥammad Rashīd. *Al-Khilāfa aw al-imāma al-cuẓmā.* Cairo, 1922. A discussion of the Caliphate and related issues by the prominent spokesman of the Salafiyya.

———. *Ta'rīkh al-ustādh al-imām al-shaykh Muḥammad cAbduh.* Cairo, 1925. Vol. 2. A panegyric biography of cAbduh by his most famous disciple. Volume 2 is an anthology of cAbduh's own writings.

al-Ṣabbāgh, Mikhā'īl. *Nashīd qaṣīdat tahāni' li-saʿādat al-qayṣar al-muʿaẓẓam Nābūlyūn sulṭān Faransā.* Paris, 1811. A *qaṣīda* to Napoleon I, on the birth of his son.

Ṣāliḥ, Nakhla. *Al-Kanz al-mukhabba' lil-siyāḥa fī-Urubā.* Beirut, 1876. An account of the writer's impressions of several European countries which he visited.

Sāmī, Amīn. *Taqwīm al-nīl.* Cairo, 1928–1936. Parts 2 and 3. A compilation of original state documents in Arabic and Turkish (the latter translated into Arabic) from Egypt in the times of Muhammad Ali, ʿAbbās, Saʿīd and Ismāʿīl.

Ṣannūʿ, Yaʿqūb. *Al-Badā'iʿ al-maʿraḍiyya bi-Bārīs al-bahiyya.* Paris, 1899. A description of Paris, with brief historical remarks.

———. *Ḥusn al-ishāra fī musāmarāt abī naẓẓāra.* Cairo, 1910. Ṣannūʿ's impressions from the 1900 international fair in Paris, with a survey of French history, culture and daily life.

———. *Maḥāmid al-Fransīs wa-waṣf Bārīs.* Paris, 1890. A translation of E. N. Felumb, *La France et Paris* (original version unavailable).

Sarkīs, Khalīl. *Riḥlat mudīr al-Lisān Khalīl Sarkīs ilā al-Asitāna wa-Ūrūbā wa-Amirīkā.* Beirut, 1893. A travel account by the editor of *Lisān al-ḥāl.*

Sharīf, Muḥammad. *Riḥla ilā Ūrūba.* Cairo, 1888. In 7 parts. An assemblage of geographical, historical and other data on Europe and its civilization.

al-Sharqāwī, ʿAbd Allāh. *Tuḥfat al-nāẓirīn fiman waliya Miṣr min al-wulāt wal-salāṭīn.* Cairo, 1864. A chronology of government in Egypt from ancient times up to Muhammad Ali, by a leading Egyptian ʿālim. Including brief but highly illuminating remarks on the French Revolution and French government in Egypt.

al-Shidyāq, Aḥmad Fāris. *al-Bakūra al-shāhiyya fī naḥw al-lugha al-Inklīziyya.* Istanbul, 1883. An English grammar book, appended with an English-Arabic word list.

———. *Kashf al-mukhabba' ʿan funūn Ūrūba.* Istanbul, 1883. An account of the author's sojourn in England and France between 1848 and 1852, with interesting observations on various aspects of European culture.

———. *Al-Sāq ʿalā al-sāq fimā huwwa al-faryāq.* Paris, 1855. An autobiography written in rich Arabic style, with occasional references to Western social and political affairs.

———. *Al-Wāsiṭa fī maʿrifat Māliṭa.* Istanbul, 1883. A summary of Shidyāq's impressions during his stay in Malta in the mid-1840s.

al-Shidyāq, Ṭannūs. *Akhbār al-aʿyān fī jabal Lubnān.* Beirut, 1859. A history of the chief landlord families in Lebanon.

al-Shihābī, Ḥaydar Aḥmad. *Lubnān fī ʿahd al-umarā' al-Shihābiyyīn.* Beirut, 1933. A history of Lebanon under the Shihābīs, including a discussion of events in Europe in the late eighteenth and early nineteenth centuries (see Introduction).

Shiḥāda, Buṭrus Ilyās. *Ta'rīkh Amirīkā*. Beirut, 1881. The story of the discovery of America, with a brief epilogue on later developments. Apparently an independent work.

Ṣufayr, Yūsuf. *Majālī al-ghurar li-kuttāb al-qarn al-tāsiʿ ʿashar*. Baʿabdā, 1898. A compilation of articles, speeches and letters by prominent nineteenth-century Arab writers, such as Adīb Isḥaq, Buṭrus al-Bustānī, and Fransīs Marrrāsh.

al-Ṭahṭāwī, Aḥmad ʿUbayd. *Al-Rawḍ al-azhar fī ta'rīkh Buṭrus al-akbar*. Cairo, 1849. A translation of Voltaire's *Histoire de l'empire de Russie sous Pierre le Grand*, n.p. 1759–1763. 2 vols.

al-Ṭahṭāwī, Rifāʿa Rāfiʿ. *Anwār tawfīq al-jalīl fī akhbār Miṣr wa-tawthīq banī Ismāʿīl*. 2 vols. Cairo, 1868. A history of ancient Egypt before and during the rise of Islam.

———. *Al-Jughrāfiyya al-ʿumūmiyya*. 3 vols. Cairo, 1843. An adaptation of C. Malte-Bruun's *Précis de la géographie universelle*, 8 vols. Paris, 1810–1829.

———. *Muqaddima waṭaniyya Miṣriyya*. Cairo, 1866. A short patriotic tract written mostly in *sajʿ* (rhymed prose).

———. *Al-Kanz al-mukhtār fī kashf al-arāḍī wal-biḥār*. Cairo, 1834. A condensed geographical, historical and political survey of the world, country by country, written in the didactic question-and-answer style.

———. *Manāhij al-albāb al-Miṣriyya fī mabāhij al-ādāb al-ʿaṣriyya*. 3rd ed., Cairo. 1912. First published in 1873 (the year of Ṭahṭāwī's death), this is a summary statement of his social and political philosophy.

———. *Al-Murshid al-amīn lil-banāt wal-banīn*. In Muḥammad ʿImāra, ed., *al-Aʿmāl al-kāmila li-Rifāʿa Rāfiʿ al-Ṭahṭāwī*, Vol. 2, Beirut, 1973. A general work on education, first published in 1872.

———. *Qalā'id al-mafākhir fī gharīb ʿawā'id al-awā'il wal-awākhir*. Cairo, 1833. One of Ṭahṭāwī's earliest translations, of G. B. Depping's *Aperçu historique sur les moeurs et coutumes des nations*, Paris, 1826. Ṭahṭāwī appended to it a detailed glossary, over a hundred pages long, providing background information on many matters of world geography, history and culture.

———. *Takhlīṣ al-ibrīz ilā talkhīṣ Bārīz*. Ed. Mahdī ʿAlān, Aḥmad Aḥamd Badawī and Anwār Lūqā. Cairo, 1958. Ṭahṭāwī's famous account of his five-year sojourn in Paris, with extensive observations on French history, political system, society and culture.

———. *Al-Taʿrībāt al-shāfiyya li-murīd al-jughrāfiyya*. Cairo, 1843. A book on world geography, compiled from various sources, which is a mine of intelligence on the history, government and religions of the world. This work, like Ṭahṭāwī's *Qalā'id*, is appended with a glossary of geographical and political terms.

———, et al. *Al-Qānūn al-Faransāwī al-madanī*. 2 vols. Cairo, 1866. A translation of *Code Napoleon*, Paris, 1807.

al-Ṭarābulusī, Nawfal Niʿmat Allāh. *Zubdat al-ṣaḥā'if fī siyāḥat al-maʿārif*. Beirut, 1879. A history of world civilization. One of the more lucid statements on the West in Arabic in the nineteenth century.

Tawfīq, Ḥasan. *Rasā'il al-bushrā fī al-siyāḥa bi-Almāniyā wa-Swisīrā*. Cairo, 1891. The author, an instructor of Arabic in Berlin, relates his impressions from travels in Germany and Switzerland.

———. *Al-Riḥla ilā madīnat Birlīn*. Cairo, 1887–1889. 13 parts. The author's impressions from his sojourn in Berlin.

al-Turk, Niqūlā. *Mudhakkirāt*. Ed. and trans. Gaston Wiet. Cairo, 1950. A chronicle of Egypt under French occupation and Bonaparte's expedition to Syria, with occasional remarks on contemporary European events (see Introduction).

al-Yāzijī, Ibrāhīm. *Mukhtārāt*. Beirut, 1950. A selection from the works of the eminent nineteenth-century Lebanese writer.

Zakī, Aḥmad. *Al-Dunyā fī Bārīs*. Cairo, 1900. An account of the author's impressions from a brief visit to the Paris international fair of 1899.

———. *Al-Safar ilā al-mu'tamar*. Cairo, 1893. Views on Europe, based on the author's travel through the continent on his way to the ninth Orientalists' Congress in London.

al-Zarābī, Muṣṭafā Sayyid Aḥmad. *Bidāyat al-qudamā' wa-hidāyat al-ḥukamā'*. Cairo, 1838. A compilation of translated French texts, originally prepared by Ṭahṭāwī, on the ancient history of Greece, Rome and the Near East.

———. *Qurrat al-nufūs wal-ʿuyūn bi-siyar ma tawassāṭ min al-qurūn*. 2 vols. Cairo, 1846. A relatively faithful Arabic rendition of C. U. Desmichels' *Histoire général du Moyen Âge*, Paris, 1835, 1837, in 2 volumes.

Zaydān, Jurjī. *Ta'rīkh Injiltira ilā al-dawla al-Yūrkiyya*. Cairo, 1899. A brief history of the English monarchy to the fifteenth century.

Newspapers and Periodicals

Details given for each item are arranged in the following order: name of source; years examined, in parentheses; name of first editor (usually the paper's founder); place of publication and year first issued; frequency of publication; remarks.

Abū nazzāra (1878–1890; 1898–1899). Ya'qūb Ṣannū'; Cairo and Paris, 1877; irregular. An illustrated political-satirical journal, which appeared variably under different titles (*Abū nazzāra zarqā, Abū zammāra, al-Nazzārāt al-Miṣriyya, al-Tawaddud, al-Waṭanī al-Miṣrī* and more). The text was handwritten, in colloquial Arabic, and usually arranged as a dialogue between the editor and imaginary figures.

al-Ahrām (1876–1900). Salīm and Bishāra Taqlā; Alexandria, 1876, (since 1898 published in Cairo); weekly, then daily. Almost from the start one of Egypt's leading newspapers.

A'māl al-jam'iyya al-Sūriyya (1852). Beirut, 1852. An organ of the Syrian Society; irregular.

al-Arghūl (1896–1897). Muḥammad al-Najjār; Cairo, 1894; biweekly. A literary and political magazine.

al-'Aṣr al-jadīd (1881). Salīm Naqqāsh; Alexandria, 1880; weekly. A political journal; ephemeral.

al-Bashīr (1870–1871; 1878–1900). An organ of the Jesuit Fathers; Beirut, 1870; weekly. An important and influential journal, which discussed European politics extensively.

al-Baṣṣīr (1881–1882). Khalīl Ghānim; Paris, 1881; weekly; ephemeral.

al-Bayyān (1897–1898). Ibrāhīm al-Yāzijī and Bishāra Zalzāl; Cairo, 1897; biweekly. A literary journal.

Birjīs Bārīs (1859–1866). Rushayd al-Daḥdāḥ; Paris, 1858; daily. A widely circulated newspaper. After 1860 appeared also in an Arabic-French bilingual edition.

Dalīl Miṣr (1889–1891). Yūsuf Āsaf and Qayṣar Naṣr; Cairo, 1889. A yearbook of general information.

Ḍiyā' al-khāfiqayn (1892–1893). A. H. Salmoné; London, 1892; monthly. Ephemeral.

al-Fayyūm (1895). Ibrāhīm Ramzī; Fayyūm, 1894; irregular. Ephemeral.

Ḥadīqat al-akhbār (1858–1868). Khalīl al-Khūrī; Beirut, 1858; weekly. The first private political newspaper in the Arab lands, and one of the most influential. Published during much of the time under Ottoman patronage.

al-Hilāl (1892–1900). Jurjī Zaydān; Cairo, 1892; monthly. One of the most important Arabic literary and cultural magazines.

al-I'lām (1885–1889). Muḥammad Bayram; Cairo, 1885; weekly. A pro-British political journal.

al-Insān (1884). Ḥasan Ḥusnī Bāshā al-Tuwayrānī; Istanbul, 1884; bi-weekly. A cultural and scientific journal; ephemeral.

al-Ittiḥād (1880). Ibrāhīm al-Muwayliḥī; Paris, 1880; weekly. An Arabic-Turkish bilingual political journal; ephemeral.

al-Jāmi'a (1902). Faraḥ Anṭūn; Alexandria, 1899; biweekly. A literary and political journal by a prominent Lebanese intellectual; ephemeral.

al-Jāmiᶜa al-ᶜUthmāniyya (1899). Faraḥ Anṭūn; Alexandria, 1899; irregular. Ephemeral.

al-Janna (1879–1884). Salīm al-Bustānī; Beirut, 1870; semiweekly. A broadly circulated political and cultural newspaper.

al-Jarīda al-ᶜaskariyya al-Miṣriyya (1865). Cairo, 1865. An official bulletin of the Egyptian army. A single issue in the collection of Dār al-Kutub, Cairo.

al-Jawā'ib (1868–1884). Aḥmad Fāris al-Shidyāq; Istanbul, 1860; semiweekly. Perhaps the most influential Arabic newspaper of the time, published by one of the more astute Lebanese intellectuals under Ottoman patronage. Selections were published between 1871 and 1880 in 7 volumes, under the title: *Kanz al-gharā'ib fī muntakhabāt al-jawā'ib*.

al-Jinān (1870–1886). Buṭrus al-Bustānī; Beirut, 1870; biweekly. One of the earliest and most important Arabic political, cultural and scientific periodicals.

Kashf al-niqāb (1894–1895). Amīn Arslān; Paris, 1894; weekly. Ephemeral.

Kawkab al-mashriq (1882–1883). ᶜAbd Allāh Marrāsh; Paris, 1882; monthly. An Arabic-French bilingual journal; ephemeral.

al-Laṭā'if (1887–1896). Shāhīn Makaryūs; Cairo, 1886; monthly. Organ of the Egyptian Free Masons. A historical, cultural and political journal.

Madrasat al-funūn (1882–1883). Ḥamīd Wahbī; Istanbul, 1882; monthly. An Arabic-Turkish bilingual, philosophical, historical and scientific journal.

al-Manār (1898–1900). Rashīd Riḍā; Cairo, 1898; 10 issues per year. An important literary, cultural and political journal, published by the ideologue of the Salafiyya.

al-Mawsūᶜāt (1898–1900). Aḥmad Ḥāfiẓ ᶜAwaḍ; Cairo, 1898; biweekly. A cultural and literary journal; ephemeral.

Miṣr al-qāhira (1879–1880). Adīb Isḥaq; Paris, 1879; weekly, then daily. An important newspaper, but short-lived.

al-Mu'ayyad (1900). ᶜAlī Yūsuf and Aḥmad Māḍī; Cairo, 1889; daily. An anti-British and pro-khedivial newspaper, of central importance in Egypt's political life of the time.

[*Muntakhabāt al-jawā'ib* (1871–1880). See *al-Jawā'ib*.]

Muntakhabāt al-mu'ayyad (1890). A collection of articles from the first volume of *al-Mu'ayyad*.

al-Muqaṭṭam (1889–1900). Fāris Nimr and Yaᶜqūb Ṣarrūf; Cairo, 1889; daily. A pro-British newspaper, of considerable influence since its foundation.

al-Muqtaṭaf (1876–1900). Fāris Nimr and Yaᶜqūb Ṣarrūf; Beirut, 1876; moved to Cairo in 1884; monthly. A cultural and scientific journal which played a major role in the region's intellectual life.

al-Mushīr (1895–1898). Salīm Sarkīs; Alexandria, 1894; weekly. A political, anti-Ottoman journal.

al-Naḥla (1870; 1877–1880). Louis Ṣābunjī; Beirut, 1870 and London, 1877; biweekly, then monthly. The London periodical was bilingual, Arabic-English. A cultural and political, anti-Ottoman journal.

Nafīr Sūriya (1860–1861). Buṭrus al-Bustānī; Beirut. Eleven issues were published between September 1860 and April 1861, during the Mount Lebanon events. The main theme was a modern type of *ḥubb al-waṭan*, defined as "Syrian" patriotism.

al-Nashra al-usbūʿiyya (1871–1873; 1877; 1885–1886; 1888; 1891–1900). Beirut, 1871; weekly. Organ of the American missionaries in Beirut, edited by Henri Jessup, which devoted much space to discussing political matters.

al-Naẓẓārāt al-Miṣriyya (1879–1880). Yaʿqūb Sannūʿ. See *Abū naẓẓāra*.

al-Nūr al-tawfīqī (1881–1889). Dimitrī Markūnas; Cairo, 1888; biweekly. A cultural and historical journal; ephemeral.

al-Qāhira (1885–1886). Salīm Fāris; Cairo, 1885; biweekly, then daily. An important newspaper, edited by Aḥmad Fāris al-Shidyāq's son. In 1886 the editor closed it down, to replace it with *al-Qāhira al-ḥurra* (see below).

al-Qāhira al-ḥurra (1886–1888). Salīm Fāris and Najīb Hindiyya; Cairo, 1886; daily. An anti-British and anti-Ottoman newspaper which offered extensive coverage of foreign affairs.

al-Ra'īs (1900). Louis al-Khāzin and Ibrāhīm al-Ḥawrānī; Junya, 1900; monthly. Ephemeral.

al-Rajā' (1895; 1898–1899). Alexius Kātib; Paris, 1895; weekly. Ephemeral.

al-Ra'y al-ʿāmm (1894; 1896–1897). Iskandar Shāhīn; Cairo, 1893; weekly. A cultural and political journal.

al-Ṣadā (1876–1877). Jibrā'īl Dallāl; Paris, 1876; biweekly. An Arabic-French bilingual journal; ephemeral.

al-Tankīt wal-tabkīt (1881). ʿAbd Allāh al-Nadīm; Alexandria, 1881; weekly. A satirical-political newspaper by the spokesman of the ʿUrābī movement; ephemeral.

al-Tawaddud (1878–1880; 1888–1889; 1894–1898; 1898–1899). Yaʿqūb Sannūʿ. See *Abū naẓẓāra*.

Thamarāt al-funūn (1875–1882; 1889–1897). ʿAbd al-Qādir al-Qabbānī; Beirut, 1875; weekly. The first Muslim newspaper in Beirut, published under Ottoman patronage. Widely circulated and influential among Muslims.

al-ʿUrwa al-wuthqā (1884). Jamāl al-Dīn al-Afghānī and Muḥammad ʿAbduh; Paris, 1884; irregular. Eighteen issues of this famous political organ were published.

al-Ustādh (1892–1893). ᶜAbd Allāh al-Nadīm; Cairo, 1892; weekly. A literary and political journal; ephemeral.

ᶜUṭārid (1858–1859). Manṣūr Carletti; Marseille, 1858; weekly. One of the earliest Arabic newspapers; ephemeral.

Wādī al-nīl (1868–1870). ᶜAbd Allāh Abū al-Suᶜūd; Cairo, 1866; semi-weekly. The first nonofficial newspaper in Egypt, which was, however, heavily supported by the Khedive.

al-Waṭanī al-Miṣri (1883). Yaᶜqūb Sannūᶜ. See *Abū naẓẓāra*.

al-Waqāʾiᶜ al-Miṣriyya (1828–1833). Official organ of Muhammad Ali's government, Cairo, 1828; semiweekly. First Arabic newspaper; bilingual; Arabic-Turkish. Discussed local matters and, to some extent, political affairs abroad.

Secondary Sources

ᶜAbd al-Karīm, Muḥammad ᶜIzzat. *Taʾrīkh al-taᶜlīm fī ᶜaṣr Muḥammad ᶜAlī.* Cairo, 1938.

ᶜAbduh, Ibrāhīm. *Taṭawwur al-ṣiḥāfa al-Miṣriyya 1798–1951.* Cairo, 1951.

Abu Lughod, Ibrahim. *Arab Rediscovery of Europe.* Princeton, 1963.

Ahmed, Jamal Mohammed. *The Intellectual Origins of Egyptian Nationalism.* London, 1960.

Alwan, Mohammed Bakir. *Ahmad Faris Ash-Shidyaq and the West.* Bloomington, Indiana, 1970.

Arnold, Thomas W. *The Caliphate.* With a concluding chapter by Sylvia Haim. New York, 1966.

ᶜAwaḍ, Aḥmad Ḥāfiẓ. *Fatḥ Miṣr al-ḥadīth aw Nābulyūn Būnābārt fī Miṣr.* Cairo, 1925.

ᶜAwaḍ, Luwis. *Taʾrīkh al-fikr al-Miṣrī al-ḥadīth.* 2 vols. Cairo, 1969.

Ayalon, Ami. "The Arab discovery of America in the nineteenth century." *MES* 20 (Oct 1984), pp. 5–17.

———. "Dimuqrāṭiyya, ḥurriyya, jumhūriyya: The modernization of the Arabic political vocabulary." *Arabica*, forthcoming.

———. "Semantics and the modern history of non-European societies: Arab 'republics' as a case-study." *The Historical Journal 28* (1985), pp. 821–34.

Ayalon, David. *The Mamluk Military Society.* Collected studies. London, 1979.

———. *Studies on the Mamluks of Egypt (1250–1517).* Collected studies. London, 1977.

ᶜAzīz, Sāmī. *Al-ṣiḥāfa al-Miṣriyya wa-mawqifuhā min al-iḥtilāl al-Injlīzī.* Cairo, 1968.

Badawī, Aḥmad Aḥmad. *Rifāᶜa al-Ṭahṭāwī bak.* Cairo, 1950.

Baer, Gabriel. *Studies in the Social History of Modern Egypt.* Chicago, 1969.

Bagehot, Walter. *The English Constitution and Other Political Essays.* New York, 1924.

al-Bāshā, Ḥasan. *Al-Alqāb al-Islāmiyya fī al-ta'rīkh wal-wathā'iq wal-āthār.* Cairo, 1957.

―――. *Al-Funūn al-Islāmiyya wal-waẓā'if, ᶜalā al-āthār al-ᶜArabiyya.* 3 vols. Cairo, 1966.

Beeston, A. F. L. *The Arabic Language Today.* London, 1970.

Beg, M. A. J. "Al-Khāṣṣa wal-ᶜāmma." *EI².*

Berkes, Niyazi. *The Development of Secularism in Turkey.* Montreal, 1964.

Blochet, E. "Apropos du Hizb." *Revue du Monde Musulman* 14 (1911), pp. 110–19.

Bodman, Herbert Luther. *Political Factions in Aleppo 1760–1826.* North Carolina, 1963.

Boseworth, C. E. "The titulature of the early Ghaznavids." *Oriens* 15 (1962), pp. 210–33.

Boustani, Saladin. *The Journals of Bonaparte in Egypt 1798–1801.* Cairo, 197–?. Vol. 9.

Bowen, Harold. 'Aᶜyān." *EI².*

Braude, Benjamin. "Foundation myths of the *Millet* system." In *Christians and Jews in the Ottoman Empire,* edited by Benjamin Braude and Bernard Lewis, vol. 1, pp. 69–88. New York, 1982.

Cahen, Claude. "Djaysh." *EI².*

―――. "L'Évolution de l'Iqtaᶜ du IXᵉ au XIIIᵉ siècle." *Annales* 8 (1952), pp. 25–52.

―――. "Iḳṭāᶜ." *EI².*

―――. "Y a-t-il des corporations professionnelles dans le monde musulman classique?" In *The Islamic City,* edited by Albert Hourani and S. M. Stern, pp. 51–63. Oxford, 1970.

Chelhod, J. "Ḳabīla." *EI².*

Davison, H. Roderic. "The advent of the principle of representation in the government of the Ottoman Empire." In *Beginnings of Modernization in the Middle East in the Nineteenth Century,* edited by William R. Polk and Richard L. Chambers, pp. 93–108. Chicago, 1968.

―――. *Reform in the Ottoman Empire 1856–1876.* Princeton, 1963.

Defrémery, M. "Mémoire sur les Emir al-Oméra." In *Mémoires présentés par divers savants à l'académie,* ser. 1, vol. 2, pp. 105–96. Academie des inscriptions et belles-lettres, Paris, 1852.

Delanoue, Gilbert. "L'Epître des huit mots' du cheikh Ḥusayn al-Marṣafī." *Annales Islamologiques* 5 (1963), pp. 1–29.

Deny, J. *Sommaire des archives turques du Caire.* Cairo, 1930.

Devereux, Robert. *The First Ottoman Constitutional Period.* Baltimore, 1963.

Dowdall, H. C. "The word 'state'." *Law Quarterly Review* 39 (1923), pp. 98–125.

Dubois, Jean. *Vocabulaire politique et social en France de 1869 à 1872.* Paris, 1962.

Duguit, L., H. Monnier and R. Bonnard. *Les constitutions et les principales lois politiques de la France depuis 1789.* 7th ed. Paris, 1952.

Dūrī, ᶜAbd al-ᶜAzīz. "Dīwān-i." *EI².*

——. *al-Nuẓum al-Islāmiyya.* Baghdad, 1950. Vol. 1.

Duverger, Maurice. *Constitutions et documents politiques.* 5th ed. Paris, 1968.

Fāris, Bishr. "Ta'rīkh lafẓat al-sharaf." In his *Mabāḥith ᶜArabiyya.* Cairo, 1939.

Findley, Carter V. *Bureaucratic Reform in the Ottoman Empire: The Sublime Porte 1789–1922.* Princeton, 1980.

——. "Madjlis al-shūrā." *EI².*

Frey, Max. *Les transformations du vocabulaire français à l'époque de la Révolution (1789–1800).* Paris, 1925.

Gardet, Louis. *La cité musulmane, vie sociale et politique.* 3rd ed. Paris, 1969.

Gibb, H. A. R. "Constitutional organization." In *Law in the Middle East,* edited by Majid Khadduri and Herbert Liebsney, pp. 3–27. Washington, D.C., 1955.

——. "Studies in contemporary Arabic literature." In his *Studies on the Civilization of Islam,* Edited by Stanford Shaw and William Polk. Boston, 1962.

—— and Harold Bowen. *Islamic Society and the West.* 2 vols. Oxford, 1950.

—— and Collin Danes. "Nā'ib." *EI¹.*

Gottschalk, Hans L. "Al-anbaratūr/Imperator." *Der Islam* 33 (1957), pp. 30–36.

——. "Dīwān-ii." *EI².*

Goubard, Amédée. *Histoire de la Révolution et de l'empire.* Paris, 1846–1851. Vols. 1–4.

Haim, Sylvia. *Arab Nationalism, an Anthology.* Berkeley, 1962.

——. "Islam and the theory of Arab nationalism." In *The Middle East in Transition,* edited by W. Z. Laqueur, pp. 280–307. New York, 1958.

Ḥamza, ᶜAbd al-Laṭīf. *Ādāb al-maqāla al-ṣuḥufiyya fī Miṣr.* 8 vols. Cairo, 1958–1963.

Hartmann, Martin. *The Arabic Press of Egypt.* London, 1899.

Haugen, Einar. "The analysis of linguistic borrowing." *Language* 26 (1950), pp. 210–30.

Heywood, J. A. *Arab Lexicography—Its History and Its Place in the General History of Lexicography.* Leiden, 1959.

———. "*Ḳāmūs.*" *EI²*.

Heyworth-Dunne, Jamal al-Din. *An Introduction to the History of Education in Modern Egypt.* London, 1938.

———. "Printing and translation under Muḥammad ᶜAlī of Egypt: The foundation of modern Arabic." *JRAS,* July 1940, pp. 325–49.

———. "Rifāᶜa Badawī Rāfiᶜ at-Ṭahṭāwī: The Egyptian revivalist," *BSOAS* 9 (1937–1939), pp. 961–67; 10 (1940–1942), pp. 399–415.

Ḥilmī, Maḥmūd. *Niẓām al-ḥukm al-Islāmī muqārinan bil-nuẓum al-muᶜāṣira.* Cairo, 1970.

Horovitz, Joseph. "Jewish proper names and derivations in the Koran." *Hebrew Union College Annual* (Cincinnati), 2 (1925), pp. 145–227.

Hourani, Albert. *Arabic Thought in the Liberal Age 1798–1939.* Oxford, 1970.

———. "The changing face of the fertile crescent in the XVIIIth century." *Studia Islamica* 8 (1957), pp. 89–122.

———. "Djamᶜiyya." *EI²*.

———. "Ottoman reform and the politics of notables." In *Beginnings of Modernization in the Middle East in the Nineteenth Century,* edited by William R. Polk and Richard L. Cambers, pp. 41–68. Chicago, 1968.

Ibn al-Khaṭīb, Lisān al-Dīn Muḥammad. *Ta'rīkh Isbāniyā al-Islāmiyya.* Edited by E. Levi-Provencal. Beirut, 1956.

ᶜInān, Muḥammad ᶜAbd Allāh. *Dawlat al-Islām fī al-Andalus.* 2 vols. Cairo, 1969.

———. *Duwal al-ṭawā'if mundh qiyāmihā ḥattā al-fatḥ al-murābiṭī.* Cairo, 1969.

Issawi, Charles. "European loan-words in contemporary Arabic writing: A case study in modernization." *MES* 3 (1966–1967), pp. 110–33.

Jeffrey, Arthur. *The Foreign Vocabulary of the Qur'an.* Baroda, 1938.

al-Jundī, Anwar. *Al-Ṣiḥāfa al-siyāsiyya fī Miṣr mundh nash'atihā ilā al-ḥarb al-ᶜalamiyya al-thāniya.* Cairo, 1962.

Kahane, Henry and Renée Kahane. "Lingua Franca: The story of a term." *Romance Philology* 30 (August, 1976), pp. 25–41.

Karpat, Kemal H. "The land regime, social structure, and modernization in the Ottoman Empire." In *Beginnings of Modernization* in the Middle East in the Nineteenth Century, edited by William R. Polk and Richard L. Chambers, pp. 69–90. Chicago, 1968.

——. "The transformation of the Ottoman state, 1789–1908." *IJMES* 3 (1972), pp. 243–81.

Kekule, Stephen. *Über Titel, Amter, Rangstufen und Anreden in der Offiziellen Osmanischen Sprache.* Halle, 1892.

Kenny, L. M. "East versus West in al-Muqtataf, 1875–1900: Image and self-image." In *Essays on Islamic Civilization, Presented to Niyazi Berkes,* edited by Donald P. Little. Leiden, 1976.

Khaddūr, Adīb. *Al-Ṣiḥāfa al-Sūriyya, nash'atuhā, taṭawwuruhā, wāqiʿuhā al-rāhin.* Damascus, 1972.

Khūrī, Ra'īf. *Al-Fikr al-ʿArabī al-ḥadīth.* Beirut, 1943.

Klausner, Clara L. *The Seljuk Vezirate. A Study of Civil Administration 1055–1194.* Harvard, 1973.

Koebner, Richard. *Empire.* Cambridge, 1961.

——. "Semantics and historiography." *The Cambridge Journal,* 7 (1953), pp. 131–44.

Kramers, J. H. "L'Islam et la démocratie." *Orientalia Neerlandica,* 1945, pp. 223–39.

——. "Sulṭān," *EI¹.*

Krymskii, Agathangel Efimovich. *Istoriya Novoi Arabskoi Literaturvi.* Moscow, 1971.

Kvastad, Nils B. "Semantics in the methodology of the history of ideas." *Journal of the History of Ideas* 38 (1977), pp. 157–74.

Landau, Jacob. *A Word Count of Modern Arabic Prose.* New York, 1959.

Lapidus, Ira Marvin. *Muslim Cities in the Later Middle Ages.* Harvard, 1967.

Levi Della Vida, G. "La traduzione Araba delle storie di Orosio." *Al-Andalus* 19 (1954), pp. 257–93.

Levi-Provencal, E. *Histoire de l'Espagne musulmane.* Vol. 3: *Le siècle du califat de Cordoue.* Paris, 1967.

Lewis, Bernard. "Başvekil," *EI².*

——. "Democracy in the Middle East—its state and prospect." *MEA* 6 (1955), pp. 101–8.

——. "Djumhūriyya." *EI².*

—— "Dustūr-ii." *EI².*

——. *The Emergence of Modern Turkey.* 2nd ed. Oxford, 1968.

——. "Hukumet and devlet." *Belleten* 46 (1982), pp. 415–21.

——. "The impact of the French revolution on Turkey." In *The New Asia,* edited by G. S. Metroux and F. Crouzet, pp. 31–59. New York, 1965.

——. *Islam in History.* New York, 1973.

————. "Meşveret."*Tarih Enstitüsü Dergisi* (Istanbul) 12 (1981–1982), pp. 775–82.

————. *The Muslim Discovery of Europe.* New York, 1982.

————. "Translation from Arabic." *Proceedings of the American Philosophical Society* 124 (1980), pp. 41–47.

————. "Turkey: Westernization." In *Unity and Variety in Muslim Civilization,* edited by G. E. Von Grunebaum, pp. 311–31. Chicago, 1955.

———— (with Ch. Pellat et al.) "Djarīda." *EI².*

Linant de Bellefonds, Y., et al. "*Ḳānūn.*" *EI².*

Louca, Anwar. *Voyageurs et écrivains égyptiens en France aux XIXᵉ siècle.* Paris, 1970.

Lozano, Luis. "The perils of the translator." In *Translation and Interpretation, the Multi-Cultural Context.* edited by Michael S. Batts, pp. 61–66. Vancouver, 1975.

Lutfi al-Sayyid Marsot, Afaf. *Egypt and Cromer.* London, 1968.

MacDonald, D. B. "Ḥizb." *EI².*

Madelung, Wilferd. "The assumption of the title Shāhānshāh by the Būyids and 'the reign of the Daylam (*Dawalt al-Daylam*)'." *JNES* 28 (1969), pp. 84–108, 168–83.

Mardin, Ebul'ülā. "Development of the sharī°a under the Ottoman empire." In *Law in the Middle East,* edited by Majid Khadduri and Herbert Liebsney, pp. 279–91. Washington, D.C., 1955.

Mardin, Şerif. *The Genesis of Young Ottoman Thought.* Princeton, 1962.

Massignon, Louis. "L'UMMA et ses synonymes: notion de 'communauté sociale' en Islam." *REI* 1941–1946, pp. 151–57.

Monteil, Vincent. *L'Arabe moderne.* 2 vols. Paris, 1960.

Mottahedeh, Roy P. *Loyalty and Leadership in an Early Islamic Society.* Princeton, 1980.

————. "The Shu°ūbīyah controversy and the social history of early Islamic Iran." *IJMES* 7 (1976), pp. 161–82.

————. "Some attitudes towards monarchy and absolutism in the eastern Islamic world of the eleventh and twelfth centuries A.D." *Israel Oriental Studies* 10 (1980), pp. 86–91.

Mu'nis, Ḥusayn. *Fajr al-andalus.* Cairo, 1959.

Muruwwa, Adīb. *Al-Ṣiḥāfa al-°Arabiyya nash'atuhā wa-taṭawwuruhā.* Beirut, 1961.

Najjar, Fauzi. M. "Democracy in Islamic political philosophy." *Studia Islamica* 51 (1980), pp. 107–22.

Nawwār, °Abd al-°Azīz Sulaymān. *Wathā'iq asāsiyya min ta'rīkh Lubnān al-ḥadīt, 1517–1920.* Beirut, 1974.

Paine, Thomas. "Dissertation on Government, the Affairs of the Bank and Paper Money." In his *Political Writings,* vol. 1, pp. 365–413. Charlestown, Massachusetts, 1824.

Paret, R. "Umma." *EI¹*.

Pérès, Henri. *L'Espagne vue par les voyageurs musulmans de 1610 à 1930*. Paris, 1937.

———. "Voyageurs musulmans en Europe aux XIXᵉ et XXᵉ siècles." Mélanges Maspéro, vol. 3, *Mémoires de l'Institut Français du Caire*, vol. 68 (1935), pp. 185–195.

Philipp, Thomas. "Class, community and Arab historiography in the early nineteenth century—the dawn of a new era." *IJMES* 16 (1984), pp. 161–75.

al-Rāfiʿī, ʿAbd al-Raḥmān. *ʿAṣr Ismāʿīl*. 2 vols. Cairo, 1932.

———. *ʿAṣr Muḥammad ʿAlī*. Cairo, 1947.

———. *Taʾrīkh al-ḥaraka al-qawmiyya wa-taṭawwur niẓām al-ḥukm fī Miṣr*. 2 vols. Cairo, 1929.

———. *Miṣr wal-Sūdān fī awāʾil ʿahd al-iḥtilāl*. Cairo, 1948.

Raymond, André. *Artisans et commerçants au Caire au XVIIIᵉ siècle*. 2 vols. Damascus, 1973–1974.

Rivlin, Helen Anne B. *The Agricultural Policy of Muḥammad ʿAlī in Egypt*. Harvard, 1961.

Rizq, Yūnān Labīb. *Al-Aḥzab al-Miṣriyya qabl thawrat 1952*. Cairo, 1977.

Rosenthal, Erwin I. J. *Political Thought in Medieval Islam*. Cambridge, 1958.

Rosenthal, Franz. "Dawla." *EI²*.

———. *The Muslim Concept of Freedom*. Leiden, 1960.

——— and B. Lewis. "Ḥurriyya." *EI²*.

Rustum, Asad. *Lubnān fī ʿahd al-mutaṣarrifiyya*. Beirut, 1973.

Safran, Nadav. *Egypt in Search of Political Community*. Harvard, 1961.

Salem, Elie. "Nationalism and Islam." *MW* 52 (1962), pp. 277–87.

Sarkīs, Yūsuf Ilyān. *Muʿjam al-maṭbūʿāt al-ʿArabiyya wal-muʿarraba*. Cairo, 1928.

al-Ṣāwī, Aḥmad Ḥusayn. *Fajr al-ṣiḥāfa fī Miṣr*. Cairo, 1975.

Schacht, Joseph. *An Introduction to Islamic Law*. Oxford, 1964.

Schölch, Alexander. *Egypt for the Egyptians!* London, 1981.

Sharabi, Hisham. *Arab Intellectuals and the West*. Baltimore, 1970.

Shaw, Stanford J. *Between Old and New: The Ottoman Empire under Sultan Selim III 1789–1807*. Harvard, 1971.

———. "The central legislative councils of the nineteenth century Ottoman reform movement before 1876." *IJMES* 1 (1970), pp. 51–84.

———. *The Financial and Administrative Organization and Development of Ottoman Egypt 1517–1798*. Princeton, 1962.

———. *History of the Ottoman Empire and Modern Turkey*. 2 vols. Cambridge, 1976–1977. (Vol. 2 written with Ezel Kural Shaw).

———. *Ottoman Egypt in the Age of the French Revolution*. Harvard, 1964.

Shaykhū, Luwis. *Al-Ādāb al-ᶜArabiyya fī al-qarn al-tāsiᶜ ᶜashar.* 2 vols. Beirut, 1924, 1926.

al-Shayyāl, Jamāl al-Dīn. *A History of Egyptian Historiography in the Nineteenth Century.* Alexandria, 1962.

――. *Ta'rīkh al-tarjama fī Miṣr fī ᶜahd al-ḥamla al-Faransāwiyya.* Cairo, 1950.

――. *Ta'rīkh al-tarjama wal-ḥaraka al-thaqafiyya fī ᶜaṣr Muḥammad ᶜAlī.* Cairo, 1951.

Shoshan, Boaz. "On the relations between Egypt and Palestine: 1382–1517 A.D.." In *Egypt and Palestine, a Millennium of Association (868–1948),* edited by Amnon Cohen and Gabriel Baer, pp. 94–101. Jerusalem, 1984.

Sourdel, Dominique. *Le vizirat ᶜAbbāside de 749 à 936.* 2 vols. Damascus, 1959–1960.

Spies, Otto. "Wakāla." *EI¹.*

Stetkevych, Jaroslav. *The Modern Arabic Literary Language: Lexical and Stylistic Developments.* Chicago, 1970.

Struever, Nancy S. "The study of language and the study of history." *Journal of Interdisciplinary History* 4 (1974), pp. 401–15.

Ṭarabayn, Aḥmad. *Lubnān mundh ᶜahd all-mutaṣarrifiyya ilā bidāyat al-intidāb, 1861–1920.* Cairo, 1969.

Ṭarrazī, Fīlīb di. *Ta'rīkh al-ṣiḥāfa al-ᶜArabiyya.* 4 vols. Beirut, 1913, 1914, 1933.

Tyan, Emile. *Histoire de l'organisation judicaire en pays d'Islam.* 2nd ed. Leiden, 1960.

――. *Institutions du droit public musulman.* Vol. 1: *Le Califat;* vol. 2: *Sultanat et Califat.* Paris, 1954, 1957.

L'Universite de Paris. Institut d'études islamiques et Centre d'études de l'Orient contemporain. *L'Adaptation des langues "classiques" aux besoins modernes dans le Proche Orient (Arabe, Turc, Persan, Hebreu et Grec modernes).* 1961. Mimeographed.

Van Arendonk, C. "Sharīf." *EI¹.*

Van Nieuwenhuijze, C. A. O. "The Ummah; an analytical approach." *Studia Islamica* 10 (1959), pp. 5–22.

al-Wakīl, Shams al-Dīn. *Al-Mujāz fī al-jinsiyya wa-markaz al-ajānib.* Alexandria, 1966.

Washington-Serruys. *L'Arabe moderne étudie dans les journaux et les pièces officielles.* Beirut, 1897.

Wendell, Charles. *The Evolution of the Egyptian National Image.* Berkeley, 1972.

Weinreich, Uriel. *Languages in Contact, Findings and Problems.* New York, 1953.

Wienner, Philip P., ed. *Dictionary of the History of Ideas.* 5 vols. New York, 1973.

Zashin, Elliot, and Phillip C. Chapman. "The uses of metaphor and analogy: Toward a renewal of political language." *The Journal of Politics* 36 (1974), pp. 291–326.

Zaydān, Jurjī. *Tarājim mashāhir al-sharq fī al-qarn al-tāsiᶜ ᶜashar.* 2 vols. Beirut, 1969.

―――. *Ta'rīkh ādāb al-lugha al-ᶜArabiyya.* 4 vols. Cairo, 1958.

Zolondek, Leon. "The French revolution in Arabic literature of the nineteenth century." *MW* 57 (1967), pp. 202–11.

―――. "The language of the Muslim reformers of the late nineteenth century." *Islamic Culture* 37 (1963), pp. 155–62.

―――― "Nineteenth-century Arab travelers to Europe: Some observations on their writings." *MW* 61 (1971), pp. 28–34.

―――. "Ash-Shaᶜb in Arabic political literature of the nineteenth century." *WI* 10 (1965), pp. 1–16.

Index

Note: The index does not include compound expressions appearing in the text; they are far too numerous to be listed. Such expressions should be looked up under their individual components, e.g. references to *majlis al-aʿyān* would be found under *majlis/majālis* and *ʿayn/aʿyān*. Exceptions are proper institutional names, such as the Egyptian *majlis shūrā al-nuwwāb* and the Ottoman *şūrā-i devlet*, which are listed in their full form.

189